Julie Jason's Guide to Connecticut Probate

What Every Connecticut Family Needs to Know About Probate

By

Julie Jason, JD, LLM

Bloomington, IN

authorHOUSE®

Milton Keynes, UK

AuthorHouse™
1663 Liberty Drive, Suite 200
Bloomington, IN 47403
www.authorhouse.com
Phone: 1-800-839-8640

AuthorHouse™ UK Ltd.
500 Avebury Boulevard
Central Milton Keynes, MK9 2BE
www.authorhouse.co.uk
Phone: 08001974150

First published by AuthorHouse 1/2/2007

ISBN: 978-1-4259-6016-2 (e)
ISBN: 978-1-4259-6015-5 (sc)

Library of Congress Control Number: 2006908024

Printed in the United States of America
Bloomington, Indiana

This book is printed on acid-free paper.

Disclaimer

While the information in this book is about legal issues, it is not legal advice or legal representation. Because of the rapidly changing nature of the law and the author's reliance on outside sources, the author can make no warranty or guarantee of the accuracy or reliability of information contained herein. Be sure to consult your lawyer before taking any action involving your estate or your property or any other matter discussed in this book.

Praise for Julie Jason's Guide to Connecticut Probate

"Julie Jason is that rare writer, a reader-friendly expert who presents vital information about law and personal finance in a clear, easy-to-grasp manner. She has not only demystified the probate process, but also given examples that show the great benefit that a little knowledge and preparation can have for your family and heirs."

Jim Zebora,
Business Editor, The Advocate/Greenwich Time

"Many writers have provided "How To" lessons for managing the probate process. Julie Jason goes beyond that. This is for the reader who has studied the "How To" and then sets out to do it. She addresses the problems of the complicated cases, the variations from the norm, and the difficult people. Her message is clear, and her style permits an easy read."

Judge James J. Lawlor,
Connecticut Probate Administrator

"This is a thoughtful and thorough review of the Connecticut Probate process. It arms readers with the knowledge necessary to undertake effective estate planning and to understand the advice they receive from lawyers and others about the choices they should make. I recommend this book without reservation."

Judge Robert K. Killian, Jr.,
Probate Judge for the District of Hartford

"A great overview of a very complex subject -- full of valuable tips and helpful advice."

Professor Jeffrey A. Cooper.
Quinnipiac University School of Law

"Probate will never be fun – think about the event that triggers it. However, it doesn't have to be a stressed-filled journey to an unanticipated destination either. Thanks to Julie Jason and her Guide to Connecticut Probate, every Connecticut family can plan for an orderly transition upon death or incapacity. Ms. Jason provides access to a range of expert tools and resources, including essential forms and official state publications. Equally important, she draws upon the experience gathered as a nationally-prominent money manager to offer succinct commentary and strategic guidance. This book is a must for everyone who cares about the well being of loved ones who will be left behind."

Christopher P. Bruhl,
President & CEO, The Business Council of Fairfield County

"Julie Jason has provided the community with a wonderful guide not only to estate settlement but also for advance estate planning."

Gayle B. Wilhelm, Esq.,
Cummings and Lockwood LLC

"A well written book that will help guide a family through the myriad of concerns in estate administration."

William Wilson, CPA,
Van Brunt, Dubiago & Company

"A valuable resource for all Connecticut citizens."

Professor Robert Whitman,
Professor of Law, University of Connecticut Law School.

"Julie Jason provides citizens of Connecticut with an easy to understand guide to the probate process. She covers topics that most people regrettably try to avoid until it is too late to recover from legal or financial disaster. This is valuable information for people with very modest means and those with abundance."

Glenn A. Cassis,
Executive Director, African-American Affairs Commission, Connecticut General Assembly

"A clearly written comprehensive review of the essentials of a critical but rarely understood zip code in estate planning."

Bill Lane,
CFP, Past President of the FPA in Connecticut

"If what you have was worth spending your lifetime to build, it MUST be worth preserving for your family. This book helps you understand how to do that in a well organized, easy to read format."

Byron Udell,
JD, CLU, CFP, ChFC, President & CEO, AccuQuote.com

Dedication

In Memory of Richard H. Stein, Esq.

Acknowledgments

I would have not been able to write this book without the help of expert trusts and estates practitioners. I am particularly grateful for the help of Connecticut Probate Administrator Judge James J. Lawlor, and his Chief Counsel, Thomas E. Gaffey, as well as Stamford Probate Judge Gerald Fox, Esq. (Fox & Fox, LLP), Greenwich Probate Judge David W. Hopper, Esq. (Pullman & Comley, LLC), Darien Probate Judge John B. Rearden, Jr., Esq. (Pullman & Comley, LLC), and Norwalk Probate Judge Anthony J. DePanfilis, Esq. (DePanfilis & Vallerie, LLC).

I am also indebted to Roselyn Ramist, Clerk of the Stamford Probate Court, and Barbara Carbino, Clerk of the Greenwich Probate Court, both of whom were kind enough to meet with me to help me understand how cases are handled in their courts.

I am most grateful to Gayle Brian Wilhelm, Esq. for his help at all stages of this project. Mr. Wilhelm is principal of the Cummings & Lockwood LLC's Private Clients Group, founder of the Lower Fairfield County Estate Planning Council, Fellow of the American College of Trusts and Estate Counsel, and lead author of Connecticut's primary legal reference source for probate lawyers and judges, a seven-volume series of treatises on wills, trusts, death taxes, settlement of estates, and probate litigation.

I thank Dianne Besunder, spokesperson for the IRS for her support and assistance, as well as the following trusts and estates attorneys, accountants, and financial experts. Again, without them, this book would not have been possible:

- John T. Bannen, Esq., Quarles and Brady, LLP (Milwaukee, WI)
- Gary Buseck, Esq., GLAD (Boston, MA)
- Samuel L. Braunstein, Esq., Braunstein and Todisco, PC (Fairfield, CT)
- Deborah S. Breck, Esq., Pullman & Comley, LLC (Westport, CT)
- Mark Chioffi, Esq., Martin, Lucas & Chioffi, LLP (Stamford, CT)
- Natalie Choate, Esq., Bingham McCutchen LLP (Boston, MA)
- Jeffrey A. Cooper, Esq., Quinnipiac University School of Law (Hamden, CT)
- Carolyn DeVore, Esq., Pullman & Comley, LLC (Westport, CT)
- Bruno Graziano, Esq., CCH Incorporated
- David Handler, Esq., Kirkland & Ellis, LLP (Chicago, IL)
- Gregory A. Hayes, Esq., Day, Berry & Howard LLP (Stamford, CT)
- Jevera Hennessey, Esq., Kaye and Hennessey, LLC (Greenwich, CT)
- Lily Lee, CPA, Thomson Tax & Accounting Professional Software Services
- Stephan R. Leimberg, CEO of Leimberg and LeClair, Inc. (Havertown, PA)
- Michael L. Millman, Managing Director of the Nutmeg Benefit Group, LLC (Fairfield, CT)
- Aoife A. Cox Rinaldi, Esq., Martin, Lucas & Chioffi, LLP (Stamford, CT)
- Lori E. Romano, Esq., Shipman & Goodwin, LLP (Greenwich, CT)
- Gregory A. Saum, Esq., Ivey, Barnum & O'Mara, LLC (Greenwich, CT)
- Michael Sem, Esq., CCH Incorporated
- Jane Shuck, Brentmark Software (Orlando, FL)

- Edward A. Slott, CPA, E. Slott & Company (Rockville Centre, NY)
- Samuel J. Starks, Esq., Law Firm of Samuel J. Starks (Stamford, CT)
- Amy E. Todisco, Esq., Braunstein and Todisco, PC (Fairfield, CT)
- Michael Vaughan, J.G. Wentworth (Bryn Mawr, PA)
- William Wilson, CPA, Van Brunt, Dubiago & Company (Stamford, CT)

I am also indebted to CCH, Brentmark Software, and the Thomson Corporation, for their help with the tax and IRA case studies provided in Chapters 4 and 11.

CCH, a Wolters Kluwer business (CCHGroup.com) is a leading provider of tax and accounting law information, software, and services. It has served tax, accounting, and business professionals and their clients since 1913. Among its market-leading products are The ProSystem fx® Office, CCH® Tax Research NetWork™, Accounting Research Manager® and the U.S. Master Tax Guide®. CCH is based in Riverwoods, Ill.

Brentmark® Software (www.brentmark.com) provides personal financial planning products and services for professionals and consumers: estate, financial, and retirement planning software; informational web sites (RothIRA.com, LifetimeSavingsAccount.com, NewRMD.com, Roth401k.com, PensionPlanners.com, and StateDeathTax.com); and online calculators (CalcTools.com). Software products include Pension & Roth IRA Analyzer, Estate Planning Tools, PFP Notebook, Pension Distributions Planner, Kugler Estate Analyzer™, Retirement Income Navigator, Charitable Financial Planner, Estate Planning QuickView, Savings Bond Toolkit, and IRS Factors Calculator.

The Thomson Corporation (headquartered in Stamford, CT) is a leading global provider of integrated information-based solutions to business and professional customers. Thomson provides value-added information, with software tools and applications that help its customers make better decisions, faster. Thomson serves more than 20 million information users in the fields of law, tax, accounting, higher education, reference information, corporate e-learning and assessment, financial services, scientific research, and healthcare. Thomson Tax & Accounting

Professional Software Services provides trusts and estates accounting software.

Finally, thank you, Julia Kisielius, for your editing prowess.

Table of Contents

Introduction

Every Connecticut family will be touched by probate at some point in their lives because of a death or incapacity of a loved one. Understanding how the probate process works in advance of a catastrophe can help you plan your life to avoid common missteps.

An orderly transition is all about anticipating what can go wrong — little things, like being unable to locate a password to the computer that containing your financial records — and big things, like a child inadvertently causing your IRA to become fully taxable.

Consider these potential problems:

- Your will doesn't say what you think it does.
- You forget to update your will after your divorce and remarriage.
- Your IRA custodian has no beneficiary designations on file.
- Your last will is missing, but your previous spouse is able to produce an earlier will that named him or her your sole heir.

And, some others

- A married childless couple without a will is exposed to the in-law factor: when one spouse dies, the survivor will share the couple's assets with his or her in-laws.
- If your children contribute to the IRA they inherit from you, the entire IRA becomes taxable.

- Unmarried couples have no rights to each other's property if there is no will.
- Estate taxes have to be paid within nine months of death, even if the house isn't sold by that date.
- A free dinner seminar on "how to avoid probate" leads you to set up a living trust you don't need.
- Heirs don't realize they can take a tax deduction on their own income tax returns for "income in respect of a decedent" in certain cases when your estate pays estate taxes.
- If you want to avoid Connecticut estate taxes by moving out of state, Connecticut will want five years worth of records showing your activity in and outside the state.

These issues and many more are addressed in this book, which began as a collection of my weekly columns in the Stamford Advocate, the Greenwich Time, and the Norwalk Advocate. Thanks to help from legal and financial professionals, the book turned into much more, evolving into a gateway to expert tools and resources.

Among other things, I am pleased to provide you with forms, commentary, and official Connecticut publications in the reference section of the book, including documents provided by the American Bar Association, the American College of Trust and Estate Counsel, and the Gay & Lesbian Advocates & Defenders. In addition, I share some of the planning techniques that I use with in my money management practice.

If you find that this book is useful to you, please let me know. If you have a question or run into a problem or can't decide on a course of action, do contact me. I meet with readers whose situations I can describe in my columns to illustrate a point with a real-life situation.

You can reach me by calling (203)322-1198 or emailing me at Julie@JacksonGrant.us. You can write to me at Jackson, Grant Investment Advisers, Inc., Two High Ridge Park in Stamford, CT 06905.

PART I –THE BASICS

Chapter 1

What Is Probate?

Probate serves a useful purpose. If the probate process were not available, a deceased person's property would rattle around in no-man's land forever.

Let me give you an example. Say your favorite great-uncle Harry tells you that he wants you to have his beloved rebuilt red Ford pickup when he passes on—one of only 116,327 built by Ford in 1953.

When Harry dies, you go to Melanie, Harry's widow, to claim the pickup. Lucky for you, Melanie knows Harry's wishes and hands you the keys and the title, which is in Harry's name.

You now have possession of the car. But do you own it? Can you sell it? Can you insure it? No. Only the owner of the car, Harry, can transfer title to you. But Harry passed away.

This is where probate enters the picture. Probate is the mechanism to transfer ownership after the owner's death. In this case, Harry's will will be "probated" in the probate court located in the town where Harry resided at the time of his death. The court will verify the validity of Harry's will and transfer property he owned at death to the beneficiaries named in his will. If there is no will, Harry's property will pass to his heirs under the laws of "intestacy," a topic we will discuss in Chapter 7.

Let's take a look at the other assets Harry owned at death.

Jointly Owned Real Estate

Harry and Melanie owned their home jointly with right of survivorship (JWROS). When Harry died, Melanie automatically became the sole owner of the house because the deed for the property was JWROS. The property transferred to Melanie outside of probate because it was held in JWROS.

If the property had been titled "Harry and Melanie, Tenants in Common," it would be probate property, since Harry's one-half ownership of the property would transfer to his heirs, not to Melanie, unless Harry left his share of the property to Melanie in his will.

IRA with Beneficiary Designation

Harry had an IRA (Individual Retirement Account). When he opened the IRA, Harry filled out and sent in to the IRA custodian a beneficiary designation form naming Melanie as the primary beneficiary of the IRA. As a result, the IRA passes to Melanie outside of probate.

Payable on Death (POD) and Transfer on Death (TOD)

Harry also had a brokerage account "payable on death" (POD) to his son, George. This asset passed to George automatically when Harry died. A POD or a "transfer on death" (TOD) account is not a probate asset.

Savings Account

Harry had a savings account titled in his name alone. Just like Harry's truck, the savings account cannot pass to a beneficiary without the help of probate court. An asset held in the name of the decedent alone is a probate asset — unless of course, as we discussed, there is a beneficiary designation or another form of death transfer, such as a TOD.

Probate assets such as the truck and the savings account will transfer first to Harry's "estate" and then to his heirs or beneficiaries after all issues are resolved, expenses and taxes paid, and the estate "settled," allowing the estate to be officially closed by the probate court.

No Probate Estate

It is possible to pass all assets directly to heirs outside of the probate process. In Harry's example, the savings account could have been registered in Harry's name "in trust for" Melanie, or as JWROS. The truck could have been registered TOD under Connecticut General Statute section 14-16 (as amended by Public Act 02-105) which permits automobiles to be registered in transfer on death form ("Harry, transfer on death to Sam"). Living ("inter vivos") trusts are another common mechanism to transfer assets directly to beneficiaries during one's lifetime. Living trusts take effect during one's lifetime. Assets held by living trusts are non-probate assets. For more information on trusts, read "Understanding Trusts: A Look at Living Trusts and Other Trusts," which is reproduced for you in Appendix 1-A.

Taxes and Debts

Even if all property passes to heirs directly because all holdings are in non-probate form, other matters must come before the court. Among other things, the estate needs to pay its bills and file appropriate Connecticut estate tax returns with the probate court, even if no Connecticut estate tax is due.

Probate fees are assessed on the gross taxable estate, whether or not the decedent's property passes through the probate process. Fees are calculated on the inventory, not just the probate estate. In my example of Harry's estate, the gross taxable estate includes all assets, while the probate estate includes just the truck and the savings account.

What Happens in Court?

If there is a will, the executor named in the will must take the following steps, irrespective of whether there are any probate assets.

1) The executor files an application in probate court for a public hearing to approve the will and confirm the executor. If someone is going to contest the will, it will happen at this stage of the process.

2) Within two months of his or her appointment, the executor takes possession of everything the decedent owned in his or her own name, transfers it into the name of the "estate," obtains the fair market value of

each asset, and prepares a list of the property and its value (an inventory) for filing with the court.

3) The executor files a "certificate of notice for land records" with the town clerk in each town the decedent owned real estate.

4) After getting appropriate approvals, the executor sells property that is not the subject of a specific bequest if necessary to raise the cash he or she will need to pay taxes and expenses.

5) Within 14 days of the executor's appointment, the court publishes a newspaper notice to creditors so that they can present their claims. Generally, creditors have 150 days to file claims with the court.

6) The executor files a Connecticut estate tax return with the probate court, whether or not the estate is taxable. There are two different Connecticut estate tax returns, one for taxable estates of $2 million and up and one for non-taxable estates under $2 million. (The Connecticut estate tax was enacted in 2005 and effectively takes the place of the Connecticut succession tax, which was repealed effective for deaths occurring after January 1, 2005.)

The applicable return must be filed within nine months of the date of death. A federal estate tax return (Form 706) must be filed with the IRS within nine months of death, but only if the estate is taxable federally. (See Chapter 4 for information on federally taxable estates.)

Federal and state taxes must be paid at the time of the filing. While extensions are permitted, penalties and interest can be hefty. Chapter 4 deals with estate taxes in more depth.

7) Along with filing the estate's tax returns, the executor must also file the decedent's last income tax returns (IRS Form 1040 and CT-1040) for the year of death. The decedent's income tax return is for the year up to his date of death, covering actual income received and expenses paid during the period. After a taxpayer's death, income received by the estate is taxed to the estate. If income due the decedent is received by a beneficiary, the beneficiary must report that income on his or her income tax return.

8) Usually within 12 months of death, the executor files a final accounting listing the financial transactions of the estate, including the payments made out of the estate (expenses, debts, taxes) and monies received (interest earned, property sold, debts collected).

9) After the final accounting is approved by the court, the executor distributes property to beneficiaries.

10) The executor files a final closing statement after all the distributions are made and the estate is closed. Anyone who is aggrieved can file an appeal (usually within 30 days) with the Connecticut Superior Court.

When There Is No Will

If there is no will, there is no "executor." Instead, someone (usually a family member) petitions the court to be appointed the "administrator" of the estate. The administrator follows the process as above, except that the property is distributed in accordance with Connecticut laws instead of the decedent's wishes. (What happens if you die without a will ("intestate") is discussed in Chapter 7.)

Probate Courts

Connecticut's first probate court was established some 300 years ago, in the late 1600s. Today, 123 of Connecticut's 169 towns have probate courts to serve town residents.

Initially, probate courts handled only post-mortem matters—the affairs of the deceased — and appointed guardians of minors. Probate court responsibilities were later expanded by the Connecticut legislature to include trusts, commitment of mentally ill adults and children, appointing conservators for the mentally impaired, and adoptions. Probate courts also hear claims of paternity of fathers, remove unfit parents as guardians of their children, grant name changes, appoint guardians of mentally retarded persons, and consider minors' applications for marriage.

The courts are run by part-time probate judges who are elected to four-year posts. Interestingly, judges need not be lawyers. In the past, the judges ran their own courts completely independent of each other, with their own budgets, and there were no requirements for uniformity of procedures or judges' compensation. Judges were not paid a salary. Instead, they took in revenues (fees charged by the court for probate services), from which they paid the expenses of the court, including salaries of court personnel, and kept the remainder for themselves as compensation for their services. However, fee schedules were extremely complex, resulting in a lack of uniformity among courts in the way fees were charged.

In 1948, judge's fees were capped and net revenues above the judge's compensation were paid into a central fund for the State of Connecticut's probate system. In 1967, the office of the Probate Court Administrator was established to oversee the operations of probate courts throughout the state. At the same time, additional measures were enacted to improve uniformity in fees and compensation.

The probate court system is being evaluated to determine the feasibility of consolidating smaller courts, moving toward more uniformity across different courts, and imposing additional changes in structure and fees, including increasing judges' hours to full time.

Your Visit to Probate Court

At some point in your process, you or your attorney will need to visit your local court. To make the best use of the court's resources, do some research before you go. Connecticut's probate court's official site is www.jud.state.ct.us/probate. There you will find forms and pamphlets that can help you prepare for your visit to probate court. Be sure to read "Guidelines for the Administration of Decedents' Estates", which is an official Connecticut booklet reprinted for you in Appendix 1-B.

Also read, "The Probate Court and You", another official Connecticut resources reprinted in Appendix 1-C, which provides a glossary of terms and answers the following questions.

1. Why Do Probate Courts Become Involved in the Settling of Decedents' Estates?
2. When Is It Necessary to Open an Estate?
3. What Does "In Survivorship" Mean, and Must Survivorship Property Be Reported to the Probate Court?
4. What Taxes Might Be Due at the Time of Death?
5. How Does the Connecticut Estate and Gift Tax Operate?
6. Is the Connecticut Estate and Gift Tax Determined in the Same Manner as the Federal Estate Tax?
7. What Is the Effect of Having Savings or Securities "In Trust For" Another Person? How Do Such Bank Accounts Differ from a Custodial Bank Account for a Minor?
8. Is There a Simple Method to Probate a Small Estate?

9. Who Can Serve as an Executor or Administrator of an Estate? What Duties Does One Have?
10. Is It Necessary to Have a Lawyer or Other Professional Help Probate an Estate or File the Required Tax Returns?
11. How Do You Make Application for the Probate of a Decedent's Will?
12. How Old Can a Will Be and Still Be Good?
13. What Can Be Done if a Person Dies and Has a Safe Deposit Box, and a Will May Be in the Box?
14. When A Person Dies, Are His Assets All "Frozen" and Unavailable to the Family?
15. What if a Person Dies Leaving No Will? What Happens to the Property?
16. How Is the Property Distributed When There Is No Will?
17. Does Death Relieve a Family from Making Payment of Monies Owed by a Decedent?
18. What Are the Various Costs Involved in Settling a Decedent's Affairs?
19. What Is the Basis for Computing Probate Charges?
20. How Are Probate Charges Used by the Probate Court?
21. What Is a Probate Court Hearing?
22. What Are Probate Appeals?
23. What Information and Documents Will You Need to Provide to the Probate Court?
24. Does a Probate Court Handle Matters Other Than Matters Associated with Decedents' Estates?

Once you have done some reading, pay a visit to the court. At the court, you can expect the staff to provide you with basic information, forms, and timelines. Remember that the staff is not in a position to give you legal advice. If you are dealing with a small estate ($20,000 or less in the name of the decedent alone), the proceedings can be handled in an expedited fashion with the help of the staff. For larger estates, disputes, or complicated matters, it would be wise to retain a lawyer who specializes in trusts and estates matters. Chapter 17 will help you find a competent lawyer if you do not have one.

Chapter 2

Should You Try to Avoid Probate?

If you believe newspaper and TV advertisements you see from time to time, you might try to do everything possible to avoid probate. But remember that those ads are selling you something—something that could be more advantageous to the seller (insurance agents, financial planners, and even attorneys and accountants) than to you.

According to Gayle Wilhelm of the Stamford, Connecticut, law firm, Cummings & Lockwood, LLC, it all started with Connecticut resident Norman F. Dacey's book, *How to Avoid Probate!*, written in the 1960s. The book described the Connecticut probate system as "one of the most viciously corrupt systems ever distorted by the inventive minds of the greedy." Ironically, however, by the 1960s any abuses in Connecticut's system were long gone, according to Wilhelm. Thus, the call to "avoid probate," which often creates a sense of urgency in the wealthy retiree, needs to be understood for what it is: a technique intended to drive business to the sellers of all sorts of financial services.

If you take a closer look at the avoiding-probate pitches, you'll notice that they are usually focused on selling a living trust along with insurance products. As with every well-polished scam, there is a slight element of truth in each of the promises made in the sales pitch.

Here is the typical sales pitch for a living trust:

1) A living trust will avoid estate taxes. *This simply is not the case.*

2) With a living trust, you can avoid exorbitant probate fees. *Again, not so. In some cases, setting up a trust may be more costly than the probate fees you are trying to avoid.*
3) Living trusts protect your assets against creditors. *This is true only in certain narrow cases.*
4) Living trusts are really easy to set up. *Only if you are working with a qualified attorney.*
5) A living trust avoids publicity. *While it is true that living trusts are not filed in probate court while wills are, the filing of a will hardly ever gets publicity.*

Avoiding the "Avoid Probate" Scam

According to watchdog groups such as the National Consumer Law Center (NCLC), "avoiding probate" scams target seniors in particular. To lend their advertisements credibility, some sellers of living trusts and similar legal services incorporate familiar names that seniors trust in their sales solicitations. Be skeptical if you see an endorsement.

You should also be aware that some scammers use the living trust as an excuse to get information about your assets to pitch highly lucrative insurance products and variable annuities. This is precisely what happened to one of my readers. She and her husband attended an "avoiding probate" seminar a few years ago. Following a free dinner, they signed up for a complimentary one-on-one consultation, during which they purchased services to help them avoid probate.

Even though their estate was insubstantial, convinced of the evils of probate, the couple paid $1,500 to form a living trust and placed all of their assets in the trust. In addition, they purchased some high, hidden-cost insurance products. When the husband died, his widow was astonished to find out that she still had to go to probate court to file the will as well as the Connecticut estate tax returns for a non-taxable estate, along with an inventory that included the trust assets. She also had to pay the probate court a fee of $150 (a drop in the bucket compared to the $1,500 cost of setting up the trust).

The couple could have saved that $1,500, because before funding the trust, all of the couple's property was in joint name with right of survivorship. None of that property would have "gone through probate" on the death of the first spouse. Further, none of the property would have been subject to estate taxes on either death, because the assets were substantially below $2 million.

Transferring Property Outside of Probate

If your estate is not subject to estate taxes (generally under $2 million), and your goal is to transfer property outside of probate, the process is very simple. Just keep in mind the following rules that apply upon your death:

1) Your surviving joint tenant will own any real estate owned in joint tenancy with "right of survivorship" (but not as "tenants in common").
2) Your "payable on death" beneficiary on your bank and brokerage accounts will own those accounts.
3) The IRA beneficiaries you named on your IRA beneficiary forms will own your IRAs.
4) The beneficiaries you name on bank accounts held "in trust for" them will own those accounts.
5) The property held in living trusts (funded while you are alive) will pass in the manner provided in the trust instrument.

To use these techniques, be sure to understand each fully. Also, if you have substantial wealth, be sure to have a good tax adviser carefully review your situation, your holdings, and your potential federal and estate tax liability in order to determine how your assets should be titled and whether trusts would be desirable in your situation. For example, if you are married, your lawyer or tax adviser may recommend some assets be held in each spouse's name alone to be transferred into a credit shelter trust at death. A credit shelter trust is a tax saving device that preserves a taxpayer's estate tax lifetime exclusion amount. (Estate taxes are covered in Chapter 4.)

This is the sort of decision that should be made based on a thorough understanding of your individual circumstances. Therefore, be sure to hire a seasoned and well qualified trusts and estates attorney to guide you through this and other important estate planning decisions. Be sure to read Chapter 17 on how to find a skilled lawyer.

Summary

The probate process itself is not something to be feared. Probate court can bring clarity to murky situations, such as when there is no will, when multiple creditors claim that the decedent owed them money, when the decedent doesn't include his current wife in his will, or when children of a former marriage claim certain property belongs to them.

Trusts can be effective planning tools in the right circumstances, but only if they serve a useful purpose in your personal situation. For more information on trusts, read Appendix 1-A, "Understanding Trusts: A Look at Living Trusts and Other Trusts," an official publication of the Probate Courts of Connecticut.

Chapter 3

Is Probate Expensive?

The general public may think that fees charged by the probate court are excessive, creating part of the marketing justification for "avoiding probate." Actually, probate fees are quite reasonable.

Probate Fees

Consider the following numbers: for a Connecticut estate of $10,000, the probate fee is $150, according to the fee schedule published by the Office of the Court Administrator. For an estate of $500,000, the probate fee is $1,865. For an estate of $1,000, the fee is $50. The most your estate will pay in probate fees is $12,500, which is the cap for estates of $4.75 million and over.

Probate fees are set by law and are based on the size of the estate. There is a 50 percent reduction for property passing to a surviving spouse.

The "estate," for purposes of computing the probate fee, is the gross estate for Connecticut estate tax purposes, less 50 percent of any property passing to the surviving spouse. There are a few other adjustments. For example, if damages were recovered for injuries that resulted in the death, those are added to the "estate" to figure the probate fee.

To figure the fee, the courts look for the "gross estate" reported in the Connecticut Estate Tax Return (Form CT-706/709, for estates of more than $2 million) or the Connecticut Estate Tax Return for Non-

Taxable Estates (Form CT-706-NT, for estates of $2 million or less). (See Appendix 3-A for a list of Connecticut probate costs and fees.) There will be additional costs, of course, if you use an attorney or have an executor (if there is a will) or an administrator (if there is no will). If a family member serves as executor or administrator, he or she may waive executor or administrator fees.

Executor's Fees

An executor is entitled to a fee that is reasonable under the circumstances of the particular estate. A large, complex estate will take more time and expertise to settle, and will therefore be more expensive in terms of executor's fees. Unlike some states, Connecticut probate courts do not rigidly apply a set percentage based on the size of estate. Instead, the courts apply a nine-factor test set out in a 1923 Connecticut case called *Hayward v. Plant*. The nine factors used in determining the executor's fee are as follows:

1) The size of the estate.
2) The executor's responsibilities involved in settling the estate.
3) The character of the work required.
4) The special problems and difficulties met in doing the work.
5) The results achieved.
6) The knowledge, skill, and judgment required of and used by the executor.
7) The manner and promptitude in which the estate was settled.
8) The time and services required.
9) Any other circumstances that are relevant and material to the determination.

Institutional Executors' Fees

Institutional executors, such as banks, charge executor fees based on a published fee schedule. Under the fee schedule for a well-known Connecticut bank, an estate of $6 million pays an executor's fee of $154,000 (an effective rate of 2.6 percent) and $34,000 for a $1 million estate (for an effective rate of 3.4 percent). An estate of $200,000 pays a 4.5 percent fee, or $9,000.

Anyone making a will needs to think about executor fees. Before choosing a lawyer, bank, or other institution as an executor, it's important to review the executor's fee schedule. However, the probate court has jurisdiction to review the executor's fee and may find the fee to be unreasonable if the fee is not justified in light of the work done for the estate. If an individual such as a family member or a lawyer serves as executor, some courts may approve the fees if they are in line with the local bank fee schedule.

Legal Fees

Legal counsel for the estate may charge on the basis of time spent, on a percentage of estate assets, or on a flat-fee basis. After discussing fees with the executor and coming to an agreement on the terms, the lawyer will provide the executor with a written engagement letter that confirms the fee arrangement in writing. The written engagement letter is a requirement in the state of Connecticut. A few examples of engagement letters are provided in the reference section of this book.

Excessive Legal and Accounting Fees

The probate courts have to approve the final accounting of the estate, including the amounts paid to the executors, lawyers, and accountants who handle the administration of the estate. The court may find that a fee is excessive and order a reduction. As an example, in a recent case, a Connecticut court reduced the accountant's bill from $11,200 to $5,500 and the attorney's fees from $11,960 to $4,500 because the bills were excessive considering the work product and the size and complexity of the estate.

If the size of a legal bill is a shock to the executor, the executor should question it. When I was preparing to write about probate in my weekly column, I heard from a reader who lost his wife in 2005. All of the couple's assets had been in joint name (husband and wife, with right of survivorship), except for the IRA, which named the husband the sole beneficiary. In addition, there were three bank accounts in the wife's name alone.

Such an estate hardly seems complicated. When this man received his first legal bill for $18,000, he was shocked. In reviewing the bill, he found that the lawyer charged $450 an hour, which came as a surprise. And at that rate, charges add up quickly. The lawyer had not provided an up-front written estimate of legal costs and the client did not know to ask for one. Unfortunately, by then, a simple matter (agreed upon billing for agreed upon services) escalated into an unpleasant conflict. No one was happy.

When a bill seems high, it's best to question the bill, and review the work done to date. Most important of all is to get an up-front written estimate and to keep track along the way of how close to the estimate the lawyer's fees are. Also, be aware that there are ways to keep costs down. For example, in the earlier example of the man with the $18,000 legal bill, he could have handled a lot of the administrative legwork, such as transferring the bank accounts and IRA to himself, on his own. One area where it's not a good idea to take the do-it-yourself approach is with the filing of the estate tax return. For this task, it's best to hire a lawyer or an accountant.

Summary

Often, a strong reaction to a legal bill could be a matter of expectations. For example, a client may have been unaware that the lawyer spent time with post-mortem planning or a complicated tax situation, and would therefore be surprised by the hefty charges this work can add to the final bill. Therefore, it pays to ask questions before a lawyer begins working to settle an estate and along the way as well. Whenever charges seem unreasonable, it's important to question them. And if the answers are unsatisfactory, you always have the option of changing lawyers. Be sure to read Chapter 17, "How to Find an Estate Planning Lawyer," if you are in the process of selecting a new or replacement lawyer. Also read, "Attorney Fee Agreements," in Appendix 3-B, provided courtesy of FindLaw, a Thompson Corporation Service.

Chapter 4

Do You Need to Worry About Estate Taxes?

There are two types of taxes that come into play when someone dies: 1) income taxes and 2) estate taxes[1].

Income taxes affect everybody. Estate taxes affect the wealthy. But beware. You may be one of the wealthy even if you don't think of yourself that way. Everything you own at death counts – your house, your 401(k), your furnishings, your clothes, your books, your jewelry, your dishes, your car, your life insurance and everything else that belongs to you is added together to see if you have a taxable estate.

Income Taxes

Because there is so much confusion about income taxes after death, let's talk about that first. Your executor will file four income tax returns: two for the decedent (IRS Form 1040 and Connecticut Form 1040) and two for the estate (IRS Form 1041 and Connecticut Form 1041. (If the

[1] Estate taxes (or "death taxes") are essentially "transfer taxes." They are imposed on the value of a decedent's estate and are to be paid by the executor from the estate's assets; if not paid, estates taxes may be imposed on the heirs on the theory of transferee liability. "Inheritance taxes" are imposed on the beneficiaries of an estate based on the amount received by the beneficiary.

estate is open for more than one year, additional Form 1041s may be required.)

As we discussed in Chapter 1, when you die, your executor has to make sure that your final income tax returns are filed with the IRS and with Connecticut to cover the period before your death. If you die on or before June 1, your final Form 1040 return will be for the period January 1 through June 1, to be filed by your executor before April 15 of the following year under the regular income tax filing schedule that applies to all individuals. Income received after the decedent's death is picked up by the estate's income tax return (Form 1041). For example, if you die on June 1, income earned from June 2 forward will go to your estate and will be taxable to your estate.

What might be considered as income? All earnings are included, such as interest, dividends, and capital gains from all sources, such as bank accounts, bonds, stocks, rental income, royalties, or your business. The estate can deduct expenses on its income tax return, such as executor's fees, legal expenses, and business expenses if the executor is managing the decedent's business.

Income in Respect of a Decedent (IRD)

Income received by the estate is called "income in respect of a decedent," or "IRD," and includes any ordinary income the decedent would have received had he or she lived. For example, salary and interest accrued at death, bonuses, proceeds from an uncompleted sale of property, and a partner's share of partnership income would all be considered items of IRD.

The estate tax attributable to items of IRD is deductible for income tax purposes, but only if the estate owes <u>estate</u> taxes. (You don't get an *income tax deduction* if the estate does not have to pay *estate taxes*.)

There are also certain items that can generate what is known as a "deduction in respect of decedent." These items would include ordinary and necessary business expenses, deductible interest, and expenses incurred in the production of income. Although typically the estate would pay these items and, thus, be entitled to the deduction, if a beneficiary receives property that is subject to a liability, he or she would be entitled to the deduction in the year the liability is paid.

A beneficiary can also have IRD, many times in connection with tax-deferred accounts, such as IRAs. Many beneficiaries miss the fact that they can take an IRD deduction on their own tax returns if the estate pays estate taxes. Learn more about the IRD and the three other potential pitfalls of tax-deferred accounts in Chapter 11.

Estate Taxes

Federal estate taxes may or may not be due, depending on the size of the estate and on credits and deductions that may be applicable. Changing year-to-year federal credits and tax rates were put in place in 2001 by EGTRRA, the Economic Growth and Tax Relief Reconciliation Act of 2001. Be sure to check with your lawyer for the tax structure in place at the time you do your planning.

Based on EGTRRA, the amount that is not subject to federal estate tax increases over time and the rate at which the estate is taxed decreases. For deaths in 2006 through 2008, the federal exemption amount is $2 million, and the top estate tax rate is 46 percent in 2006, and 45 percent in both 2007 and 2008. (Congress is considering raising the federal exemption to $5 million.)

In 2009, the exemption increases to $3.5 million and the top tax rate is 45 percent. For deaths occurring in 2010, the death tax is due to be completely eliminated. However, the death tax will be reinstated at pre-EGTRRA levels in 2011 ($1 million exemption, with tax rates between 41 percent and 55 percent, depending on the size of the estate), unless Congress acts to make estate tax repeal permanent.

Estate tax law changes will probably continue, as they have many times since federal estate taxes were first enacted some 200 years ago. Connecticut estate taxes differ from federal estate taxes and are covered later in this chapter. If you own property in more than one state, each state can tax the property located in the state and income attributable to that state.

Basis

Assets you own at death receive a new income tax basis, which is tied to the market value that is used on your estate tax return (the fair market value at death or six months after death, if the executor elects). For example, if you purchased your home for $50,000 in 1970, and upon your death it was worth $2 million, the basis is stepped up from $50,000 to $2 million. That means that your beneficiary can sell the house for $2 million without paying a capital gains tax, since there is no gain ($2 million sales proceeds – $2 million basis = $0 gain).

If the basis were not stepped up, the taxable gain would have been $1.995 million. Items of IRD, however, do not receive a stepped-up basis. (You should be aware that under current federal law, a different basis rule applies for death occurring in 2010.)

Married Decedent

If you are married to a U.S. citizen, everything that you leave to him or her will be free of both Connecticut and federal estate taxes. There is no limit – even if you have a $1 billion.

Assets you leave to your spouse fall under the "unlimited marital deduction." The effect of the deduction is to exclude any assets you leave to your spouse from your taxable estate. Essentially, the marital deduction defers the payment of estate taxes on those assets until your spouse dies. (Special rules apply to non–U.S. citizen spouses.)

However, leaving everything to your spouse may be a bad idea if your estate is worth $2 million or more. Why? By leaving everything to your spouse, you are giving up a valuable tax planning tool, your "estate tax applicable credit amount" which used to be called your "unified credit," before EGTRRA.

The estate tax applicable credit is a credit against estate taxes. In 2006, 2007, and 2008, the estate tax applicable credit of $780,800 effectively shelters a $2 million estate from estate taxes. In 2009, the estate tax applicable credit shelters $3.5 million. Consider the following example. To simplify, this example does not include Connecticut estate taxes.

First Death

Say you and your spouse jointly own $6 million of property with right of survivorship (JWROS). At your death, the entire estate passes to your spouse free of estate taxes. Since there is no estate tax liability, your estate tax applicable credit – worth $780,800, enough to offset $2 million in assets — goes unused.

Second Death

When your spouse dies, his or her estate tax applicable credit of $780,800 (assuming death in 2007) effectively excludes $2 million from his or her taxable estate. That leaves $4 million of the $6 million estate subject to estate taxes upon your spouse's death. That $4 million will be taxed at a top rate of 45 percent (2007), for an estate tax of $1.8 million. This leaves a net inheritance of $4.2 million ($6 million less $1.8 million) after taxes for heirs.

Better Planning

Your heirs could have done much better if you had not lost your estate tax applicable credit at your death. With two credits of $2 million apiece (yours and your spouse's), you could have sheltered $4 million instead of just $2 million. Using both credits would increase their inheritance by almost $1 million.

Protecting Both Spouse's Applicable Credits

As you can see from the above example, couples can pass along larger estates to their heirs if they protect both spouses' estate tax applicable credits. How can this be accomplished while avoiding estate tax on the first spouse's death? The technique is called a "credit shelter trust" (also called an "A-B trust" or a "bypass trust").

Here is a simplified example of how a credit shelter trust works: your lawyer creates a credit shelter trust in each of your wills. He directs you to transfer $4 million of the joint property into two $2 million accounts owned by each spouse in their own names.

When the first spouse dies, the $2 million in the deceased spouse's name becomes the property of the credit shelter trust, which has the effect of preserving the first spouse's estate tax applicable credit for heirs.

Let's review how this happens. The federal estate tax on the $2 million in the credit shelter trust is $780,800 (2007). The estate tax applicable credit of $780,800 reduces the tax to zero. Thus, the $2 million in the credit shelter trust escapes federal estate tax on the first death.

Further, because the credit shelter trust is not considered part of the surviving spouse's estate, the $2 million in the trust would not be part of his or her taxable estate. Thus, when the second spouse dies, the heirs receive the full value of the credit shelter trust (no matter how much it has grown since the first spouse's death) free of estate taxes.

The remainder of the surviving spouse's estate of $4 million is taxed as follows. The tentative tax on $4 million is $1,680,811 less the estate tax applicable credit of $780,800 for a federal estate tax of about $900,000. That leaves a net after tax inheritance for your children of $2 million plus $4 million minus $920,000, netting over $5 million for your heirs, instead of $4.2 million if everything you owned stayed in JTWROS ownership. Your kids would be ahead by $880,000, with just the minimum of planning on your part. If you include Connecticut taxes, the savings would be even greater.

Typically, credit shelter trusts, which are used in conjunction with the marital deduction, are set up to pay income and, perhaps, principal to a surviving spouse and to pass the assets to one's heirs after the second spouse's death.

Non-spouse Beneficiaries and Unmarried Decedents

If you are married and leave property to someone other than your spouse, or if you are single, your estate gets to claim your estate tax applicable credit against your federal estate tax. The credit essentially frees up $2 million from federal estate taxes if death occurs between 2006 and 2008 or $3.5 million if death occurs in 2009, or an unlimited amount if death occurs in 2010, when the estate tax is repealed for that year only. Connecticut estate taxes are treated differently.

Connecticut Estate Taxes

If your estate is worth more than $2 million, your estate will be subject to Connecticut estate taxes. Connecticut tax rates begin at just over 5 percent and top out at 16 percent. Connecticut's current estate tax was signed into law on June 30, 2005 by Governor Jodi Rell. The law eliminated the Connecticut Succession Tax but restored the Connecticut Estate Tax effective for decedents dying on or after January 1, 2005.

The Connecticut tax is a cliff tax, which means that the tax is figured on the entire estate, not just the amount above $2 million. If you own

$1 above $2 million at death, the entire $2,000,001 is taxed. If you own $2 million or less, your Connecticut estate tax is zero. The $2 million threshold includes gift amounts reported on any cumulative gift/estate tax returns filed during the person's lifetime.

The Connecticut estate tax unifies gift and estate taxes. One tax schedule and tax return applies to both estate and gift taxes. Each year you make a gift (except for annual gifts of $12,000 or less per donee (see Chapter 12 for more on annual gifting)), you need to file a cumulative gift and estate tax return irrespective of whether a tax is due. Connecticut tax forms are available online at www.ct.gov/drs for forms. You can also obtain forms by calling 1-860-297-4753.

Another Example

I highly recommend that you read the case study in Appendix 4-A, which is an official IRS example that demonstrates how to calculate a decedent's income tax and estate tax returns for the IRS. Pay particular attention to the interplay between income taxes and estate taxes.

Tax Planning Tips

As you think about ways to protect your estate from death taxes and leave your heirs a bigger share of the wealth you've accumulated in your lifetime, consider the following tips.

First, find a good lawyer. Talk to him or her about your goals. Don't limit yourself to saving taxes. Among other things, consider philanthropic goals and asset protection. For example, you can protect the inheritance of a child from creditors or in the event of a future divorce.

Second, review the ownership of each asset. Don't forget to look at the deeds to your real estate holdings to see how they are titled, as well as your life insurance policies and your IRA beneficiary designations.

Third, assuming you are married, consider creating a "credit shelter trust. This is a basic estate planning tool that gives you the ability to take advantage of both your and your spouse's credits, as explained above.

Fourth, consider an insurance trust. If you are healthy, you may be able to gift money to a trust for the purpose of buying life insurance that would be payable to your heirs outside of your taxable estate. Structured properly, you can pass along these assets free of gift, estate, and income taxes. See Chapter 13 for more on insurance trusts.

Fifth, if you have a large estate, consider maximizing your annual tax-free gifts. For example, because an individual can gift $12,000 each year tax free, a couple with three married children and three grandchildren can gift $216,000 free of federal and state estate, gift, and income taxes. (Each spouse gives $12,000 a year to each of nine people—three children and their spouses plus three grandchildren—for a total of $108,000, or $216,000 for both spouses.)

Gifting at or below the $12,000 threshold does not trigger a requirement to file the Connecticut tax return and is not counted when totaling the Connecticut $2 million lifetime gift and estate tax exemption. See Chapter 12 for more on annual gifting.

Summary

Remember that you have a choice when it comes to estate planning. You can pay Uncle Sam or you can pay your beneficiaries. With thoughtful planning and competent legal counsel, you can protect your assets for your family.

Chapter 5

Moving Out of State to Avoid Connecticut Estate Taxes

There is no question that wealthy Connecticut residents are moving out of state to avoid Connecticut estate taxes. One popular state for such a move is Florida, where there is no income tax and no estate tax.

A move to Florida can mean considerable tax savings for wealthy Connecticut residents. For example, a Connecticut resident with a $10 million estate can save about half a million dollars by changing his or her residence to Florida. (A Connecticut resident would be taxed roughly $4.2 million ($1 million to Connecticut plus $3.2 million to the IRS, using 2006 – 2008 rates), while a Florida resident would owe only federal estate taxes of about $3.6 million. (The federal tax bill for Connecticut is not identical to Florida in this example, since the Florida resident does not get a deduction for Connecticut estate taxes.)

That's a substantial enough savings to encourage people with a lot of money to move out of Connecticut. For those with estates of $2 million or less, such a move would not make economic sense, since there is no Connecticut estate tax for estates under $2 million (and no federal tax). However, if you are near the $2 million dollar mark, you don't want to dismiss the merits of changing your domicile — Connecticut's estate tax is a cliff tax (if you have a dollar above $2 million, Connecticut taxes the full $2,000,001). The IRS only taxes the $1.

Proof of Domicile

If you do decide to move to Florida (or any other state) to avoid Connecticut estate taxes, your heirs will have to prove you were no longer a resident of Connecticut, and this takes more than simply proving that you lived out of state for more than six months, as many people mistakenly believe.

Form C-3

If you are thinking of changing residence from Connecticut to another state, you should study "Connecticut Domicile Declaration" (Form C-3). The Connecticut Department of Revenue Services (DRS) requires that this form be filed when residency is in issue for estate or income tax purposes.

Normally, Form C-3 is filed in probate court along with the estate tax return when the estate is over $2 million and the non-resident owns Connecticut real estate. Connecticut property belonging to non-residents passes to heirs through a probate proceeding called "ancillary administration."

Form C-3 calls for a lot of detailed information about what the decedent was doing in and outside of Connecticut for five years before his or her death. Specifically, the state of Connecticut wants to know:

1. Where the decedent voted,
2. Where income tax, property tax, and intangible tax returns were filed and taxes paid,
3. Whether the decedent filed resident or non-resident returns,
4. The address the decedent used on federal tax returns,
5. The business activities he or she engaged in inside and outside Connecticut,
6. Whether he or she was a party to a lawsuit in Connecticut,
7. Whether he or she held any memberships in religious organizations, clubs, or societies in Connecticut or outside Connecticut,
8. The name and address of the bank where the decedent's safe deposit box was located,

9. Professional licenses, drivers licenses, business licenses, and boat licenses, including the date of issuance, the state of issuance, and the license numbers,
10. Automobile registrations,
11. Hospitalizations and medical treatment or examinations in Connecticut, along with the name and address of the doctor and dates of treatment,
12. The place of death and burial,
13. Copies of obituaries printed in newspapers in Connecticut and elsewhere,
14. The name and address of the bank to which the decedent's Social Security payments were deposited,
15. The number of days the decedent "actually stayed" in Connecticut
16. The number of days the decedent actually stayed in the state he or she is claiming as a residence, and
17. Whether the decedent executed a declaration of domicile in another state.

Documentation

Assuming Connecticut's DRS claims the decedent is a Connecticut resident, you will need to prove otherwise by providing appropriate documentation, such as voter registration card; logs of incoming and outgoing visits to a gated community, if the decedent resided in one; records of doctors' appointments; and credit card statements showing restaurant bills, gas, flights, car maintenance, and the like.

If you look at the list, you may wonder if any particular item has any more weight than another. For instance, what if the decedent met all the other requirements but died in Connecticut in a car accident while visiting friends? One can expect that no one factor will weigh more heavily than others and that all the circumstances will be taken into account when a determination is made by the DRS. However, you can be sure that owning real estate in Connecticut will always attract additional scrutiny, since one would suspect that there is additional activity in the state that might give rise to a finding of domicile.

Summary

Moving out of state to avoid Connecticut estate taxes is a big step. Before attempting to change your residence, review your plan with your accountant or attorney. If you need help understanding Form C-3, call the DRS at 800-382-9463 if you are in Connecticut. From out of state, call 860-297-5962. You can find Form C-3 online at www.ct.gov/drs.

PART II – PROBLEMS TO AVOID

Chapter 6

What Happens If You Die Without a Will?

Only one out of every two American adults has a will. I would venture that most people without wills a) don't want to face up to their mortality, b) don't think they need a will, or c) don't realize that after they are gone, their families will need to wind up their affairs for them, sometimes with unforeseen results, costs, delays, and unnecessary frustration.

In Connecticut, when a person dies without a will, the laws of "intestacy" determine who gets what. The results depend on your family structure (see the chart at the end of this chapter).

Let's consider a few hypothetical examples beginning with married couples with and without children, followed by unmarried individuals.

Married Couple with Children

John and June are in their 30s, having been married five years. They have two young children, an infant and a 3 year old. John and June have equity of $200,000 in a home worth $600,000 that they own in joint name "with right of survivorship," a joint bank account with $20,000, and a brokerage account in John's name alone with $240,000 of stocks that he inherited from his grandmother.

There is employer life insurance of $90,000 on John's life, with an additional death benefit of $90,000 in the event of accidental death. June is the beneficiary named in the policy.

In addition, John has a 401(k) at work valued at $3,000, naming June his beneficiary, and another $50,000 IRA that he started with a 401(k) rollover before he got married, naming no beneficiaries. June, a stay-at-home mom, has a $4,000 IRA naming John her beneficiary. The $400,000 mortgage is in John's name alone. John also has a checking account in his own name with a balance of $3,000. Both own cars in their own names.

Neither Has a Will

John and June are driving home one Saturday evening and their car is hit by a drunk driver. John is killed. June survives.

Even though John has no will, certain assets will pass directly to his widow, June: the house, because it is in joint name with right of survivorship; the life insurance benefit of $180,000 (June is the beneficiary); and John's $3,000 401(k), because June is his beneficiary.

To access these assets, June will have to get copies of the death certificate from the town clerk and submit them, along with the appropriate paperwork, to the custodians of the assets.

The insurance company will require a claim form. John's 401(k) administrator will require notification and instructions on what June would like done with the 401(k). The real estate will have to be re-titled in June's name alone and a new title recorded at the town clerk's office. All of these assets will pass directly to June outside of the probate process.

The remaining assets are John's checking account of $3,000, his car (worth $8,000), his $50,000 IRA (no beneficiary), and his $240,000 brokerage account. Together these total $311,000. These holdings will pass to John's heirs through probate in accordance with the laws of intestacy.

Under the Connecticut laws of intestacy, June will receive the first $100,000 plus one-half of the remainder. Thus, June will receive $100,000 plus ½ of $211,000 ($105,500), less fees that the probate court will charge for the settling of the estate (approximately $1,150) and legal fees. The remainder will pass directly to the children, even though they are very young.

The court will appoint a guardian to manage the children's assets for them. The guardian may be June, but not necessarily so. When the children reach the age of 18, the guardian's authority will cease and the assets will be placed under the children's direct control. For more information about guardianships in Connecticut, read "Guidelines for Guardianships of Minors," which is reprinted in Appendix 6-A.

Neither federal nor Connecticut estate taxes will be due for this estate. No federal estate tax return will have to be filed with the IRS. However, a Form CT-706 NT (Connecticut Estate Tax Return for Non-Taxable Estates) must be filed with the probate court within nine months of the date of death. This return is used by the probate court to calculate probate fees.

Married with No Children

Childless married couples with no wills need to be alert to the *in-law factor.* According to Connecticut law, when one spouse dies and the couple has no children (or grandchildren), and the deceased spouse has no will, the surviving spouse gets the first $100,000 plus 75 percent of the remainder of the estate. The rest of the estate goes to the deceased spouse's parents.

Some people feel motivated to draw up a will when they have children, in order to name a guardian for the children in the event of their death. But clearly, married couples without children have an even greater reason to have a will: without a will, a surviving spouse will have to share the deceased spouse's property with his or her in-laws.

Avoiding the in-law factor should be a great incentive to have a will.

Single

According to Connecticut law, if you are single with children, upon your death everything goes to them. If you have no children, your parents are your heirs. If you have no will, no spouse, no children (or descendants), and no parents living at the time of your death, your estate goes to your brothers and sisters equally. If they are not living, then everything goes to your next of kin (aunts, uncles, cousins, etc.), and if you have none, the state of Connecticut gets your estate.

The Probate Process

When someone dies, whether with or without a will, potential heirs need to be identified for the court. If the deceased was married at the time of death, the names and addresses of the surviving spouse and living and deceased children (and children of any deceased child) will need to be provided. If there is a surviving spouse but no children, the names and addresses of the deceased's parents will need to be provided.

For those who are not married and have no children, the names of the parents need to be provided to the court. If the parents are deceased, then the names of brothers and sisters and children of deceased brothers and sisters must be provided. If there are none, then the names of uncles and aunts must be provided; and if none, then first cousins; and if none, then second cousins, and so on.

Finding the Decedent's Will

If a relative dies and no one in the family is aware of a will, be sure to search for one. Look for safety deposit boxes and check with the relative's lawyer. If you run into a dead-end, go to the lawyer who handled the closing on the relative's house, no matter how long ago that might have occurred. Chances are good that if the relative has a will, the same lawyer who handled the closing on his or her home also prepared the will – a will does not expire unless it is replaced with a new will.

If you do find a safety deposit box, the bank will not give you access unless you provide an order from the probate court. When you take the order to the bank, an officer of the bank will open the box for you and take an inventory of the contents. If you find a will, you will need to take it to probate court immediately for probating. It is a crime to withhold a will.

Naming an Executor

There are many reasons why it is important to draw up a will, not the least of which is naming an executor to handle your affairs after your death. It is not unusual for family members to feud over who should handle this responsibility and the probate court may well appoint a bank or other disinterested party in lieu of a family member.

Summary

If you would like to review the Connecticut laws of intestacy, go to the reference section of this book and read "The Probate Court and You," an official publication of the Connecticut Probate Courts (see Appendix 1-B). For an overview of the importance of wills, read "Wills: Why You Should Have One and the Lawyer's Role in Its Preparation," which is reproduced for you in Appendix 6-B.

The following table summarizes how Connecticut intestacy laws work.

If the decedent is survived by:	The property goes to:
Spouse, and children of both decedent and spouse	Spouse takes first $100,000 and ½ of the remainder. Children take the other ½
Spouse, and children of the decedent, one or more of whom is not the child of the spouse	Spouse takes ½. All the children share in the other ½ equally
Spouse and parent or parents (no children)	Spouse takes first $100,000 plus ¾ of the remainder. Parent(s) take the other ¼.
Spouse only (no children, no parents)	Spouse takes all
Children only (no spouse)	All goes to the children
Parent(s) (no spouse, no children)	All goes to the parents
Brothers and sisters (no spouse, no parents, no children)	All goes to the brothers and sisters
Next of kin (no spouse, no children, no parents, no brothers, no sisters)	All goes to the next of kin

If there is no next of kin, but there is a step child, he or she will be next in line. If there is no step child, then all goes to the state of Connecticut.	
"Children" = if the child died before the decedent, his or her descendants may take instead.	

Chapter 7

What Happens If You Become Disabled or Incapacitated?

Who would take care of you and your financial affairs if you suddenly become incapacitated and unable to make health care decisions, to work, or even to sign a check? A debilitating stroke or even a bicycle accident can leave you in that position.

Everyone over the age of 18 (legal age in Connecticut) would benefit from executing an "advance directive," a legal document that sets out an individual's wishes and protects his or her rights in the event of incapacity.

An advance directive tells your physician whether to provide life support and authorizes the person you appoint to make health care decisions for you if you are unable to do so ("health care attorney-in-fact" or "health care agent"). The directive should also contain a HIPAA release (Health Insurance Portability and Accountability Act of 1996), giving the health care agent access to your medical records when needed.

The advance directive should be signed in the presence of two witnesses. You should keep the original in a safe place and give copies to the health care representative you named in the directive, your doctor, and appropriate family members. If you are scheduled for a medical procedure, bring a copy to the hospital.

An advance directive alone is not enough. You also need to talk with your family about your wishes so that they are prepared to act on the directive. To help you prepare for a talk, take a look at the recommended scripts on the American Bar Association's Web site at www.abanet.org/aging/toolkit/home.html (see tool #6). That site will also help you through the decision-making process, from how to select a health care agent to setting personal priorities. You will also see guidelines for health care agents on the site.

Power of Attorney

You may also need a "power of attorney," a document you sign to give authority to your agent ("attorney in fact") to act on your behalf. It's best to state in the document that your agent is authorized to act on your behalf even if you are incapacitated ("durable power of attorney")[2]. To meet the requirements of the Connecticut statute on the subject, include the following language: "This power of attorney shall not be affected by the subsequent disability or incompetence of the principal."

Living Trust

Instead of a durable power of attorney, your lawyer could establish a trust for you that springs into action should you become incapacitated. There would have to be a means of transferring your property into the

---

[2] **Sec. 45a-562. (Formerly Sec. 45-69o). Power of attorney to survive disability or incompetence.** (a) The subsequent disability or incompetence of a principal shall not revoke or terminate the authority of any person who acts under a power of attorney in a writing executed by the principal, if the writing contains the words "this power of attorney shall not be affected by the subsequent disability or incompetence of the principal," or words of similar import showing the intent of the principal that the authority conferred shall be exercisable notwithstanding the principal's subsequent disability or incompetence; provided the power of attorney is executed and witnessed in the same manner as provided for deeds in section 47-5.

(b) If a conservator of the estate of the principal is appointed after the occurrence of the disability or incompetence referred to in subsection (a) of this section, the power of attorney shall cease at the time of the appointment, and the person acting under the power of attorney shall account to the conservator rather than to the principal.

trust at incapacity, or the trust would have to be in existence and funded before incapacity.

Trusts are more costly than powers of attorney, but assuming the trust is drafted and executed properly, there may be more certainty in a trust. A financial institution will recognize a trustee's authority, no matter how old the trust. That may not be the case with a power of attorney – the issue is whether the power was subsequently revoked. Be sure to talk to your attorney before deciding which option is best for your circumstances. There are advantages and disadvantages to each.

When There Is No Provision for Incapacity

If you become incapacitated but have made no provisions for your care, the probate court may be required to step in and appoint a "conservator." A conservator will supervise your affairs if you are incapable of doing so. Once a conservator is appointed, the conservator takes over under the watchful eye of the court.

Conservators can be traced back to English Common Law, when the king would authorize a writ to summon a commission to undertake an inquiry, usually in cases of "lunacy" or "idiocy," explains Erin Arcesi in "Conservatorships and Marriage," 16 Quinnipiac Probate Law Journal 296 (2003). The proceeding established the right of the Crown to take over the person's property and provide for his or her care.

After 1875 the standard for appointing a conservator was a finding that the person is incapable of taking care of himself or herself or managing his or her affairs and may arise from debauched habits or habitual drunkenness.

The definition was modified over the years, and after 1977, "incapacity" meant a person who cannot manage his affairs due to a mental, emotional, or physical condition resulting from mental illness or deficiency, physical illness or disability, chronic use of drugs, alcohol, or confinement (Connecticut General Statutes section 45a-644(c)).

If a person is incapable of caring for himself or managing his affairs, someone (usually a family member) applies to the court to be appointed conservator. In Connecticut, anyone who believes someone is incapable of caring for him or herself may file an application for appointment of conservator in the probate court where the incapable person (respondent) resides.

A state marshal visits the respondent and serves him or her with a notice of the hearing. The respondent's spouse also receives a notice. An attorney is appointed to represent the respondent, if he or she cannot afford one of his or her own. The respondent has a right to be present.

The hearing usually takes place within 30 days of the application. At the hearing, the judge considers medical evidence presented by the applicant and other evidence, such as testimony of family, friends, and caretakers. The court can also order a fresh examination by another physician.

The standard for a finding of incapacity is quite high. There must be clear and convincing evidence of incapacity. If the court finds that the respondent cannot take care of him or herself, the court appoints a "conservator of the person." If he or she cannot manage his or her financial affairs, the court appoints a "conservator of the estate." The appointment nullifies any existing powers of attorney.

Once a conservator is appointed, the respondent is referred to as the conservator's "ward." The conservator is considered a trustee under the law and must act in the sole interest of the ward. The probate court oversees the relationship through hearings and periodic accountings.

Bond

The conservator must obtain a probate bond in the amount of the ward's estate to guarantee protection of the ward's assets. The court can accept a lower amount if the conservator agrees to a restriction on the control of some of the assets. A bond can be purchased through an insurance agent. The amount of the bond is set by the court, taking into account the financial wherewithal of both the applicant and the ward and their relationship. Depending on the size of the bond, some insurers require the applicant to supply his financial statement to the insurer.

What can the conservator do? A "conservator of the person" is an arm or agent of the court and has the duty and the responsibility for the general custody of the ward, including the duty to provide the care, comfort, and maintenance of the ward, to care for the ward's personal effects, and the duty to report to the probate court on the ward's condition.

A "conservator of the estate" has the authority to manage the estate and the net income required to support the ward. The conservator can sue for collection of debts. He or she is required to file an inventory of the estate with the probate court.

A conservatorship ends when the ward recovers and can take care of him or herself, at which time the court enters an order to terminate the conservatorship and the property is returned to the ward.

Summary

The Probate Court Administrator for the State of Connecticut publishes a pamphlet called "Guidelines for Conservators," which I recommend you read. You can find a copy in the reference section of this book (see Appendix 7-A).

If you want more information on how to write an advance directive, go to http://www.abanet.org/publiced/practical/directive_writing.html. A sample advance directive prepared by Cummings & Lockwood, LLC, is provided in the reference section of this book (see Appendix 7-B).

For more information on powers of attorney, go to http://www.abanet.org/rppt/public/power-of-atty.html#powerofattorney. A sample Connecticut durable power of attorney that springs into effect at incapacity is provided in the reference section (see Appendix 7-C).

Chapter 8

Will Your Will Cause a Lawsuit?

When someone dies, heirs, beneficiaries, and creditors all have a stake in how that person's estate is wound up. If any of these stakeholders feels his or her interests are not represented fairly in the administration of the estate, conflicts can surface.

Here are a few examples of the types of conflicts that are brought before probate courts for resolution.

- Upon a husband's death, the wife knows that the husband had a lawyer draft a will a couple of years before, but no one can find the will. In a will that he executed before their marriage, he left everything to his brother. Now the brother is filing the earlier will in probate court.
- A divorced woman remarried, but never got around to putting her new husband into her will or naming him as the beneficiary of his or her life insurance policy.
- Jim and Mary live together but never marry. Jim dies without a will.
- John's will provides for three of his four children. When John dies, the fourth child challenges the will.
- The executor of Jane's will divides her jewelry in a way that is unacceptable to one of Jane's children.
- Heirs wonder if the executor is paying him or herself too much.

- The beneficiaries of a decedent's testamentary trust don't like the trustee.

Avoiding Challenges to Your Will

One of the best ways to avoid a lawsuit challenging your will is to make your estate planning documents crystal clear, leaving no room for interpretation. (See Chapter 20, "What Can Be Wrong with a Will?" for more on this topic.)

Careful drafting of a will can eliminate a lot of confusion and avoid some lawsuits, but not all. For example, if you want to leave a smaller bequest to one child, that child may want to challenge your will. Were you of sound mind when you executed the will? Did your other children put pressure on you to favor them?

Another challenge can simply be that the lawyer made a mistake when drafting the will. To negate such an argument, specifically state your intentions in the will. For example, if you want to disinherit a child, specifically name that child and state that it is your intention to leave him or her out of the will.

Successful Challenges to a Will

In Connecticut, if a will is successfully challenged and invalidated in its entirety, your probate assets would pass as if you had no will, and your heirs would receive their share based on the laws of intestacy.

For example, if you are widowed with two children but you disinherited one child, the disinherited child could claim one-half of your probate estate. If you are married with no children, your spouse receives the first $100,000 plus three-fourths of the remainder. Your parents would receive the rest. (For more information on intestacy, read Chapter 6 and refer to Appendix 1-B, "The Probate Court and You.")

Some attorneys will warn their clients about potential challenges if they are making unequal distributions to their children. While steps can be taken to minimize the chances of litigation, you can never really eliminate the possibility.

Leaving a Spouse Out of a Will

If you leave your spouse out of your will, expect a challenge. Surviving spouses are protected under a Connecticut statute that provides for an "elective share" or a "statutory share" (Connecticut Generate Statutes 45a-436), providing the disinherited spouse with lifelong income on one-third of the *probate estate*.

As you know from Chapter 1, you can easily put most if not all of your assets in non-probate form and circumvent the protection of the statutory share. For example, if you re-titled all of your assets into joint name with your children, you would have no probate estate. With no probate estate, the spouse's elective share is zero.

Because of the potential for completely and easily disinheriting a spouse, members of the Connecticut Bar Association are proposing legislative changes to broaden the base off of which the elective share is computed.

Poorly Drafted Wills

Poorly drafted wills can also cause lawsuits. In a Connecticut case *(Cornell v. Cornell)*, the issue revolved around the meaning of this provision in the testator's will: "I give, devise, and bequeath one-third in value of all my estate, both real and person, wherever situated . . . to my wife."

You would think this provision was clear enough, but consider this: did the testator mean to give one-third of the net estate (net of taxes) or one-third of the gross estate? The taxes were over $700,000.

The wife's attorney's position was that the one-third should not be reduced by taxes. In support of his argument, he pointed to another article of the will which seemingly provided the answer: "all estate, succession, inheritance, and transfer taxes . . . shall be paid out of the residuary estate as an expense of the settlement of my estate."

The probate court did not agree. Because of the ambiguity, the court looked to evidence outside of the will and concluded the "one-third" meant one-third of the estate diminished not only by the federal and Connecticut taxes but also by its share of the debts, executors' and attorneys' fees, funeral, and administration expenses.

To resolve ambiguities, a good tax clause should expressly state 1) what gifts or beneficiaries are freed of the burden of taxes, 2) what taxes are affected, and 3) where the burden of taxes is shifted.

The use of a vague clause invites a lawsuit. Careful drafting of all clauses of a will can go a long way toward avoiding disputes and litigation.

Appeals

A benefit of the probate system is that anyone who has an interest can be heard. Any interested party not satisfied with the decision of the probate court may have a second chance to litigate the matter in Connecticut Superior Court by filing an appeal within 30 days of the probate court's decision. As with any litigation, the expenses of such an action can add up.

Undue Influence

One common reason for contesting a will is a claim of "undue influence." Let me give you a real life example of a will contest based on undue influence. As you read on, you will notice the type of evidence the court considered. Notice the stakeholders' interests.

Undue influence is the "exercise of sufficient control over a person in an attempt to destroy his free agency and constrain him to do something other than he would do under normal control." To show undue influence, you need: 1) a person who is subject to influence, 2) an opportunity to exert undue influence, 3) a disposition to exert undue influence, and 4) a result indicating undue influence. Let me illustrate through an example.

Consider this recent case (the parties' names have been changed). Marcia (the plaintiff) alleged that her husband, George (the testator), was under the undue influence of his daughter Anne when he executed a codicil to his will in anticipation of his marriage to Marcia. The codicil did not provide for Marcia.

If Marcia won the will contest by showing the codicil was executed under undue influence, she would get one-half of the estate under the laws of intestacy. If she lost, Marcia would get nothing.

Let's review the facts. On December 4, 1997, two days before his marriage to Marcia, George executed a codicil to his will stating, "I am executing this instrument in anticipation of my marriage to Marcia on December 7, 1997 and direct that my marriage subsequent to the execution hereof shall not be construed to revoke my will—except as previously specified in my codicil, my will shall continue in full force and effect." The will did not provide for the contingency of marriage and it left all of George's estate to his daughter, Anne, and his three grandchildren.

George died on June 21, 2000.

At trial, Marcia testified that she was unaware that her husband executed the codicil until their honeymoon. When counsel for Marcia inquired further as to the conversation, counsel for Anne objected and the jury was excused. Marcia made the following offer of proof:

[Marcia's Counsel]: "Could you ··· tell the court what the conversation was with [George] when you found out about the codicil ··· the evening after you got married?" ···

[Marcia]: "He said to me, I made a power of attorney to (a relative) and I did a codicil to my will. And I said, how come? And he said, well, in case anything happened to me, he said, I had to give somebody the authority, and I didn't want to give it to Anne. And he said that Anne raised such holy hell about making a codicil that I had to make the codicil. He said a couple of more things after that, but...."

[Marcia's Counsel]: "What else did he say?"

[Marcia]: "He said that she threatened him. She wouldn't come to the wedding. She wouldn't bring the grandchildren to the wedding. She was never going to see him again. She wouldn't let the grandchildren have any contact with him or see him. She wouldn't give him the papers that he needed because there was a problem at the [convalescent home George owned]. The state was investigating and the state's attorney's office was getting involved."

[Marcia's Counsel]: "She had records of his?"

[Marcia]: "Yes, she did."

[Marcia's Counsel]: "And she said she wouldn't—and he told you that she told him that she wouldn't give him the records?"

[Marcia]: "That's right. And [George's attorney] had problems getting the documents from her that were needed to protect [the convalescent home] from payback to the state of Connecticut for the problems that she [Anne] had created." ····

[Marcia's Counsel]: "This was told to you on Sunday night?"

[Marcia]: "Sunday night."

Anne's counsel objected to this testimony, arguing that George's statements were inadmissible. Marcia's counsel responded that George's statements were being offered not for the truth of the matter asserted, but as proof of George's state of mind when he executed the codicil several days before making the statements.

After the jury returned, Marcia was allowed to testify as follows regarding the conversation she had with George:

[Marcia's Counsel]: "Did [George] say he had a conversation with [Anne]?"

[Marcia]: "Yes."

* * *

[Marcia's Counsel]: "Did he say how he felt or what he feared or anything of that nature as a result of these conversations with [Anne]?"

[Marcia]: "He was afraid that she would—he would not see her, he would not see his grandchildren, she would not give him the documents that he needed because the state was investigating [the convalescent home] .... He was frightened and he said [that] that's what he was afraid of."

[Marcia's Counsel]: "And did he say that fear had anything to do with signing the codicil?"

[Marcia]: "Yes, that's the reason he did."

* * *

[Marcia's Counsel]: ... "Did you have any further conversation about that on the honeymoon?"

[Marcia]: "He said he was sorry he did it."

[Marcia's Counsel]: "Okay. Anything else?"

[Marcia]: "He said that he'd take care of it when we came back from the honeymoon."

Marcia's counsel sought to introduce testimony by a handyman and driver frequently employed by George, recounting the substance of a conversation he testified that he had overheard between George and Anne in George's office during the days immediately preceding the execution of the codicil. Anne previously had testified that she had not been to see George for at least three months prior to his executing the codicil.

The court allowed the handyman to testify as to what he had observed, but again excluded testimony about words Anne actually used. Then the handyman testified that he had observed a loud argument between George and Anne, and that George used words to the effect of "don't threaten me, don't yell at me."

Marcia did not succeed in proving undue influence and lost her case. There was also testimony at trial that George drafted and executed a later will leaving one-half of his estate to Marcia. Unfortunately for Marcia, that will never was found.

Summary

Understanding some of these cases may help realize the importance of good drafting and anticipating will challenges. It is of utmost importance that you read your will and trusts to be sure that you understand what your lawyer drafted. If something is not clear to you, in all likelihood it will not be clear to an interested party who may lay a challenge.

Chapter 9

What If Your Executor Has Problems Settling Your Estate?

Many people name their spouses or children as executors of their wills, or even their lawyers. To give you an idea of what can go wrong, let me tell you about a 2005 New Hampshire case involving stock losses.

Monsignor NB, a 48-year-old New Hampshire resident, was killed on September 30, 2000 while riding his motorcycle to church to celebrate mass. At the time of his death, he held securities in fifteen publicly traded companies valued at over $6.5 million, subject to margin debt of nearly $4 million. (Margin debt is a loan from the brokerage firm used to fund the purchase of the stock.) Nearly $3 million represented two stocks, Cisco Systems and Sun Microsystems.

In his will, Monsignor NB left all his property to his parents. He named his best friend, Father S, executor of his will. When the value of the stocks fell dramatically, Father S's actions (and inaction) as the executor were challenged by the beneficiaries, Monsignor NB's parents.

Here is a chronology of the events. Father S was notified by the Diocese that he was nominated executor on October 2, just a few days after Monsignor NB's death. The Diocese informed Father S that he would be hearing from the law firm representing the estate to set up a meeting with him.

On October 23, having not heard anything from the law firm, Father S placed a call to the firm and made an appointment to meet on October

26, taking with him a stack of Monsignor NB's unopened mail to open and review with the law firm. Included in the unopened mail were urgent notices of margin calls from the brokerage firms holding the rapidly declining stocks.

The law firm prepared a petition for estate administration and mailed it to the court on November 1. The petition was received by the court on November 3. On November 13, the will was allowed and the petition granted to appoint Father S the executor, on the condition that Father S obtain a fiduciary bond for $2.2 million. (At the time, the law firm thought that $2.2 million was the size of the estate.) The bond was received by the court for filing on December 1 and a certificate of appointment was mailed to Father S on December 6.

By the end of November, the law firm had started communicating with the brokerage houses. However, the law firm, according to court records, "frequently sent the wrong paperwork to the brokerage houses, or sent the correct paperwork to the wrong brokerage house address. To further compound matters, on at least one occasion, a brokerage house failed to respond once it had finally received the correct paperwork and then later lost the package altogether."

Throughout this time, mail containing margin calls kept coming (nine notices were delivered in October, eight in November, and thirty-seven in December). Father S brought the unopened mail to the firm representing Monsignor NB's estate for their review.

All of the accounts were finally liquidated about six months after Monsignor NB died. In the end, the value of the stock accounts had fallen to just under $500,000 from $6.5 million at the date of death (September 30). The greatest devaluation took place between early November and mid-December 2000—within six weeks of Monsignor NB's death, the period during which Father S was petitioning for authority to act as executor.

Monsignor NB's parents went to probate court arguing that Father S did not act in time to prevent losses, given the state of the stock market.

The probate court agreed with the parents and "surcharged" Father S in the amount of $1,256,000 with interest of 5 percent calculated from November 27, 2000 through April 15, 2005 (the date of the court's order). A surcharge is the penalty for failure to exercise common prudence, common skill, and common caution in the performance of the fiduciary's duty and is imposed to compensate beneficiaries for loss caused by the fiduciary's lack of care.

The court reasoned that Father S did not act with urgency, even after prodding by the attorneys in late November to sell the stocks. The court concluded that at the latest, by November 27, 2000, Father S should have completely assessed the situation and disposed of the securities.

Father S claimed that he should be shielded from the surcharge because he relied on the law firm representing the estate. The court disagreed, stating that Father S could not be relieved from liability because he did not "properly supervise" the law firm. The court agreed that the law firm failed to act "as it should have," but nonetheless determined that Father S was not relieved of his responsibility as a dutiful executor. He never transitioned from his role as a friend of Monsignor NB into his role of "captain of the estate," said the court.

Father S and the company issuing the bond both challenged the court's decision, arguing the court "created an unrealistic and unattainable standard for all executors of estates." The court disagreed. In November of 2005, the court issued an order affirming the decision, reasoning that special or expedited administration should have been sought by the executor because of the unique circumstances—namely that margin calls for thousands of dollars, ultimately totaling millions of dollars, were issuing with frequency.

"But for Father S's failure to timely collect and review (Monsignor NB's) mail . . . his attorneys' failure to assess the urgency of the situation and more aggressively seek authority to administer the estate beyond the routine, the loss to the estate for which he has been surcharged would not have occurred," said the court in its November 8, 2005 order. "After a (friend) dies, an executor often must labor over hard decisions and work diligently toward resolution, despite natural and understandable feelings of loss and devotion to the confidant and close friend," said the court. Thus, Father S was held liable for $1,256,000 (called a "surcharge"), plus 5 percent interest.

Father S paid himself $4,000 out of the estate for his services as an executor. However, the court found this amount excessive, and reduced his fee to $1,500. The court also found the law firm's fees excessive, reducing them from $55,074 to $35,000.

Summary

Whether you have been named executor of an estate or are making a decision about whom to name as executor of your estate, it's important to be as informed on the topic as possible. For a good resource explaining the legal responsibilities of executors, administrators, and trustees, skip the bookstore. Books written for the layperson tend to be too simplistic when it comes to this topic. Instead, read "Fiduciary Liability Issues," by Dominic J. Campisi of Evans, Latham, and Campisi, P.C., San Francisco in the February 10, 2005 issue of *The American Law Institute.* This article discusses such concepts as the executor's duty to take reasonable care in selecting and overseeing agents, including accountants and legal counsel. You can get a copy of the article online at www.ali-aba.org.

Chapter 10

How to Deal with a Dissatisfactory Trustee

If you are the beneficiary of a trust, you should expect your trustee to be responsive to your concerns, questions, and needs. If you are unable to communicate with the trustee or are unsatisfied with the trustee's responsiveness to your concerns, the trustee may not be right for you.

Example

Take this example based on a dilemma described to me by one of my readers. Mary (not her real name) and her sister, Joan, are the sole beneficiaries of a trust their mother set up in her will. The mother named her local bank as trustee because she knew and respected the trust officer, whom I will call Frank.

After the mother's death, the bank was acquired by a large bank, and its character changed from a friendly local organization that knew its customers to a large impersonal institution.

Before the acquisition, Mary would talk to Frank whenever she had any concerns or questions about the trust. After the acquisition, Frank was reassigned. Now Mary found that she had to leave numerous messages before someone would return her calls and no one seemed to know the status of the trust.

Soon Mary and Joan were dissatisfied with how they were being treated by the bank. After unsuccessfully attempting to improve the situation, Mary read the trust documents to see if the trustee could be removed. No such luck. The trust document did not provide for the removal and replacement of the trustee. Until recently, Mary would have had no recourse unless the trustee could have been persuaded to resign.

New Laws Permit Removal

Until recently, the general rule was that you could not remove the trustee unless the trust document itself provided for removal and replacement. The rationale behind this rule was that if the grantor had wanted the beneficiary to have the power to remove the trustee without cause, he or she would have written that into the trust document. The probate court could always remove a trustee for cause, such as fraud or breach of fiduciary duty.

Since 2001, when the Connecticut legislature broadened the situations under which a trustee could be removed, it is now possible for a probate court to remove and replace the trustee for beneficiaries in the position of our two sisters.

The sisters would have to show that they met the requirements of Connecticut General Statutes Section 45a-242(a)(4), which allows removal of a trustee if "there has been a substantial change of circumstances or removal is requested by all of the beneficiaries, the court finds that removal of the fiduciary best serves the interest of all the beneficiaries and is not inconsistent with a material purpose of the governing instrument, and a suitable co-fiduciary or successor fiduciary is available."

Under this statute, removal of an uncommunicative and non-responsive trustee is possible if all the elements of the statute can be met. If you do proceed to have a trustee removed under this statute, both current *and* future (yes, future) beneficiaries need to be involved in the request to seek a replacement trustee.

What is a future beneficiary? Let me give you an example. A trust can provide for "income to my wife, Theresa, for as long as she lives, and at her death, principal to my daughter, Caroline, or, if not then living, to her children then living in equal shares." Caroline may not survive Theresa, but may have children who do survive Theresa. These unborn children are the future beneficiaries that could be remainder beneficiaries of the trust. Their interests need to be protected.

Virtual Representation

A future beneficiary can be represented by another beneficiary under the concept known as "virtual representation." In my example, Caroline could represent her future children. Under section 45a-487d of the Connecticut General Statutes, "A minor, incapacitated or unborn individual, or a person whose identity or location is unknown and not reasonably ascertainable, may be represented by and bound by another person having a substantially identical interest with respect to the particular question or dispute, but only to the extent there is no conflict of interest between the representative and the person being represented."

The Removal Process

If you find yourself working with a trustee with whom you are dissatisfied, consult an experienced trusts and estates attorney to advise you of your options. If your dissatisfaction arises out of a change in income – perhaps your checks stopped coming – you will definitely want to talk to a lawyer if you don't get satisfactory answers from the trustee. Payment stoppage could arise out of an administrative matter (a change of address or undelivered mail), excessive expenses, poor judgment (bad investments), grave conflict of interest (excessive payments to the trustee), or outright lawlessness (theft or embezzlement).

Depending on the problem and the type of trust, your attorney will suggest different options. While removal might be the best solution in some cases, the probate courts have other mechanisms in place short of removal. Keep in mind that one of the probate court's functions is to address wrongs done to beneficiaries and to supervise fiduciaries.

Testamentary Trusts and Accountings

In the case of testamentary trusts (trusts that are set up in a will and become effective at death), Connecticut requires judicial accountings every three years, unless accountings are waived in the will. (When the will is drafted, the testator can add a provision that says statutory accountings are waived.)

Trusts that take effect during one's lifetime (*inter vivos* trusts) are not subject to this accounting requirement, but any interested party (beneficiary, trustee, or creditor) can file a petition with the court to request an accounting.

Legal accountings give beneficiaries protection. The trustee is responsible for filing the accounting and reporting on all activity in the trust during the accounting period, including all principal and income, gains and losses, expenses, fees, and distributions made to beneficiaries. The court reviews the accounting, gives notice to beneficiaries and other interested parties, holds a hearing, allows parties to file formal written objections, supervises discovery, holds evidentiary hearings, and after deliberation, issues decrees. When satisfied that all is in order, the court enters a decree that discharges the trustee's responsibilities for the period under review.

Preventing Removal

If you are contemplating setting up a trust and want to prevent your beneficiaries from successfully petitioning the court to remove the trustee sometime in the future, add a clause in the trust making it clear that your intent is to prohibit the replacement of a trustee. Such a clause might state: "I have selected my trustee with care and as a material purpose in creating this trust, having taken into account my trustee's familiarity with my objectives in creating the trust, my trustee's personal interest in assisting me to attain those objectives, and my trustee's qualifications for doing so. Therefore it is my intent herein and I hereby direct that my trustee not be removed except for cause as determined by a court of competent jurisdiction."

Summary

If you are the beneficiary of a trust, you need to be able to effectively communicate with the trustee – after all, the trust was set up for your benefit. Of course, the trustee has to consider the interests of all the beneficiaries, and if your interests are not in alignment with the interests of others, you may feel you are not being treated fairly. You will not be able to replace that trustee, unless there has been a breach of fiduciary duty.

PART III – ESSENTIAL PLANNING FOR EVERY FAMILY

Chapter 11

Warn Your Heirs: Tax Deferred Accounts Need Special Handling

If you are like many investors, you have been busy saving for retirement at work through 401(k)s, 403(b)s, or 457 plans and on your own through traditional and Roth IRAs and tax deferred annuities. If you are retired, you may have rolled over your 401(k) or a pension distribution into an IRA.

Your tax deferred accounts may be substantial. In fact, they may be your largest assets. I would imagine that after all that effort building your retirement nest egg, you probably want your heirs to hold onto as much as possible for their own retirement by continuing tax deferral for as long as possible.

Before we begin, I should mention that this Chapter deals with the highly technical requirements of the laws that govern tax deferred accounts. While this Chapter is updated for the Pension Protection Act of 2006, be sure to check with your tax adviser before taking any action with respect to your tax deferred accounts. The figures in the examples have been provided by the tax experts at CCH and Brentmark. (You can read more about CCH and Brentmark in the acknowledgements.)

First, let's review some basics. *Keep in mind that Roth IRAs are treated differently, since they are essentially free of income taxes. You do not get a tax deduction when you open a Roth and earnings are tax-free, not tax deferred.*

Basics: How Tax Deferred Accounts Pass to Heirs

There are two ways to pass your tax deferred accounts to your heirs: 1) outside of probate using a beneficiary designation, which is normally preferred or 2) through your will, which is normally less advantageous.

Beneficiary Designation

Preferably, you will transfer the accounts outside of probate by using a "beneficiary designation form." If you take this route, your beneficiaries will be able to continue the tax deferred status of the account over their lifetimes, while taking out minimum required distributions each year based on their life expectancy.

Beneficiary designation forms are provided to you by the custodian of the tax deferred account. They need to be filled out carefully, reviewed by your lawyer, updated periodically, and kept in a safe place.

Your Will

The second way to pass your tax deferred accounts to your heirs is to put your intentions into your will instead of completing a beneficiary designation form. This method is not desirable in most cases, because the accounts will lose their tax-advantaged status more quickly. That is, the accounts will be treated as if you withdrew all the money soon after death: the entire account will be subject to income taxes. You will get the same result if you fill out the beneficiary designation form by writing "my estate" into the blank for the beneficiary.

Because most people should not be giving up the benefits of tax deferral, you should not pass a tax deferred account to an heir through your will unless your lawyer gives you a very good reason to do so. For example, you have no living relatives or friends and you want to leave your entire estate, including your tax deferred accounts, to charity.

Income Taxes

No matter how large or small your estate, *your beneficiaries will have to pay income taxes* on the money you leave them in an IRA, either all at once or stretched out over the beneficiary's lifetime if you plan things right.

The income taxes are triggered by withdrawals from the account after your death, whether they are voluntary, mandated by law, or mandated by a retirement plan.

a) Voluntary Withdrawals

A beneficiary may want to buy a car with his or her inheritance and use your IRA to pay for it, not knowing that each dollar that he or she takes out of your IRA will trigger an income tax.

b) Withdrawals Mandated by Law

If you are over 70-1/2, your beneficiary will have to make sure that you withdrew your final RMD (required minimum distribution) in the year of your death. If not, your beneficiary needs to make the withdrawal before 12/31 of that year. (When you are over 70-1/2, you have to withdraw a certain amount from your IRA each year based on a formula applied to the prior year-end value of the IRA.)

If the withdrawal is done <u>after</u> your death, the amount withdrawn will be taxable as income to your beneficiary and reported on the beneficiary's income tax return. The beneficiary will receive an IRS Form 1099–R showing the withdrawal as income to the beneficiary.

Each year, beneficiaries (except surviving spouses under the age of 70-1/2) must withdraw a minimum amount from the tax deferred account in accordance with an IRS schedule based on the beneficiary's life expectancy. (I'll go through an example later in this Chapter.) This type of withdrawal is mandated by law and there are severe penalties for failure to take the withdrawal (a tax of 50 percent of the amount that should have been withdrawn).

c) Withdrawals Mandated by a Retirement Plan

Some 401(k)s and other company retirement plans do not permit a beneficiary to stay in the plan. For example, your 401(k) plan could provide that at death, a participant's account will be paid out to the beneficiary upon death, or within one year or five years of death. We'll call this type of withdrawal a "death distribution."

Before 2007, a non-spouse beneficiary had to pay income taxes on the full amount of the death distribution. Rollovers into an IRA were not permitted. Since the passage of the Pension Protection Act of 2006, beginning in 2007, a non-spouse beneficiary is permitted to preserve tax deferral, by rolling over the retirement plan to an IRA that meets certain technical requirements. (The IRA has to be in the correct form to preserve tax deferral and the "rollover" is technically a trustee-to-trustee transfer.) This is a significant benefit for non-spouse beneficiaries.

Four Traps to Avoid

While tax deferred investments such as 401(k)s, IRAs, and 403(b)s are terrific tools for accumulating retirement wealth, heirs can lose these assets as quickly as they received them. Warn your heirs about four potential problems to avoid: I) inadvertently triggering income taxes and losing tax deferral, II) forgetting to start required minimum distributions (RMDs), III) overlooking income tax deductions, and IV) paying taxes twice.

I) Inadvertently Triggering Income Taxes and Losing Tax Deferral

Your beneficiary can inadvertently trigger income taxes and lose tax deferral of your IRA and other tax deferred accounts after your death in a number of ways. You need to warn him or her not to: a) re-title the inherited IRA, b) combine it with his or her own IRA, or c) take money out for purchases. While these warnings apply to anyone who inherits a tax deferred account, as you'll see in the discussion, special rules apply to spouses.

Non-spouse Beneficiary

Let's go through an example of a non-spouse beneficiary. John named his only son, Jeremy, as the sole beneficiary of his IRA when he filled out his IRA beneficiary designation form. After his death, Jeremy has the power to continue to grow the IRA tax deferred over his own lifetime while taking out just the annual minimum required by law under the RMD ("required minimum distribution") rules for non-spouse beneficiaries.

Because of the beneficiary designation, the IRA is not a probate asset, so it does not have to go through probate. (If John had written "my estate" into the blank, the IRA would have been a probate asset, passed through the will, and lost tax deferral.)

At John's death, Jeremy will provide the IRA custodian with a copy of the death certificate (and a copy of the beneficiary designation, if the IRA custodian can't locate it.) The custodian changes the Social Security number on the IRA account from John's to Jeremy's. However, the IRA is not titled in Jeremy's name. Instead – and this is key – the custodian changes the title of the IRA from "John's IRA" to "John's IRA (deceased)" or "Jeremy's Inherited IRA."

a) Re-titling the Inherited IRA

If Jeremy tells the IRA custodian to re-title the IRA from "Jeremy's Inherited IRA" into his own name ("Jeremy's IRA"), which custodians will do upon request, a funny thing happens. The inherited IRA is considered fully "distributed," which is another word for withdrawn.

Bingo, Jeremy generates taxable income for himself in the amount of the inherited IRA. If the inherited IRA is worth $100,000 at the time of the re-titling, the IRA custodian will send Jeremy an IRS Form 1099-R at the beginning of the following year showing a $100,000 fully taxable withdrawal. If the inherited IRA is worth $3 million, Jeremy will receive a Form 1099-R for $3 million, all of which will be subject to income taxes on the federal and state level.

b) Combining the Inherited IRA with Your Own

You have the same problem if Jeremy decides to organize his affairs by consolidating his own IRA with the IRA he inherited from John. The inherited IRA is considered distributed and is fully taxable. If Jeremy keeps the consolidated IRA, he has another problem. If he doesn't undo the transfer, the inherited IRA is considered an "excess contribution," which is a violation of another law and subject to an additional tax of six percent of the excess each and every year until the error is corrected.

c) Taking Money Out For Purchases

Another way to wipe out your hard earned retirement savings is to forget to warn Jeremy that any money he takes out of the inherited IRA is subject to income taxes. If Jeremy wants to buy a $30,000 car with IRA money, he will need to withdraw

$40,000 to pay for the car and the taxes on the withdrawal (assuming Jeremy's effective income tax rate is 25 percent).

If Jeremy realizes he made a big mistake after the deed is done, he has no recourse. The law is merciless. There is no turning back. If you are thinking the solution might be an IRA rollover, no such luck. (Taxpayers generally have a 60 day grace period to move money from one IRA to another through a "rollover.") Unless you are a spouse, there is no such thing as a rollover for an inherited IRA. Under current law, a non-spouse beneficiary cannot rollover an inherited IRA into another inherited IRA.

Do not be confused by non-spouse "rollovers" of inherited qualified retirement plans, such as 401(k)s, which are permitted under the Pension Protection Act of 2006. The latter type of "rollover" is technically a transfer from the plan trustee to the IRA custodian and as such is not governed by the 60 day rule.

Under the Act, beginning in 2007, a non-spouse can make a trustee-to-trustee transfer of a 401(k) ("John Jones, Participant") to an inherited IRA ("John Jones, Deceased IRA f/b/o Jim Beneficiary"). Under current law, the beneficiary cannot take a withdrawal from the 401(k) and roll it over into an IRA.

Different Rules for Spouses

Different rules apply to spouses. A spouse can turn the inherited IRA into his or her own IRA without suffering a taxable event. However, the surviving spouse should not re-title the inherited IRA into his or her own name before seeking counsel. If the surviving spouse is under age 59-1/2 and wants to take money out of the inherited IRA, he or she can avoid the 10 percent premature withdrawal penalty. He or she will not avoid the penalty if the IRA is treated as his or her own IRA.

If the surviving spouse is significantly younger than the deceased, the survivor could be better off re-titling the IRA into his or her own name. That way, the survivor will not be subject to required minimum distributions (RMDs) until he or she is 70-1/2. Otherwise, the survivor would have to begin RMD's when his or her deceased spouse would have reached 70-1/2.

II) Forgetting RMDs

If you are over 70-1/2, warn your beneficiaries that they will need to be sure that the full amount of your RMD was withdrawn in the year of death. If your beneficiary does not withdraw the RMD before December 31 of the year of death, expect a hefty 50 percent "excess accumulation" penalty. If $50,000 is the RMD and it is not withdrawn on time, the penalty is $25,000. Spousal beneficiaries are not exempt from this year-of-death RMD or penalty.

That's the first RMD. There are more. Each and every year, the beneficiary must withdraw (and pay taxes on) the appropriate RMD. The amount (based on a life expectancy table included in IRS regulations) varies depending on whether the beneficiary is a spouse, non-spouse, or non-person (such as a charity, your estate, or a trust).

RMD Example

To give you an example of a non-spouse beneficiary, consider this situation: Jenny was born on January 1, 1935 and died in 2006 at the age of 71. Her son, Tom, was born on February 15, 1969 and was 37 when Jenny died. Jenny's IRA was worth $100,000 on December 31, 2005, and Jenny withdrew her full 2006 RMD of $3,774 before she died.

To arrive at the RMD figure of $3,774, Jenny used the "Uniform Lifetime" RMD table (Table III of Appendix C of IRS Publication 590) to locate the divisor for her age (the divisor is 26.5 at age 71). For his divisor, Tom will use a different table, the "Single Life Expectancy Table for Use by Beneficiaries" (Table I of Appendix C of IRS Publication 590). Both tables are provided in Appendix 11-A (Table III) and 11-B (Table I).

Tom's first RMD must be withdrawn during the year following Jenny's death (2007). Assuming the IRA is worth $102,000 on December 31, 2006, Tom would withdraw a minimum of $2,237 in 2007 based on a divisor of 45.6 for a person his age (38 in 2007). The following year, the divisor will be one less 45.6 (44.6) and the following year, it will be one less again (43.6) and so on.

To learn more about RMDs, I suggest you visit www.brentmark.com, www.newrmd.com, and www.calctools.com (free RMD calculator), all of which are hosted by Brentmark Software, Inc. Brentmark publishes software that calculates RMDs for account owners and beneficiaries.

III) Overlooking an Income Tax Deduction

Make sure your family knows that your beneficiary MAY get to take a tax deduction on the beneficiary's income tax return against post-death distributions from the inherited IRA based on the amount of federal estate tax paid because of the inclusion of the IRA in your estate. You can spot a post-death distribution on IRS Form 1099-R. For traditional IRAs, look for "Code 4" on the Form 1099-R. This type of income is referred to as "income in respect of a decedent" – "IRD" for short. The IRD deduction is available to the beneficiary ONLY if your estate is actually subject to federal estate taxes.

Authorized under section 691(c) of the Internal Revenue Code, *the IRD deduction is often overlooked, even by the beneficiary's accountant.* Why? Two reasons: first, the estate tax return is usually prepared by a different accountant and second, tax preparation software does not normally include IRD deductions.

Example of an IRD Deduction

Let's go through an example of an IRD deduction based on a death in 2007. Say the Connecticut estate tax is about $638,000 and the federal estate tax is $1,962,900 on a $7 million estate of which $3 million is a 401(k). (The federal estate tax is reduced somewhat because of a deduction (not a credit) for the Connecticut estate tax on the federal estate tax return.) The net federal and Connecticut tax bills combined are $2,600,900.

You are the child of the IRA owner and sole heir and beneficiary of the $3 million 401(k), which is distributed to you by the plan pursuant to its death provisions. (Some plans will not allow a beneficiary to remain in the plan and send out a distribution check to the beneficiary. For purposes of this example, I am assuming that the non-spouse beneficiary cannot avoid the taxes on the distribution by transferring it over to an IRA via a trustee-to-trustee transfer, as allowed under the Pension Protection Act of 2006 beginning in 2007)

The distribution results in $3 million of taxable income that you will need to report on your 1040. Your income tax bill will be about $1,029,860 million for a single person, assuming no other income.

You can reduce your $1 million income tax bill by taking an IRD deduction. You can't deduct the entire $3 million distribution. You will be limited to your proportionate share of the estate taxes paid on the IRA.

To compute this figure it is necessary to compare the estate taxes payable on the estate both with and without the IRD item. For a $7 million estate that includes a $3 million IRA, the total federal estate tax is $1,962,900. Without the IRA, the estate tax would be $773,820. Accordingly, in this case, $1,189,080 of estate tax is attributable to the 401(k).

Because there are no other beneficiaries in this example, 100 percent of this amount is attributed to you. You enter $1,189,080 on Schedule A, line 25 "Federal estate tax paid on decedent's income reported on this return" under "Other Miscellaneous Deductions – Not Subject to 2 percent limitation"). This amount is reduced by a haircut (in this case about $57,000 to $1,132,080) and carries over to line 40 of your return, along with other itemized deductions. The IRD deduction will reduce your federal taxes from about $1,029,860 million (before the deduction) to about $633,632 (after the deduction). Be sure to tell your beneficiaries to watch out for IRD deductions, since they are often missed by the beneficiary's accountant. For more information on IRD, read IRS Publication 590 (pages 18 and 19 of the 2005 edition) and IRS Publication 559 (pages 11 and 12 of the 2005 edition).

IV) Avoiding Double Taxation When Paying Estate Taxes

Another way to lose tax deferral (and assets) in a hurry is to be stuck having your estate pay estate taxes with your IRA or other tax deferred account. (Roth IRAs are another story, since withdrawals are income-tax-free, not merely tax deferred.) Why? When you withdraw cash from the IRA to pay estate taxes, you also need to account for income taxes on the withdrawal. Each dollar you withdraw from your IRA (or any tax deferred account) is subject to income tax. You're paying income taxes in order to pay estate taxes. You never want to paint your heirs into this corner.

Let's consider the example we discussed before with a twist: the estate is $7 million as before, with a $3 million IRA and the only other assets is a $4 million house. You inherit the IRA, which you would like to keep growing tax deferred for as long as possible. As the beneficiary of an inherited IRA, you are required to take out a minimum amount each year, based on your own life expectancy. If you limit withdrawals to the minimum amounts each year, you can stretch out the inherited IRA over your lifetime (and beyond, if you name your own beneficiary).

But, here is the dilemma. The house can't be sold in time to pay the estate taxes. As in the previous example, the combined federal and Connecticut estate tax bill will be about $2,600,900.

The executor of the estate will have nine months from the date of death to come up with the cash. The executor will have three choices: sell the house, take out a mortgage on the house, or take the money out of the IRA.

The best option is to sell the house, but the executor may not be able to make the sale within the nine month window. Getting a mortgage is only a temporary solution.

The worst option is using the inherited IRA to pay the estate tax bill. Here's why. You don't actually have $3 million in the IRA. You really have $3 million less the income tax you will have to pay if you withdraw the money to pay the estate tax. In my previous example, your income tax (even after the 691(c) deduction) would be $633,632. That means that you are unnecessarily accelerating the payment of a large amount of income tax when using the IRA funds to pay the estate tax bill. The lesson here is to avoid using IRA dollars to pay the estate tax.

What's the real solution here? Put the house on the market. Ask the IRS for an extension to file your return and for a waiver of the tax penalty. You will still have to pay the interest on the estate tax due at a rate of eight percent per year (this is the rate applicable in 2006). If the house can be sold during a reasonable time, you might be able to save more money by paying the interest until the house is sold instead of taking the money out of the IRA.

Second, if the decedent is over 70-1/2, the IRA beneficiary will have to make sure the final required minimum distribution (RMD) is taken out of the IRA before the end of the year in which the IRA owner died. That RMD will be taxable to the beneficiary at ordinary income tax rates. The RMD is <u>not</u> deductible as an expense of the estate and does <u>*not*</u> reduce the size of the estate.

Summary

If you have substantial assets in tax deferred accounts, bells and whistles should go off. Extra planning needs to be done. Family members need to be apprised of the need for extra care should they inherit an IRA, 401(k), 403(b), variable annuity, or other tax deferred account. Your attorney and financial adviser need to be on board with a view to helping your family protect those assets for as long as possible.

To help your family understand the issues, encourage them to read two books by Ed Slott, "The Retirement Savings Time Bomb" (Penguin Publishers 2003) and "Parlay Your IRA into A Family Fortune" (Viking 2005). I also recommend "IRA's, 401(k)s, and Other Retirement Plans: Taking Your Money Out," by Twila Slesnick and John Suttle (Nolo Press 1999). You will also find IRS Publication 590 to be helpful. You can get a copy online at www.irs.gov or by calling 1-800-TAX-FORM.

For a free "Warn Your Heirs Checklist," email me at Julie@JacksonGrant.us.

Chapter 12

How to Transfer Wealth Tax Free Through Annual Gifting

Anyone with a sizeable estate who wants to avoid or reduce estate taxes upon his or her death can take advantage of the annual gifting rules to transfer money to heirs. An individual can make an unlimited number of tax-free gifts of no more than $12,000 per year per donee (the $12,000 was increased from $11,000 in 2006). This $12,000 figure is called the "annual gift tax exclusion."

Annual exclusions do not affect lifetime gifting, which I'll explain below. An individual can also pay certain educational and medical expenses for other people without triggering a gift tax.

Example of Annual Gifting

I recently met with a widowed client and her attorney to discuss annual gifts the widow wanted to make to her three children. One of the issues we discussed is the maximum amount that can be gifted without triggering the filing of a federal or state gift tax return (or the payment of a gift tax).

The widow can give each of her three children up to $12,000 a year for a total of $36,000. She can also give $12,000 to each child's spouse, totaling another $36,000 and another $72,000 to her six grandchildren ($12,000 x 6 = $72,000).

In this example, the total gifting for this group of family members would be $144,000. None of these gifts is taxable to the widow or to the recipients. A couple with the same family structure could double these amounts, making $288,000 of non-taxable gifts each year.

Annual Gifting and Insurance Trusts

Living in Connecticut, it is likely that you or a family member or friend has an insurance trust. The idea behind an insurance trust is to remove life insurance proceeds from an individual's taxable estate. The trust owns the insurance and pays the premiums.

Let's assume the widow mentioned earlier has an insurance trust, naming her three children as beneficiaries. (See Chapter 13 for more on insurance trusts.) The trust owns the widow's life insurance policy and pays the premiums for the policy ($9,000 a year). Each year, the widow writes a check to the trust for $9,000, so that the trust can pay the premium to the insurance company, thus protecting the ownership of the policy.

The widow's payment to the trust is a gift. To qualify for the annual gift exclusion, the trust must permit the beneficiaries to make withdrawals against the $9,000, in an amount specified in the trust. If the beneficiaries do not exercise their right to withdraw, the trustee is free to use the contribution to pay the premium.

This all seems very simple, but here's the wrinkle that many taxpayers miss. When the money is placed into the trust, it is actually considered a gift of that amount to the beneficiaries of the trust due to the right of withdrawal (their "Crummey powers," as described in Chapter 13). This reduces the annual tax-free gift that can be made to each beneficiary by the amount of their share of the gift to the trust.

In the case of the widow and her three children, her $9,000 gift to the trust equals a gift of $3,000 to each of her three children ($3,000 x 3 = $9,000), meaning she can now only make an annual gift to each child in the amount of $9,000 ($12,000 less $3,000 = $9,000). If the widow forgets that she has made that $3,000 gift to each of her children, she may inadvertently make additional gifts of $12,000 to each child. If she does, she will exceed her annual exclusion by $3,000 per child. Those amounts will be subject to gift tax.

Therefore the widow should now limit her annual gifting to her children to $9,000 ($12,000 less $3,000) to each of her three children. Other family members to whom she chooses to make annual gifts can still receive $12,000 each.

Lifetime Gifting

If you want to gift more than your annual gifting limits permit, you can give away more without triggering a gift tax, but there is a price to pay. Essentially, you can give away any amount up to your estate tax credit without paying a gift tax, but once you use up that credit, it cannot be applied against your estate tax bill. For example, you can give away up to $1 million without triggering the need to pay a federal gift tax ($2 million in Connecticut). However, when you die, the amount of the gift will reduce the amount that is sheltered from federal estate taxes through the federal estate tax applicable credit (discussed in Chapter 4). In 2006 – 2008, the credit shelters $2 million. For example, if you give away $1 million and die in 2008, your federal estate tax credit will effectively shelter $1 million instead of $2 million. See Chapter 4 for a more complete discussion of estate taxes.

Summary

Annual gifting is a good way to reduce the size of a taxable estate. As with any tax planning technique, the more you know, the better off you will be. For more information on the taxation of gifts, a good resource is the instruction booklet to IRS Form 709, "United States Gift (and Generation-Skipping Transfer) Tax Return," available online at www.irs.gov or by calling 1-800-TAX-FORM.

Another recommended IRS resource is Publication 950, *Introduction to Estate and Gift Taxes,* which explains gift and estate taxes and helps taxpayers eliminate or reduce estate taxes. For a copy, see Appendix 12-A.

Chapter 13

How to Transfer Substantial Wealth Tax Free Through Insurance Trusts

After you build wealth, it's natural to want to protect that wealth for your family after your death. Your wealth can be diminished substantially by taxes, or through simple mistakes (such as paying estate taxes with your IRA), or being forced to sell an asset (real estate or a business) below market value in order to pay taxes on time. This is the problem with illiquid estates.

Life insurance is probably the easiest and sometimes the best way to transfer substantial wealth to heirs free of <u>income</u> taxes (the death benefit is income tax-free). The death benefit can also be free of <u>estate</u> taxes, but only if you are not the owner of the policy. (If you own the policy (or exercise any incidents of ownership, such as paying the premiums), you own the death benefit. When you die, the death benefit is no different from any other asset you own and is subject to estate taxes.)

If *someone else* owns a life insurance policy on your life, the asset is not yours, is not part of your taxable estate and escapes estate taxes.

To keep the death benefit out of your taxable estate, lawyers recommend setting up a trust (an "irrevocable life insurance trust" or "ILIT") for the purpose of owning the policy, paying the premiums, and receiving the death benefit.

You would be the "grantor" or "settlor" of the ILIT. You would decide how you want the death benefit paid at the time of your death and to whom. Some ILITs provide that the trust will pay the estate taxes and other costs of administration of the estate and pay what is left over (the "remainder") to family members. In those cases, the ILIT terminates when the death benefit is fully distributed.

Other ILITS direct that the trustee invest the death benefit for the lifetime of the surviving spouse and paying him or her income from the investments, with the remainder to the children. There are other possibilities – you control the terms of the ILIT.

Selecting Life Insurance

When choosing a life insurance policy to fund your trust, consider how long you want the ILIT to last. If the purpose is to pay off estate taxes, you will want permanent insurance instead of term insurance. Permanent insurance such as "universal life" or "whole life" covers you *when you die*, whereas term insurance only covers you *if you die* during the term period. Universal life is more flexible in terms of premiums and death benefits and usually less costly than whole life. Leading edge universal life contracts offer death benefits that are guaranteed through age 121 and generally have premiums that are 10-20 percent less per year than the whole life alternative.

The outlay for permanent insurance is greater than term when you are younger. The premiums for term increase as you get older. As I mentioned before, term covers you if - and only if - you die during the term. The cost of term insurance becomes prohibitive after age 70. Since most people actually live to achieve their life expectancy of 82-86, few death benefits are paid by term contracts. If you ever doubt the accuracy of the actuarial tables, just read the obituary pages of you local newspaper and check on the ages of most of the people listed. Very few are under 80.

Before you buy the insurance, be sure to ask the insurance agent about guarantees. Newer policies can be purchased with three guarantees: 1) the premium will not increase, 2) the death benefit will not decrease, and 3) the number of premium payments will not exceed a certain number. An example of this type of policy is a "no-lapse universal life policy."

Insurance proposals are not that easy to understand and insurance agents are persuasive. You definitely don't want to buy the least expensive policy without understanding why it is less expensive. If the "illustration" (the agent's proposal) shows interest earned by the policy at 8 percent and you are comparing another policy that illustrates interest at 4 percent, the 8 percent policy will appear to be less expensive (premiums will be lower). But reality may not match the more optimistic interest rate assumption. Misrepresentation is against the law. But confusion is not. Be skeptical and alert when buying insurance.

Example

I can share an example of a real life situation that caused havoc later in life. Judy (not her real name), bought universal life insurance on her husband's life. The death benefit was $250,000. She deposited $35,000 into the policy and subsequently paid premiums of $1,000 per year.

Judy continued paying the $1,000 annual premiums for about 10 years. Then, she received a letter from the insurance company: the premium was going up to $14,000 a year.

This is not a unique situation. Insurance regulators will tell you that insurance proposals can be (1) misunderstood by the client (should Judy have known that the premiums would be going up as her husband aged?) or (2) in some cases, manipulated by the agent (winning the client's business by manipulating the interest rate in the proposal to arrive at a low premium).

You do not want to find yourself in Judy's situation. Clarify the terms of the policy before you buy it. If the terms as set out in the proposal and in the insurance contract are not effected as promised, contact the Connecticut Department of Insurance's Department of Consumer Affairs. If the policy was misrepresented, the department will intercede with the insurer on your behalf.

Setting Up an ILIT

After you are convinced that you understand the insurance policy you are buying, talk to your lawyer about setting up the ILIT. You cannot be the trustee of the ILIT. One of your beneficiaries can be trustee or an independent trustee can be appointed. The trust is irrevocable, meaning you cannot terminate it or change it except as described in the trust document.

In addition to purchasing a new life insurance policy for the purpose of setting up an insurance trust, you can also transfer an existing life insurance policy into the ILIT. However, if you die within three years of the transfer, the death benefit does not escape estate taxes.

Paying the Trust's Premiums

The trust has to pay the premiums to keep the life insurance in force (unless the policy is fully paid up). The money to pay the annual premiums comes from you; however, the payment to the insurance company must be made through the trust so that the trust is considered the owner of the policy, protecting the estate tax-free status of the death benefit. (As mentioned before, if you pay the premiums yourself, you would be considered the owner of the policy; the death benefit would be included in your taxable estate.)

Essentially, you make annual gifts to the ILIT so the trust can pay the annual insurance premiums. Unlike gifts to an individual, say a child or grandchild, transfers to the trust are gifts of a future interest and don't qualify for the annual gift tax exclusion that we discussed in Chapter 12. However, if the beneficiaries of the ILIT have the right to withdraw the gift, the gift takes on a present interest that does qualify for the annual gift tax exclusion.

In order to qualify, the trust's beneficiaries need to be notified by letter that they have an unrestricted right to withdraw the money you intend to give to the trust, as long as they withdraw during a certain period of time. The letter is called a "Crummey letter," which is named after a Ninth Circuit Court of Appeals case, Crummey v. Commissioner, 397 F.2d 82 (9th Cir. 1968).

Example

Say a widowed father of two children sets up an ILIT, naming his children as the beneficiaries. The annual premium for the life insurance is $8,000. Each year the father makes a payment of $8,000 to the trust for payment of the premium, and the trust pays the premium to the insurance company. In order for that $8,000 to be considered as a tax-free gift because of the annual gift tax exclusion, the trust sends both children a Crummey notice, alerting them that they can each withdraw $4,000 each from the trust.

This withdrawal right is a general power of appointment. If the two children do nothing, the power lapses and that creates a gift to the ILIT that qualifies for the annual gift tax exclusion. Essentially, that means that you can arrange to pay for the premiums by following the Crummey procedures each year.

Summary

Before setting up an insurance trust, consider your health (you have to be in good enough health to be able to purchase life insurance) and the pros and cons of setting up an ILIT. Don't buy life insurance without your lawyer's help because the ILIT needs to be the owner of the policy, not you. Ask the lawyer about restrictions on the life insurance owned by the trust. For example, you will not be able to borrow from the policy, you will not be able to change the beneficiaries of the trust, and you will not be able to remove and replace the trustee. Make sure the insurance you are going to buy has the necessary guarantees. Keep in touch with your lawyer to ensure that the trust is operated properly.

Chapter 14

Divorced and Remarried: How to Protect Your Heirs

Blended families are now more common than traditional families, according to the U.S. Census Bureau. Estate planning can be a challenge for these families, considering the potentially differing interests of the children of the current marriage, the children of the prior marriage(s), and the current spouse and his or her children. Former spouses may also assert claims—successfully, if you don't change the ownership of jointly-owned property or beneficiary designations on life insurance or tax deferred accounts.

First, let me warn you about unintended consequences with 1) non-probate assets, 2) intestacy, 3) new wills, and 4) prior wills. Then, we'll discuss some planning techniques.

Non-Probate Assets

Let's say you have thought about how you want to arrange your affairs and your lawyer drafts a will that takes care of your blended family. You think you're in great shape, but you don't realize that your non-probate assets don't pass under your will (or under the laws of intestacy).

If you have a blended family, review each and every one of your beneficiary designations (IRAs, 401(k)s, life insurance), each piece of real estate, and each bank account and brokerage statement. (Look for joint accounts with your previous spouse, accounts in trust for your previous spouse, and payable on death or transfer on death accounts.) Any beneficiary designations or transfers on death take these assets out of the jurisdiction of the probate court and do not pass under your will. They pass to the person you name as beneficiary or joint owner, even if your will provides otherwise. Your will only governs your probate assets.

Intestacy

Let's say you recently remarried, but haven't yet gotten around to writing a will and neither has your spouse. If you or your spouse dies without a will, property will transfer by the laws of intestacy (see Chapter 6).

If your spouse has no children and dies without a will, you will receive 100 percent of his or her probate assets. If your spouse has children from a prior marriage, one-half of his or her assets will go to you and the rest will go to the deceased spouse's children. If you have children in common, all the children (including the deceased spouse's children) will share one-half of the assets.

New Wills

If you remarried and forgot to put your new spouse in a will that you executed after your marriage, the new spouse cannot claim against the will under the usual "elective share" provision for spouses (discussed in Chapter 8) under Connecticut General Statutes Sec. 45a-436).

Instead, another Connecticut law (General Statutes Sec. 45a-257a), provides for that forgotten spouse. The surviving spouse receives the same share of the estate the surviving spouse would have received if the decedent left no will unless: 1) it appears from the will that the omission was intentional; or 2) the testator provided for the spouse by transfer outside the will and the intent that the transfer be in lieu of a testamentary provision is shown by the testator's statements, or is reasonably inferred from the amount of the transfer or other evidence.

Effect of Divorce

If you have a will that you executed during a previous marriage and you die without having made a new will after remarriage, your new spouse would be in trouble, except for another Connecticut law that protects the forgotten spouse.

Connecticut General Statutes (Sec. 45a-257c) revokes any disposition made by the will to the former spouse (and any nomination of the former spouse as executor, trustee, conservator, guardian, or other fiduciary), unless the will expressly provides otherwise. Property prevented from passing to a former spouse due to this statute passes as if the former spouse failed to survive the testator.

Estate Planning After a Divorce

What should you do if you have children from a previous marriage and want to make sure that you provide for your present spouse as well as the children of your previous marriage? Let's consider the possibilities. As you will see, some offer better solutions than others.

First, you can leave your entire estate to your current spouse with the understanding that he or she will take care of your children (his or her step-children). Even if he or she agrees to do so, there is no guarantee that that will happen.

Would there be any more protection for your children (the spouse's step-children) if you each provided for the step-children in your wills? Perhaps. However, there is no stopping your spouse from changing his or her will before or after you die.

Second, you can provide in your will for a trust to take effect upon your death (a "testamentary trust"). The will would provide that some (or all) of the assets you own at your death will be paid into the trust at death.

The will can provide that the trustee will pay all of the income generated by the trust to your spouse for as long as he or she lives. The will can provide that when the spouse dies, the remaining assets held in the trust are paid to your children. Your children would be effectively disinherited, however, if they are close in age to your spouse. In that case, the solution is to buy life insurance for the children.

If choosing this option, do not name your spouse or your children as trustees. Instead, consider using an institutional trustee for this job.

Although this option offers more protection than the first, and is less costly and disruptive of your lifestyle than the following options, it is not foolproof, since a will (and the testamentary trust in it) can always be challenged by a disgruntled heir and if successful, the testamentary trust defeated.

Third, set up a living trust to accomplish the same result as the testamentary trust. To make this work, you would have to actually move assets into the trust during your lifetime. The trust can be written to be irrevocable, so that it cannot be challenged after the fact.

Fourth, another option for the affluent is to have your will provide that your children receive the "applicable exclusion amount" which is free from federal estate taxes. (See Chapter 4). The remainder can go to the spouse. .

Fifth, you can buy life insurance. You could have one policy pay a death benefit to your spouse and another policy pay your children. If you do buy life insurance, you are the owner of the policy. Even if the beneficiary is another person (your spouse or your kids), the law considers the death benefit part of your estate along with everything else you own at death. If your estate can one day be large enough to trigger an estate tax when you die, your estate will have to pay estate taxes on the death benefit. You can avoid that problem by setting up an irrevocable living trust to buy the policy on your life, as discussed in Chapter 13. You will need to consult an attorney to do that properly.

Sixth, you can make gifts to your children during your lifetime. Gifts of $12,000 a year per child are not subject to gift taxes (2006 figure). (See Chapter 12 for more information about annual gifting.) You can make additional gifts totaling $1 million during your lifetime free of federal gift taxes, but that $1 million will reduce "applicable exclusion amount" by the $1 million gift. (See Chapter 4 for more information on federal estate taxes.) If you don't want your children to spend that money, you can pay the gifts into a living trust set up for their benefit.

Seventh, you could set up the ownership of some or all of your assets in "transfer on death" form, naming your children as beneficiaries. However, there is always the possibility that a surviving spouse will mount a challenge after your death, claiming a spousal elective share against those assets. (See Chapter 6 for a discussion of elective shares.)

Summary

Depending on your circumstances, some of these options will be better than others. A testamentary trust set up in your will may be most cost-effective and least disruptive of your current lifestyle. However, a will can always be challenged, so this is not an iron-clad solution.

Funding a living trust would probably give your children and your spouse the most protection. You could fund the trust with assets or leverage those assets by having the trust purchase life insurance.

Chapter 15

Unmarried and Gay Couples: How to Protect Your Partner

A married person has a number of privileges under the law that an unmarried person does not.

First, for married couples, there are no estate taxes on a spouse's inheritance due to the "unlimited marital deduction."

Second, there are no gift taxes on gifts to a spouse.

Third, intestacy statutes protect a spouse's right to all or part of the deceased spouse's estate if he or she dies without a will.

Fourth, elective share statutes give a disinherited spouse a right to a portion of the deceased spouse's estate.

Fifth, a spouse (or next of kin) has the right to take possession of the deceased's body. An unmarried partner has no right to remove the body or make funeral arrangements.

Sixth, a married couple has the right to file a joint income tax return.

Seventh, a spouse has the right to inherit a 401(k) and IRA from a spouse and roll it over into an IRA of his or her own.

None of these protections extend to unmarried couples, nor do the multitude of other laws that protect or govern married people. Unmarried couples are not "spouses" or "next of kin" and they do not have any right to inherit. Same-sex couples can avail themselves of some protection and be treated as "spouses" under Connecticut's civil union laws passed in 2005, which I will discuss at the end of this chapter

While the law does not protect couples who are not married and not in a civil union, you can take action to protect yourself. Actions you can take include:

1) Take extra precautions when drafting your will. To prevent your estate going to your next of kin, both partners need to make wills. The will may be challenged, of course, so you want to be especially careful in your drafting. Be clear if you are leaving someone out of your will. If you are living with your partner but are still legally married to someone else, your spouse can successfully challenge your will and will have a right to claim an elective share at your death.
2) Take advantage of non-probate asset transfers. Consider passing property to your partner through non-probate transfers. As discussed in Chapter 1, property can pass to your partner outside of probate court through non-probate forms of ownership. For example, you can record your home as follows: "James, transfer on death to Rebecca." You can register your bank account as "James, payable on death to Rebecca."
3) Review company retirement plans. You can name your partner the beneficiary of your company retirement plans at work (assuming you are not still married to someone else). At death, those accounts will become your partner's property. However, many plans do not permit a non-spouse beneficiary to continue to participate in the plan: some plans provide that a non-spouse beneficiary's account will be paid out at the death of the participant, which would result in immediate income tax liability for the partner.
4) Name beneficiaries to your tax deferred accounts. You can name your partner the beneficiary of your IRA or other tax deferred accounts. At death, the account becomes the property of the partner, but needs to be titled "Inherited IRA, Deceased Partner." Unlike a surviving spouse, the

surviving partner cannot rollover the inherited IRA into his or her own (it will lose tax deferral status).

5) Reconsider joint ownership. Some advisers will tell you to put your property in joint name with right of survivorship (JWROS); however, JWROS for unmarried couples leads to potential pitfalls and possible challenges. For example, when you set up the JWROS, you are making a gift to your partner that is subject to gift taxes. If the property is real estate, you will need both signatures to sell it. If your partner wants to leave, you will have to get him or her to sell you his or her share. If your partner becomes incapacitated, a conservator, probably his or her relative, will be appointed by the probate court. If your partner dies, the property will transfer directly to you outside of probate. If the value of the estate is more than the applicable exclusion, there will be estate taxes.
6) Consider life insurance. Unmarried couples can buy life insurance on themselves, naming their partners beneficiaries. On death, the partner will receive the death benefits free from income taxes. Whether there is an estate tax will depend on the size of the estate. To protect the proceeds against estate taxes, you will need an insurance trust. (See Chapter 13 for more information on insurance trusts.) You can generally avoid estate tax liability if each partner buys life insurance on the other partner, but in order to buy the insurance, there must be an "insurable interest," such as joint ownership of property.
7) Choose a designator. Consider appointing a "designator" under the Connecticut designator statutes (Public Act 02-105[3]). Under Connecticut law, you can designate your partner to handle certain situations on your behalf, such as health care, life support, psychiatric care, and nursing home care.

---

[3] Sec. 3. (NEW) (*Effective October 1, 2002*) (a) Any person eighteen years of age or older may execute a document that designates another person eighteen years of age or older to make certain decisions on behalf of the maker of such document and have certain rights and obligations with respect to the

8) Give your partner power of attorney. You can appoint your unmarried partner your attorney-in-fact to act on your behalf at present or in the future if, for example, you become disabled. The power needs to be in writing, notarized, and witnessed by two people (not you or your partner).
9) Name your health care agent. Consider appointing your unmarried partner your health care agent.
10) Designate custody of your remains. While this is open to challenge, each unmarried partner can put together a written document that gives custody and control of his or her remains to his or her partner. Make sure the signatures are notarized.
11) Consider a relationship agreement. Since there is no such thing as divorce for an unmarried couple, consider a written agreement laying out your joint understanding of how earnings and assets will be shared during the partnership. Such an agreement was held enforceable in a 1987 Connecticut Supreme Court case (Boland v. Catalano) where an unmarried heterosexual couple agreed to share their earnings and the fruits of their labor.

---

maker of such document under section 1-1k, subsection (b) of section 14-16, subsection (b) of section 17a-543, subsection (a) of section 19a-279c, section 19a-550, subsection (a) of section 19a-571, 19a-580, subsection (b) of section 19a-578, section 31-51jj, section 54-85d, section 54-91c, section 54-126a of the general statutes, as amended by this act, or chapter 968 of the general statutes.

(b) Such document shall be signed, dated and acknowledged by the maker before a notary public or other person authorized to take acknowledgments, and be witnessed by at least two persons. Such document may be revoked at any time by the maker, or by a person in the maker's presence and at the maker's direction, burning, canceling, tearing or obliterating such document or by the execution of a subsequent document by the maker in accordance with subsection (a) of this section.

(c) Any person who is presented with a document executed in accordance with this section shall honor and give effect to such document for the purposes therein indicated.

Same-sex Couples

Connecticut legalized "civil unions" (not marriages) for same-sex couples in 2005 (see Appendix 15-A for a copy of the statute). Marriage for same-sex couples is currently recognized in the United States only in the state of Massachusetts.

Under the law, partners in a Connecticut civil union have the same legal benefits, protections, and responsibilities as married couples under Connecticut law. These rights derive from statute, administrative regulations or court rules, policy, common law, or any other source of civil law, generally falling into the following categories: family law, intestate distribution, wills, title, survivorships, transfer of real or personal property during life or at death, state and municipal taxation, probate courts and procedure, family leave benefits, and state public assistance benefits, among others.

State law governs state income and state estate taxes, local property ownership, guardianship, and so on. State law does not extend to federal issues. That is, the Connecticut civil union law does not extend to benefits, protections, and responsibilities under federal laws that govern Social Security, federal income taxes, federal estate taxes, and the like.

Summary

Having no protection under the law, couples who are unmarried or not in a civil union need to be pro-active to protect their partners. To bring a measure of certainty to your partnership, consider using some of the planning tools we've discussed in this Chapter.

For more information on the Connecticut civil union statute, see Appendix 15-B for a copy of "Connecticut Civil Unions," provided courtesy of Gay & Lesbian Advocates & Defenders (GLAD). For more information on Connecticut civil unions, go to www.glad.org.

Chapter 16

How to Organize Your Records

A few years ago, I found myself assisting a client after her mother's untimely death. Together, we searched through her mother's Florida home to locate important documents and valuables. We found some records in the desk, some in the sock drawer, and some in a shoe box in the closet, including old stock certificates and bearer bonds. Some accounts were identified much later at tax time, when tax reports (IRS Forms 1099s and K-1's) arrived in the mail.

The mother was a business woman who always handled the finances for the family. I'm sure she knew exactly what she was doing and where her important papers were located. Her family did not know, however, and that lack of knowledge opened them up to unnecessary frustration and uncertainty at a vulnerable time.

This is not an unusual situation. After all, who wants to face the fact that life, by definition, will end?

The person who actually does some organizing and planning has a different mindset. The best analogy is a successful entrepreneur. Before he invests in a business venture, he develops contingency plans and an exit strategy.

The investment in your life is already made. It makes sense to have a contingency plan that would take effect in the event of death or disability – a sort of "personal affairs contingency plan."

Survivor's List

Let me start you off with a simple assignment that everyone should undertake, no matter how large or small the estate. Prepare a "Survivor's List," which you can do with a piece of paper and a pencil or software such as WillMaker Plus, a Quicken product. The list should have three parts: people, documents, and financial resources.

People

First, list all the people who may need to be informed or called upon as resources, along with their telephone numbers and addresses. List your spouse (and former spouses) and family members, noting the relationship to you. List your doctors and people who are aware of your health care wishes. Also list your personal and business advisers, including your attorneys, accountants, trustees, executors, and financial advisers.

Documents

List the location of important documents, such as your will, powers of attorney, trusts, health care directives and end-of-life instructions, prenuptial agreements, deeds, life insurance, medical and disability policies, liability insurance policies, home owner's insurance, tax returns, IRA beneficiary forms, pension information, business interests, medical records, and military records.

Financial Resources

List sources of income, such as wages, pensions, annuities, and Social Security benefits. List your direct deposit information, banks, and other financial institutions where you have accounts, and credit and debit cards. List your assets and your debts, such as mortgages and car financing (or note that you have none), as well as money you lent to others. Be sure to identify property that is jointly held with another. List your creditors and the expenses for running your household, passwords, and safe places such as safe deposit boxes.

Creating a survivor's list may seem like a pretty big project. It is. But, imagine how much bigger the job will be for family members when they have to go it alone without your help. Think of the frustration you will save if you prepare that list for them, put it in a safe place, update it periodically, and inform them of its existence.

Reading

The next step is to do some reading. I highly recommend "The Executor's Handbook: A Practical Guide for Settling Connecticut Estates" (3rd Ed 2006), published by Cummings & Lockwood LLC (Telephone: 203-351-4248), and "The Executor's Guide," written by attorney, Mary Randolph, published by Nolo Press (www.nolo.com).

Both of these books are simply the best step-by-step guides available, giving you a very good idea of what to expect and some planning insights.

Here are some additional resources that I recommend: "Estate Planning Basics, What You Need to Know and Nothing More," by Denis Clifford (Nolo Press); the AARP's "Crash Course in Estate Planning," by Michael Palermo (Sterling Publishing Co., Inc.); "Tools and Techniques of Estate Planning" (The National Underwriter Company (www.nuco.com)); and "The Inheritor's Handbook - A Definitive Guide for Beneficiaries," by Dan Rottenberg (Bloomberg Press).

Another excellent resource is the American Bar Association website at www.abanet.org/ppt/public/home.html, where you will find answers to common questions about probate and estate planning. And, of course, don't forget the resources of your local probate court. In Connecticut, go to www.jud.state.ct.us/probate/default.htm.

Summary

You can leave your survivors prepared (with a Survivor's List) or perplexed (without one). It's your choice.

Chapter 17

How to Find a Trusts and Estates Lawyer

Because the stakes are high when you are doing estate planning or settling an estate, proper legal advice is essential. The level of skill you need will depend on how wealthy you are and the complexity of your financial and family situations.

Finding the right attorney may take some time. You will need to identify an attorney who specializes in "trusts and estates," which is broken down further into three practice areas: 1) estate planning, 2) estate and trust administration, and 3) probate litigation. Trusts and estates is a highly specialized practice area and knowledge and skill are not easily attained.

Practice Segmentation

First, let's discuss how lawyers segment their practices. Then we'll talk about how to go about your search.

Some lawyers' practices fall into certain wealth segmentations, either by design or by accident. Each has its own set of planning issues. All estates over $2 million will need estate tax planning, using such techniques as credit shelter trusts which we discussed in Chapter 4. (If you have any doubts about the need for expertise, read "Estate Administration – Practical Planning Concerns and Opportunities," by

Steve Akers, Esq. of Bessemer Trust. You can obtain a copy by emailing akers@bessemer.com.)

All estates with significant assets in tax deferred accounts will need special tax expertise, as we saw in Chapter 11. The larger the tax deferred account, the greater the potential tax liability.

Over $10 Million

With estates worth over $10 million, individuals engage in proactive estate planning. Among other things, these individuals might look into establishing foundations and setting up trusts that benefit charities and enable gift and estate tax free transfers of wealth to heirs.

Between $5 million and $10 million

With estates worth between $5 million and $10 million, people generally want to know how to take advantage of the federal lifetime gifting exemption ($1 million for the IRS and $2 million in Connecticut) and their annual exclusions ($12,000 per recipient), but generally, that's probably as far as they want to go in terms of lifetime wealth transfers to lower the taxable estate.

Between $2 million and $5 million

The $2 million to $5 million estate raises estate tax-planning issues. However, people in this situation are not willing to make significant transfers to save on estate taxes. Accordingly, tax planning may be minimal.

Under $2 Million

If everything you own, including your life insurance, is worth less than $2 million, the primary concerns will be how and to whom assets are distributed.

Any Size Estate

One exception that runs across all segments is the establishment of a life insurance trust, the purpose of which is to eliminate estate taxes on the insurance proceeds. As we discussed in Chapter 13, an insurance trust is a mechanism to place assets out of your estate, which makes those assets estate-tax free. The idea is to have the trust (not you) buy life insurance on your life. At death, the death benefit is paid to the trust. Because you did not own the policy, the death benefit is not part of your estate.

Finding a Good Fit

When searching for legal help, be sure to hire a skilled and competent attorney who fits your personality, can meet your objectives, and is free from conflicts of interest. If you have a large estate, you'll want a lawyer who specializes in trusts and estates law and tax planning. (You do not want a generalist.)

A special note: the average person is not aware of the potential conflicts of interests in a lawyer-client relationship. To give you an insider's view of how lawyers handle such conflicts, be sure to read Appendix 17-A ("Engagement Letters: A Guide for Practitioners. Representation of Fiduciaries"), a guide written for lawyers who represent executors, administrators, or trustees.

When you interview lawyers to determine who you would like to represent you, be aware of potential conflicts, which are highlighted below in the following list of interview questions.

1) *What is your experience and background in estate taxes and planning?* You are looking for 10 years of experience or more, unless you're willing to have the lawyer learn on your nickel.
2) *What types of clients do you normally work with?* Look for a lawyer with clients who have assets, situations, ages, and needs similar to yours. A lawyer whose practice is built around hundreds of small clients will have a different focus than a lawyer who specializes in large estates.
3) *If you were referred by an adviser, explore the nature of the relationship.* For example, if your insurance agent referred you to the attorney, you don't want to have the lawyer recommend an insurance solution just to return the favor to the agent.
4) Ask about referral fees. Simply ask: *Are you paying a referral fee to the person who told me to call you?* You need to

know, since you want to understand any potential conflicts of interest.

5) *Do you sell insurance?* Since insurance trusts need to be funded with life insurance policies, you need to know if the firm sells insurance directly or indirectly through an affiliate. If the answer is yes, tell the lawyer that you won't be buying insurance from him or her or anyone who would share commissions with the lawyer for a sale.
6) *Do you sell investment services?* Some firms provide investment services for trusts. Others may have affiliates that provide investment services to trusts and others. You want to be informed to be able to judge any potential conflicts of interest. As a general rule, you would want your lawyer working toward his or her strengths – legal services – and staying clear of any other services.
7) *Do you act as trustee or executor in wills that you draft for your clients?* Some lawyers offer to serve as your trustee or executor, while others feel doing so creates an inherent conflict of interest. Consider this: if the lawyer drafting the trust also serves as trustee, how can the lawyer represent the beneficiaries in the event of a dispute? Because the lawyer serves his or her own interests when he or she files an accounting for the trust, the lawyer-trustee will normally want you to sign an acknowledgment that you understand the conflict.
   If the lawyer acts as executor, what happens if the will he or she drafted contains ambiguities that are challenged? What if the will he or she drafted is declared invalid?
   If you agree to the lawyer acting as a trustee or executor, both of which are fiduciary positions, be sure you get a letter from the lawyer explaining how he or she will handle the engagement and calculate the compensation for those services and for the services he or she provides as a lawyer In large complex situations, this agreement is best included in the will (or trust) itself. In *any* situation (no matter how complicated or simple), if there is to be no or limited

fiduciary compensation, that should be specified in the will (or trust). Silence means full compensation.
The issue of compensation is only one potential conflict: be sure to read Appendix 17-B ("Engagement Letters: A Guide for Practitioners. Estate Planning Lawyer Serving as Fiduciary") for an inside view of how lawyers see these issues when asked to serve as trustee or executor.

8) *How do you charge for estate planning? What would you estimate the bill to be for my estate plan?* These are fair questions. Expect straight answers. Under Connecticut law, you are entitled to this information in writing.
9) *How do you charge for acting as counsel to an executor with an estate similar to mine?* The attorney should be able to provide you a few examples of cases he or she is working on at present.
10) *If there are multiple beneficiaries of a trust, how do you normally address potential conflicts of interest?* There is a good chance that the interests of the beneficiaries or trustees will diverge at some point in the future. The attorney needs to be attuned to these issues and discuss them with you. If you are a beneficiary, you must understand if you are being represented by the attorney or if the attorney is representing the trustee.
11) *If you are representing spouses for estate planning and discover that the spouses have conflicting or divergent interests, how do you handle the situation?* Here again, you want to hear a logical response that gives you comfort about the lawyer's ethics. (This explanation should also be included in the engagement letter.) Ask the lawyer to give a few examples. For example, you might ask what the lawyer would do if he or she represents a married couple and the husband tells the lawyer to put a provision in his will that is not in his wife's will. (Usually a married couple's wills are identical and reciprocal.) If you would like to get a good understanding of the potential for conflicts, see Appendix 17-C ("Engagement Letters: A Guide for Practitioners. Spousal Representation"), a guide for attorneys who

represent spouses. The guide gives lawyers a checklist to follow to determine the conflict disclosures he or she should make when representing spouses and what to do if a future conflict does arise.

12) *Have any of your tax planning techniques been challenged by the IRS?* If the answer is yes, explore further. Aggressive tax planning techniques are not that uncommon, especially with estates over $25 million. You need to be aware of whether the lawyer you are interviewing takes these types of risks and be sure to understand the potential costs of working with this lawyer.
13) *Have any provisions of your estate planning documents been challenged in court?* Some challenges come up because of contentious family situations. Some are a result of thoughtlessness or poor drafting. In either case, try to ascertain the reason for the challenges, and steer away from a lawyer who seems to be responsible for such challenges because of ineffectiveness in drafting estate planning documents.
14) *Ask for a few client references.* An attorney should be happy to give you a few names of clients – of course, he or she will need to get their consent. You want to be sure to talk to people who are similarly situated. Here, you're looking for clues about the attorney's working style. Find out from his or her other clients whether the attorney is good at returning phone calls (a must!), answering questions, and coordinating with other advisers.

Resources for Finding the Right Attorney

If I were in the market for a trusts and estates attorney, I would turn to two resources: The American College of Trust and Estate Counsel (ACTEC) and my local bar association.

ACTEC is an association of lawyers "skilled and experienced in the preparation of wills and trusts, estate planning, probate procedure, and administration of trusts and estates of decedents, minors, and incompetents." This is a closed association whose members are invited to join based on their expertise. You can get a list of Connecticut lawyers who are ACTEC members from ACTEC. For more information, see Appendix 17-D.

Local Bar Associations. Your local bar association is a good starting point for finding trust and estate practitioners. Lawyers sign up if they are interested in the practice area; membership does not necessarily mean expertise.

The Connecticut Bar Association publishes a list of members who joined their "wills and trusts" sections and their "estate planning" sections, that you can find online at www.ctbar.org. The Fairfield County Bar Association's Web site is www.regionalbar.com. The New Haven Bar Association's Web site is at www.newhavenbar.org. The Web site for the Hartford Bar Association is www.hartfordbar.org.

Hiring an Attorney When Someone Dies

If your spouse or parent dies and you are responsible for coordinating matters with the deceased's attorney, first consider whether you want to work with him or her. Many people think they are obligated to stay with the attorney who planned the estate. Not so. You are hiring the attorney to represent yourself. It's a fresh engagement. As such, you need to interview the lawyer and assure yourself that he or she is the best lawyer for the job of estate administration (as distinguished from estate planning).

Before you meet with a lawyer to talk about the estate, be sure to prepare by reading, "Intake Questionnaire: Initial Meeting with Probate Lawyer," in Appendix 17-E, provided courtesy of FindLaw, a service of Thompson Corporation.

The lawyer should offer you an engagement letter explaining the administration and settlement of estates and how the law firm will charge for its services. If the firm will not provide an engagement letter, move on with your search for a lawyer you can work with.

Engagement Letters

Different types of engagement letters are used for different types of estates. If the lawyer is acting as trustee or executor, he or she will explain the inherent conflicts of interest in the letter and ask you to consent to the appointment notwithstanding. Essentially, you are being asked to waive your right to sue the lawyer if the conflict comes to a head, something you should not do lightly. Also, as mentioned before, both fiduciary fees and legal fees need to be described and explained in the engagement letter.

Here is some sample conflict language from an engagement letter for an attorney who will be serving as an executor (the letter is reproduced in full in Appendix 17-B):

"I can serve as your executor if that is your desire. Several potential conflicts of interest may arise with regard to my services as your executor. One of these conflicts of interest relates to the fact that my law firm will serve as legal counsel for me as executor. A lawyer's independence may be compromised when he or she acts as both executor and lawyer for the executor. The normal checks and balances which exist when two unrelated parties serve separately as executor and lawyer for the executor are absent.

"Unless the probate court is asked to intervene at the time, there may not be an independent, impartial review to determine if the executor in exercising an appropriate level of care, skill, diligence, and prudence in the administration of your estate, and there may not be an independent, impartial evaluation as to whether or not the fees and expenses charged by the executor and the fees and expenses charged by the law firm are reasonable, until the executor files his final account with the probate court for allowance."

Summary

Not only do you have to find a lawyer who is skilled and responsive to your needs, you also need to understand how the relationship can go off track. Interviews are important as are client references, but be careful of choosing an attorney because of a friend's recommendation. Friends may not have any idea of how skilled an attorney is and with estate planning in particular, problems don't arise until after death.

While conflicts of interest are hard to judge, they are important to understand and should not be underestimated. For a good discussion of conflicts of interest, I suggest you read "Ethical Problems for Lawyers upon Trust Terminations: Conflicts of Interest," by Joel Dobris, published in University of Miami Law Review (November 1983).

Chapter 18

Why You Need to Integrate Your Financial and Estate Plans

"Getting an inheritance isn't as easy as it looks," said Rachel Silverman in a May 27, 2006 Wall Street Journal story, "Inheritance Planning Without Grief." "Inheriting money is already an emotional and financial minefield. But in the past decade or so, amid the popularity of complex retirement investments and other assets – and the increasing complexity of tax laws – it's gotten trickier to avoid the pitfalls. Transfer a parent's IRA the wrong way and you can cause a massive tax hit. Take a treasured painting off their wall before its accounted for in the estate and you could be illegally avoiding estate taxes. In some cases, it may even be smart to decline an inheritance altogether."

Silverman couldn't be more right. When someone dies, survivors may find themselves without direction, knowledge, or wherewithal to handle the affairs of the deceased or to take care of themselves. The uninformed can step into a tax trap, especially with IRA accounts, as discussed in Chapter 11.

Another pitfall is failure to integrate a financial plan with an estate plan. For example, if you have a perfectly drafted will and all your assets are in joint name, nothing will pass under your will.

To avoid these problems, let me share with you a review that I use in my money management practice. This process picks up on many of the issues we dealt with in the earlier chapters of this book and touches on some of the material that goes into Survivor's Lists discussed in Chapter 16. It also assumes that you have read about estate planning lawyers in Chapter 17.

Step 1: Consider Family Dynamics

Most couples I know delegate finances to one spouse who takes the lead with financial decisions. That works well as long as both spouses are attuned to the overall strategy and actively participate in the ongoing review process.

I see red flags if one spouse is unavailable or disinterested. There is simply no way the surviving spouse can gain the knowledge and skill needed to manage the family's financial affairs without making some mistakes in the learning process. Why would you want to assume that extra risk? There are two risks here: "learning-curve" risk and dependency. Without any understanding of finances, that spouse becomes naively dependent on friends, family, and advisers, some of whom might be well-meaning but unskilled.

Working with an adviser requires an understanding of desired results, costs, and potential pitfalls, including conflicts of interest inherent in all relationships with service providers, even those who go to your church or synagogue or belong to your club. We all know the problems that can cause.

In some cases, the family may decide to arrange for a fiduciary to care for the spouse. You can set up a trust for the benefit of the spouse to be managed by an institutional trustee (usually a bank or trust company). The trustee is a fiduciary under the law, which means the trustee must manage the trust under a high standard of care. There can be no self-interest.

When considering family dynamics, it would be best if both spouses engage in the dialogue. Sometimes, it helps to involve the children, especially if you expect them to act as executors or trustees. Affluent families and business owners will want to engage their attorneys, accountants and financial advisers in the discussions as well.

Step 2: Read Your Will

You would be surprised at how many people do not read their estate planning documents. Read your will, your trusts, living wills, powers of attorney, health care directives, and other estate planning documents to make sure that they accomplish what you want. Read them for accuracy. Read them for clarity: if there is any ambiguity, evidence will have to be presented to probate court to determine your intent as discussed in Chapter 8. Read them for your children, especially if you name them as executors in your will or trustees of your trusts. Your children need to be able to understand your intentions without interpreting the text. If something you put in the will can have more than one meaning, clarify the language. If you recall, we saw the problems a poorly drafted will can cause in Chapter 8, "Will Your Will Cause a Lawsuit." Read Chapter 19, "Questions and Answers on Wills," and Chapter 20, "What Can be Wrong with a Will?" Resist the temptation to rely on your lawyer to tell you what is covered in your will.

When reviewing trusts, consider whether the trust is in operation now or scheduled to become effective in your will. Check to see if the trust is revocable or irrevocable. What does the trust currently own? Who does the tax returns? Who are the beneficiaries? What benefits do they receive? Who are the trustees? Importantly, you need to understand whether the trust assets will be included in your taxable estate. Generally, assets held in irrevocable trusts are not. Don't forget to read trusts of which you are beneficiary.

Step 3: Review Your Life Insurance

Check the death benefits of any life insurance policies you or anyone else (an employer or other family member) owns on your life. Check the ownership, current death benefit, projected premiums, and beneficiaries. As discussed in Chapter 13, watch out if you are the owner: the death benefit will enlarge your taxable estate.

Also take the opportunity to review the insurance policy itself. As discussed in Chapter 13, newer policies guarantee that the premium will not increase and the death benefit will not decrease.

Step 4: Review Your Sources of Income

Make a list of current or future payments, such as pensions, Social Security, and loans that will be repaid. Social Security checks received in the month of death need to be returned to Social Security, while other payments, such as pensions, may continue in full or as a reduced spousal benefit or not at all, depending on the pension plan. Will survivors receive any of these income streams? Or, will they end at your death?

Step 5: Review Your Holdings

You would be amazed at how easily one can subvert a well thought-out estate plan if your financial plan and estate plan are not integrated. Example: You and your spouse are used to holding all of your property in joint name. Your estate plan calls for you to hold $2 million in your own name to preserve your "estate tax applicable credit amount" (discussed in Chapter 4). You forget to make this change. Or, you make the change but switch back to a joint account later.

Periodically review your holdings to determine ownership and make a copy of the document you are relying on to prove ownership. Keep copies in a safe place, along with your Survivor's List (see Chapter 16).

What do you own in your name alone, such as your car, for example, checking and savings accounts, IRAs, 401(k)s, company pensions, real estate, collectibles, life insurance policies, and any other property? What do you own jointly with your spouse or others?

When you do this review don't skip anything. Include trusts, real estate deeds, bank accounts, safety deposit boxes, checks, IRAs, pensions, life insurance policies, stock in closely held businesses . . . everything. Make a copy of all tax forms you received for the last tax year, including W-2s, 1099's, and anything evidencing payments received or capital sold. Put this all in a file ready to review as necessary.

Step 6: Create a Personal Estate Ledger

Use the information you collected above to create your personal estate ledger. List your holdings and calculate the current value of your personal estate. Do the same for your spouse. If your property is jointly held with one other person, only one-half the value appears on your side of the ledger.

Step 7: Figure Out What Passes Outside of Your Will

Review each holding to see if it passes under your will or outside of your will. As discussed in Chapters 1 and 2, these bypass your will: 1) an asset held jointly with right of survivorship, 2) holdings that pass directly to a beneficiary, such as IRA or 401(k) accounts with written beneficiary designations, or bank or brokerage accounts or stocks or bonds registered in your name as "TOD" or "Transfer on Death" accounts to a specific beneficiary, 3) property owned by a trust, and the like.

On your personal estate ledger, add a column to show how each holding will pass to your heirs. Next to each item on your ledger, write down how it will transfer. For example, next to IRA, write "IRA Beneficiary Designation," if your custodian has an IRA beneficiary designation on hand naming a beneficiary. Next to home, write "By Will," if you own the property in your own name.

If you think your IRA will pass to your children, be sure to review your beneficiary designation forms to make certain. If the custodian can't find the beneficiary designation, the IRA will pass under your will.

Step 8: Understand Post-Mortem Planning

Be attuned to post-mortem planning. Here is an example. The executor will be able to elect whether to value the decedent's property as of the date of death or six months after death, if the property is still on hand. Another post-mortem device is a disclaimer, under which a beneficiary can refuse to accept property left to him or her under a will. The disclaimer must be timely (within nine months of death) and in the proper form.

Step 9: Manage the Risk of a Long-Term Illness.

Someday, someone in your family will likely need to be cared for due to an infirmity. The wealthy self-insure against this risk. The impoverished rely on government welfare programs, such as Medicaid. Many in the middle buy long-term care insurance to protect their financial assets from being used up in the event of a protracted illness. Some play roulette and if they lose the bet, spend down their assets to qualify for Medicaid. (Any one considering this route needs to read Appendix 18-A, "Medicaid Estate Planning: A Review of the Ethical Considerations of Practicing Medicaid Estate Planning in the Area of Elder Law.")

Blended families should give the issue of long-term care special attention: since spouses are financially responsible for one another, the healthy spouse can be left penniless and his or her heirs can be effectively disinherited.

Step 10: Review Your Advisory Relationships.

Who are your financial and legal advisers and what do they do for you? Will they continue in those roles if you become incapacitated or die? How will those roles change, if at all? How are your investment accounts monitored and who will perform that function? What sort of reports do you rely on now? What reports and services would you expect your spouse to rely on after your death? Who does your taxes? Would he or she do your estate tax return? Would one adviser take the lead over others after your death? Are your advisers coordinating with each other to ensure that your estate plan is integrated with your financial plan?

Summary

After we go through these steps with our clients and their attorneys and accountants, we suggest a family meeting, especially if children are to serve as executors or trustees. The agenda is set in advance and can vary depending on how much the client wishes to involve the children. In some families, the purpose of the meeting is limited to meeting the advisers face-to-face, so that the children know whom to call if the need arises. Other families want more involvement. For example, if the family is charitably inclined, the family may wish to have the children serve on the board of a private foundation.

Following these 10 steps will put you on the road to integrating your estate and financial plans. If you do not work with an adviser who will help you coordinate this effort, consider involving a trusted family member.

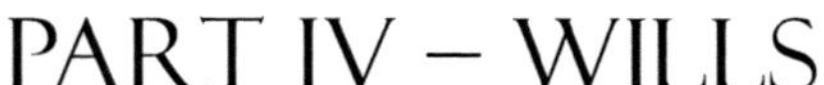

PART IV – WILLS

Chapter 19

Questions and Answers on Wills

This Chapter is provided courtesy of the American Bar Association, Reprint Rights Granted.

Q: What is a will?

A: A will is an instrument by which a person provides for the disposition of his or her property after death.

Q: Who may make a will?

A: Generally, every person of sound mind and memory, 18 years of age or over, may dispose of his or her property by will.

Q: May a person dispose of property by will in any way he or she wishes?

A: Generally speaking, yes, but with a few exceptions. For example, a surviving husband or wife may have the right to elect to take a fixed share of the estate regardless of the will. Children may be disinherited, although children born after a will is made generally will inherit as if there were no will unless the will shows an intent to disinherit children born after the will was drawn.

Q: What else can be done by a will?

A: By use of a will, an individual may designate as executor someone who is qualified and in whom he or she has confidence. An individual may establish a trust or trusts for the management of assets, the protection of family members, and for the savings of taxes in connection with an overall family estate plan. He or she may give discretionary powers to the executor and to a trustee to spend income or principal according to the changing needs of children or other relatives. An individual may select the persons to receive property and leave it to them in designated proportions. He or she may select a person to be guardian of his or her minor children

By supplementary documents, an individual may provide instructions regarding burial or cremation or anatomical gifts. Even in those cases where a testator desires to leave property to the same persons who would inherit it if he or she left no will, the testator may, by the use of a will, simplify the administration of the estate.

Q: Can a will be changed?

A: A will may be modified or added to or entirely revoked at any time before the maker's death as long as the maker is competent and able physically to change it. An amendment to a will is called a codicil. In some states, the will may refer to a memorandum disposing of tangible property (such as household items, jewelry, automobiles, etc.) which may be changed from time to time without the formalities of a will.

Q: What happens where there is no will?

A: If there is no will, the court will direct the distribution of the estate in accordance with state law. In general, this means to the immediate family—that is, the surviving husband or wife and children. Often the state law does not reflect commonly held attitudes regarding provisions for the spouse as primary and does not provide the spouse adequate means of support. If there is no surviving husband, wife, or children, other blood relatives become entitled to the property and in many cases the situation becomes very complicated. The law is rigid and gives no consideration to the needs or circumstances of the individual heirs. The law further designates who may administer the estate and may require a surety bond at the expense of the estate.

Q: Is the cost of administering an estate greater with or without a will?

A: A skillfully drawn will generally reduces expenses by giving the executor authority to act efficiently without unnecessary delay and expense. It may provide that there need be no surety bond and thus save the estate considerable expense and in many states it can direct that the intervention or involvement of the probate court can be kept to a minimum. If the will is "self-proved," court proceedings for its proof may be avoided.

Q: Is joint tenancy a substitute for a will?

A: Joint tenancy may be a useful method of transferring property, such as the family automobile and the family checking account, at death. In other situations, especially where tax considerations are involved, it can sometimes produce very unfortunate results. Even where joint tenancy is desirable, it does not take care of the situation on the death of the surviving joint tenant or a common disaster, so the necessity for a will is not eliminated. Because joint tenancy property passes outside the will, having too much property in joint tenancy may frustrate the basic family estate plan reflected in the will. Joint tenancy may also produce unexpected results when the "wrong" joint tenant dies first and has led to many disputes, including litigation, between the estate of the original owner and the surviving joint tenant as to whether the survivor's name was added as a matter of convenience or management or whether a gift was intended. A decision to put property in joint tenancy should never be made without consulting a lawyer.

Q: What is the effect of a will on life insurance?

A: If a life insurance policy is payable to an individual, then the will of the insured has no effect on the proceeds. If the life insurance policy is payable to the estate of a person, then the disposition of the proceeds can be directed by will in the same manner as any other kind of property.

Q: What is the effect of marriage or divorce on a will?

A: In many states a will is revoked by marriage unless the will expressly states that it was executed in contemplation of the particular marriage and that it shall not be revoked by such marriage. Divorce or dissolution of marriage either revokes the entire will or those provisions in favor of the former spouse. This depends on the details of your state's law.

Q: Can taxes be saved by a will?

A: Under certain conditions, definite savings can be made by the carefully planned disposition of a family estate in accordance with provisions of a skillfully drafted will. In this regard, the will may provide especially for the surviving spouse (by trust or otherwise) to minimize or eliminate taxes payable on the death of the survivor.

Q: When should a will be made?

A: A will should be made while the maker is in good health and free from emotional stress. A will that is hastily planned and drafted under pressure seldom does credit either to the maker or the drafter. The "deathbed" will is often the subject of long, expensive, and sometimes bitter litigation. Because of changing conditions in family, in size of estate, and in tax laws, a will should be reviewed periodically. A will should always be reviewed when there is a change in marital status.

Q: Who should prepare the will?

A: Generally, a will must be written and witnessed in a special manner provided by law. The drafting of a will requires learning, skill, and experience obtained only by study, training, and practice. Only a practicing lawyer can perform this service.

Chapter 20

What Can be Wrong with A Will?

The following is reprinted with permission from Chapter 9. "How to Review a Will" of "Tools & Techniques of Estate Planning," published by The National Underwriter Company. While "Tools & Techniques" is a resource for advisers (hence the use of the terms "client" and "planner," it will give you special insight on how to read a will.)

The chapter is organized in 13 parts:

1) *Introduction*
2) *Introductory Clause*
3) *Debts Clause*
4) *Tax Clause*
5) *Tangible Personal Property Clause*
6) *Devises of Real Estate Clause*
7) *Specific Bequests of Intangibles and Cash*
8) *Residuary Clause*
9) *Powers Clause*
10) *Appointment of Fiduciaries Clause*
11) *Attestation Clause*
12) *Other Clauses*
13) *Summary*

Introduction

First, it is necessary to coordinate the will properly with other dispositive documents such as employee benefit plans. For example, if the will is not synchronized with an executive's pension, group insurance, and 401(k) or other retirement plan, there is no way to minimize overall death taxes and provide for a smooth and efficient estate administration.

Second, it is impossible to know if there will be appropriate liquidity unless the will and its various dispositive schemes are examined.

Third, wills become outdated and tax laws change for instance, a marital deduction provision in a will drafted before September 13, 1981, may not qualify for the unlimited marital deduction; TRA '97 increased the unified credit in a series of steps and introduced a family-owned business exclusion; and EGTRRA 2001 introduced a slow but steady increase in the unified credit, a gradual reduction in the top estate tax rates, and a repeal of the estate tax for one year in 2010). The circumstances, needs, and desires of the parties are always in flux. The attorney who drafted the will may have died and it may have been many years since the will was revised or reviewed by either the client or attorney.

Every professional in the estate planning team must therefore be able to examine a will and spot — in general terms at least — what's wrong.

"What's wrong" with a given will is more often a question of what has been omitted or what has changed or what are the present objectives of the client than what has been improperly drafted. "What's wrong" is even more often the failure of the draftsman to match the facts of the case or the circumstances or desires of the parties with the documents. "What's wrong" may be something the accountant, for instance, knows that no other professional knows. "What's wrong" may be that the will has not been updated for years and no longer addresses the current circumstances or client goals or latest tax law. "What's wrong" may be that a will alone—without a trust or the use of other tools or techniques—is inadequate or does not maximize the possibility to accomplish the client's objectives with greater certainty and lesser cost.

The following is a (by no means complete) checklist designed to give each member of the estate planning team the tools needed to examine a will:

Introductory Clause

Start with the introductory ("exordium") clause, which should be the first paragraph in the will. The purpose of this preamble is to

1. identify the testator, the person disposing of property at death;
2. establish domicile, the county that will have legal jurisdiction for purposes of determining the validity of the will and interpreting will provisions, for purposes of state inheritance taxation (technically, what is said in a will about the testator's domicile is not dispositive but is evidence which will usually be considered even if subordinated to proof of facts to the contrary);
3. declare that the document in question is intended to dispose of the testator's property at death and no matter how many wills have been written in the past, this is meant to be the last will; and
4. revoke all prior wills. This is designed to nullify old and forgotten wills — and "codicils" (legally effective modifications of existing wills).

An example of this introductory clause is:

"I, Edward Grieg, a resident of and domiciled in the city of Bryn Mawr in Montgomery County, Pennsylvania, declare this to be my last will. I revoke all wills and codicils made prior to this will."

Planners should check:

1. Is the spelling of the client's name correct? Has the client's full name been used?
2. Is the client "A/K/A" ("also known as"), i.e., is there some other name by which the client is known and should that name be listed?
3. Is the domicile correct? For tax or other planning purposes, would it make sense to begin to document a different domicile? Will the will meet all the statutory requirements of the stated domicile? If the client spends a great deal of time in more than one residence, could the

address mentioned in the will trigger a "double domicile" problem (e.g., where more than one state claims the decedent was a domiciliary of the state and therefore has the right to impose an inheritance tax)?

4. Is there a reason prior wills and codicils should not be revoked? Instead of a new will, should the present document be a codicil making a small change but otherwise ratifying an existing will? For instance, if there is a potential for an attack on this will on the grounds of mental incompetency, fraud, or undue influence, a prior will providing a similar disposition will help prove the mental capacity of the testator and may discourage would-be contestants from attacking the current will. Conversely, if a beneficiary has been deleted, a new will should be drawn rather than a codicil to avoid the mention of the eliminated beneficiary.

After the introductory clause, the will can take either of two directions. It can (1) describe the steps that take place in administering the testator's estate (such as payment of debts and taxes and then payment of legacies) or it can (2) dispose of legacies first and describe obligations later. We will take the former approach in formulating this checklist.

Debts Clause

The next clause usually pertains to the payment of debts, expenses, and costs. The purposes of this clause are:

1. To state the source from which each debt will be paid. (This is an extremely important point because of the death tax implications. For instance, if a surviving spouse rather than some other beneficiary must pay debts, to that extent the marital deduction will be decreased and taxes may be increased. Furthermore, if the burden falls on the wrong person(s), the testator's goals may not be met.)
2. To establish as debts items that might not otherwise be considered the testator's obligations.

An example of the payment of debts clause is:

"I direct all of my debts (including any expenses of my last illness) and my funeral expenses be paid."

Planners should check:

1. Does the testator have any rights to property held in the trust of another person (a so-called "power of appointment") and, if so, what effect does the debts clause have on that property? Does it expose that property to the claims of creditors?
2. Will the beneficiaries receive more or less than the client intended when the will was drawn because of the operation of this provision? Has the size of the debt changed since the will was drawn? What will be the federal and state death tax impact of the clause?
3. What is the effect of the Equal Rights Amendment in the state of domicile? In some states the will of a married woman should contain a direction to pay debts and taxes. Otherwise, the burden of her funeral and medical expenses will be placed on her surviving husband —thus barring a deduction for payment of those expenses by her estate.
4. Did the will provide detailed funeral arrangements? Most authorities feel this is inadvisable since the will may not be found or may not be accessible in sufficient time after the testator's death. Should such provisions be placed in a "Letter of Instructions," an informal and nonlegal list of requests, suggestions, and recommendations that should not be placed in the will?
5. Does the client intend that "payment of debts" include the mortgage on property left to a specific individual? In some states, absent an express direction to the contrary, when specific property is left to an individual (a "specific bequest"), any debt on that property will not be paid off. In other states, such a clause will require the executor to satisfy the mortgage. Does the named beneficiary of a life insurance policy that has been pledged as the collateral for a loan have the right to have the loan paid off because

of the "pay my [just] debts" clause? The planner must check state law. In at least one state the answer depends on who the lender is. The result, absent specific direction to the contrary, is one way if the lender is the insurance company (the beneficiary takes only the net proceeds) and another (the beneficiary is entitled to have the estate pay off the debt out of other estate assets) if the creditor is an independent lending institution.

Tax Clause

The clause pertaining to the payment of death taxes can either be stated next or appear after the provisions disposing of property.

The purpose of the tax clause is to establish the source for the payment of the federal estate tax, the state inheritance and estate tax, and any federal or state generation-skipping transfer tax.

This is an example of a tax clause:

"I direct that all inheritance, estate, transfer, succession, legacy and other death taxes upon property required to be included in my taxable estate whether or not passing under this Will [except (1) transfer taxes levied pursuant to the provisions of Chapter 13 of the Internal Revenue Code of 1986, relating to "generation-skipping transfers," or any similar state law, and (2) taxes on property held in trust under the Will (or any revocable trust) of my spouse], and any interest and penalties thereon, shall be charged against and paid from my residuary estate passing under Article FOURTH of Part I of this my Will."

Planners should check:

1. State "apportionment" statutes. If there is no tax clause in the will or if it does not adequately address the payment of a particular death tax, state law will allocate the burden of taxes among the beneficiaries. Many states require beneficiaries to pay a share of estate taxes unless the will provides otherwise. The result is often an inappropriate or unintended reduction of the shares of certain beneficiaries or adverse tax consequences. (For example, there may be a spiraling reduction of the estate tax marital deduction. The deduction is allowed only for the net amount

passing to the surviving spouse. If that amount is reduced by an estate tax burden, the tax increases —further reducing the amount passing to the spouse, etc.) An "anti-apportionment" tax clause maybe the solution. For instance, suppose you wanted a child to receive $100,000 of your client's $2,000,000 estate free and clear. Without special provision, that child would be forced to pay his share of taxes, or 1/20 of the total federal and state death taxes. With a special tax clause, the child will receive the entire $100,000.

2. Does the client expect or want property passing outside the probate estate to pay its share of tax if it in fact generates tax? For instance, assume $1,000,000 of pension proceeds (or life insurance) is payable to the client's two oldest children and $1,000,000 of cash is payable to the client's two youngest children. Who is to pay the tax on the $2,000,000? What if the $1,000,000 of pension proceeds (or life insurance) is state inheritance tax exempt but the cash is not? Unless the will provides to the contrary, estate taxes must be paid by recipients of property passing outside the will. The will should specify who pays taxes on both probate and nonprobate property.
3. Assume a sizable amount of property will pass through a revocable living trust. Is the tax clause in that instrument coordinated with the tax clause in the will or are they incompatible? What if assets under the will are to "pour over" into a previously funded trust which itself will generate significant estate taxes. Is there (should there be) a will provision calling upon the trust to help the estate pay taxes? Does the trust have a provision recognizing and empowering a "call" on its assets to pay the probate estate's taxes?
4. Who is to pay the tax on a generation-skipping transfer? Absent a contrary direction, the taxes will probably be payable from the assets of the fund subject to the tax. Some draftsmen specifically provide that

such taxes are not to be imposed on the "skip person's" estate.

5. Assume the facts indicate that very large taxable gifts have been made by the client. The taxable portion of these gifts — to the extent not included in the client's gross estate — will be considered "adjusted taxable gifts." They will increase the rate of federal estate tax payable on the taxable estate remaining. Will an unexpectedly high burden be placed on the assets remaining because of these prior gifts and should the tax clause take such gifts into account in apportioning the tax burden?
6. Should certain beneficiaries be insulated from tax for either tax reasons or to accomplish the dispositive goals of the client or better meet the needs of the beneficiaries? For example, should a child to whom property has been given be exempted by the will from paying the estate tax on that property?

Tangible Personal Property Clause

A clause pertaining to the disposition of tangible personal property is often next. The purposes of this clause are:

(1) to provide for who will receive personal property and the terms under which they will receive it; and
(2) to make special dispositions among the persons and the organizations of the testator's choice.

An example of the tangible personal property clause is:

"I give to my daughter, Eva Grieg, all of my clothing, household furnishings, jewelry, automobiles, books, pictures, and all other articles of tangible personal property owned by me at the date of my death. If my daughter, Eva Grieg, does not survive me, I give the property mentioned above in equal shares to my grandchildren, Gretta and Gail Grieg or the survivor who is alive at the date of my death."

Or

"I give the Philadelphia Museum of Art my painting of "Helga" by Andrew Wyeth."

Planners should check:

1. Does (or should) the client make specific bequests of all "intimate" items such as a watch or ring. Absent such provisions, if personal property has been left to several individuals, the result is often needless expense in determining who gets what or reducing the estate to cash (not to mention the potential for bitter intra-family) fights). If specific bequests have been made, has each item been described in enough detail so that there will be no confusion as to which diamond ring the testator meant? (Use the same description as is found in the insurance policy covering the loss or theft of the item).
2. Has provision been made in case the item specifically left to a beneficiary is not owned by the decedent at death? For instance, what if one ring is sold and the proceeds are used to purchase a second. Does the named beneficiary receive the second ring?
3. If the item specifically bequeathed has been lost, stolen, etc. and the loss has been covered by insurance, would the client want the named beneficiary to receive the insurance? In many states the bequest of an item of personal property does not — absent specific direction to the contrary — also pass the insurance covering the item.
4. Does the client intend to pass — under the category of personal property — cash in a safe deposit box, travelers' checks, and cash found in his home or on his person? Does the client know that cash on deposit is typically not considered tangible personal property?
5. If the client has property in many different places, consider allowing the executor — at the expense of the estate — to take possession of the property "as and where is" (a provision which will permit the beneficiary to receive the property free of delivery costs and protect the fiduciary and beneficiaries during administration from the risk that specific assets will be lost).

6. The phrase "personal effects" may not encompass items of household use or even a car. Consider specific mention of items of tangible personal property.
7. Is there a "catchall" phrase that passes the residue of tangible personalty? The phrase, "all other tangible personal property" should dispose of any residual property.
8. Should the will confirm that certain property such as household furnishings, silverware, etc. belongs to someone else?
9. Does this clause dispose of property by referring to an instrument outside the will? This "incorporation by reference" is not recommended since it often leads to litigation.
10. The use of the term "contents" should be avoided. Personal property should not be described by its location.

General checkup of legacies:

1. Has property been left outright to a minor who is legally incapable of handling it or to a person under a physical, mental, or emotional handicap who does not have the physical or intellectual capacity?
2. Are all beneficiaries named alive? Are there "backup" beneficiaries (at least two) for each beneficiary? Are they the beneficiaries the client currently desires?
3. Are any of the gifts conditioned on events or circumstances that are impossible, "against public policy," or in violation of the Constitution? For example, a bequest would be invalidated by the courts if it were made on the condition that the recipient first divorce her spouse.
4. Are there gifts to "my issue" (which would unintentionally disinherit an adopted person)?
5. Do gifts to charities meet state law requirements? Has the charity's full legal (corporate) name and address been stated? (The popular name is often different from the full legal name). Have you checked the IRS's "Cumulative List of Organizations" or obtained assurances from the charity itself to make sure the gift to the charity will qualify for

a tax deduction? Has the client named a backup charity? Check to be sure the will specifies that taxes are to be paid from the portion of the residue not passing to charity. Otherwise, what should be a tax-free bequest must bear its portion of the total taxes. That reduces the charity's share and therefore increases taxes. This in turn creates a new cycle of problems.

6. If someone is intentionally omitted, have you checked state law to see if such an omission is permissible? Are there defamatory statements in the will concerning an heir? (At the probate of the will, such statements may become libelous and expose the client's estate to an action for damages.)
7. Does the will make so many specific bequests of cash that the residuary estate doesn't have enough left to pay estate taxes? Keep in mind that the IRS can attach the assets of any beneficiary for the unpaid estate tax. Check to be sure the executor will have a sufficient reserve of funds for paying estate tax and all the bequests to residuary beneficiaries.
8. Note that a tangible personal property clause should nearly always be used where the residue of the estate will be paid to a trust. Few clients want trusts involved in handling personal effects such as jewelry, or household furniture, antiques, or cars.

Devises Of Real Estate Clause

The next clause pertains to "devises," testamentary grants of real property. The purposes of the devises clause are:

1. to specify which real estate is to be disposed of under the will and to dispose of that real estate, and
2. to handle the problems where the property has been sold or destroyed prior to the testator's death.

An example of a devise is:

"I leave my residence located at 207 Rawles Run Lane, Bryn Mawr, Pa. to my daughter, Larrissa Grieg. If, at the time of my death, I am no longer using the property at 207 Rawles Run Lane as my residence, then this devise is to be void and of no effect; however, if I own any other real estate which I am using as my residence at that time, then, in such an event, I devise such other real estate to my daughter, Larrissa Grieg. If my daughter, Larrissa Grieg, does not survive me, this devise shall lapse and such real estate shall become part of my residuary estate."

Specific Bequests of Intangibles and Cash

After disposing of tangible personal property and real estate, the will may then cover specific gifts of intangibles (property where the item itself is evidence of value) such as gifts of cash or accounts receivable. An example of a gift of an intangible asset is:

"I give 100 shares of Rohm and Haas stock to my niece, Danielle Green."

Or

"I give the sum of Five Thousand ($5,000) dollars to my sister, Sara Black, if she survives me."

Planners should check:

1. Has provision been made in the event the primary beneficiary does not survive the decedent?
2. Does the will spell out what gift, if any, is made if the decedent does not possess, at the time of death, the stock mentioned in the will? What if the stock had been sold but new stock was purchased with the proceeds? What if there was a stock split and only a specified number of shares were given?

Residuary Clause

The next clause is called the "residuary clause." The purposes of the residuary clause are to:

1. transfer all assets not disposed of up to this point,

2. (in some cases) provide a mechanism for "pouring over" assets from the will to a previously established (inter vivos) trust (if a pour over is made, it is important to review the trust as carefully as the will itself), and
3. provide for an alternative disposition in case the primary beneficiary has died or the trust to which probate assets (assets passing under a valid will or by intestacy) were to be poured over was for some reason invalid, previously revoked, or never came into existence.

An example of a residuary clause is:

"All the rest, residue, and remainder of the property that I own at the date of my death, real and personal, tangible or intangible, regardless of where it is situated, I leave to my daughter, Larrissa Grieg. But if Larrissa Grieg does not survive me, then I leave the said property in equal shares to my grandchildren, Ronald Reimus and Reginald Reimus or to the survivor of them."

Planners should check:

1. Has a spouse been disinherited? If so, is the client aware of the "elective rights" (rights to a portion of the probate estate and perhaps certain other property owned by the decedent at death regardless of what the will provides) the surviving spouse has even if the will is valid? (It may be possible to control the surviving spouse to some degree by inserting a provision at least as attractive as the spouse's intestate share or by a provision reducing or eliminating the share of a person in whom the spouse is interested if he exercises his right of election. An alternative is a pre- or post-nuptial agreement).
2. Has the client, inadvertently, exercised a "power of appointment" (a right to direct the disposition of property in a trust established by someone else)? In some states, a residuary clause automatically exercises a general power of appointment unless the trust requires that it must be specifically referred to in order to make a valid exercise or unless the will itself states that no exercise is intended.

3. Is there a disposition to a young adult, minor, or a person legally, mentally, or emotionally incompetent that should be made in trust? Is there provision for the executor to retain the property during the minority of such a person or to use income or principal for that person's benefit? Has the right person been named as the custodian of a child's property and are there backups in case that person is unwilling or unable to serve?
4. Is there a default provision in case a trust into which the residue was to have poured is for any reason revoked or never came into existence?
5. If a child dies, will that child's share pass to the parties desired by the client?
6. Does the will address the possibility of the birth of a child to the client (it's never too late)?
7. Has the client, in lieu of leaving his residuary estate outright to his spouse, created a marital deduction formula disposition through a so-called formula clause?

Marital deduction formula clauses are very important to review and analyze. They are often found in the wills of clients who own assets of at least the unified credit equivalent ($1,500,000 in 2004, scheduled to increase to $3,500,000 by 2009). Such clauses typically divide the client's estate into two parts, one "marital" and the other "nonmarital." The marital portion passes property to the client's surviving spouse as part of the marital deduction and may contain an outright or trust disposition. The nonmarital portion is designed to set aside property exempted from federal estate tax by reason of the client's available unified credit and passes property to persons other than the surviving spouse (or to a credit equivalent "bypass trust" for the benefit of the surviving spouse that will not be included in the spouse's estate on his death).

Particular care must be taken not to inadvertently over pack the bypass trust and pay less than expected or desired into the marital trust. This underfunding of the marital trust could easily occur due to increases in the unified credit exemption equivalent.

The language used in the formula typically takes the form of a fixed sum (a "pecuniary marital deduction") or a fraction of the client's residuary estate (a "fractional share marital deduction"). The formula clause (especially if it is a pecuniary one) will also have to contain a provision for funding the marital deduction when assets are distributed to it.

If the marital deduction clause directs that the property is to be held in trust, the surviving spouse must generally be entitled to all of the trust's net income in each year and no other person may be interested in the income or principal during the survivor's lifetime.

Any planner who regularly reviews client wills should familiarize himself with marital deduction requirements, or, at least, direct inquiries to persons who have expertise in this area.

Powers Clause

The next clause is often one pertaining to the powers of the executor (and trustee if the will establishes a "testamentary trust," a trust created at the testator's death under the will). The purposes of the powers clause are to:

1. give the executor (and trustee) specific power and authority over and above those provided by state law to enable the executor to conserve and manage the property, and
2. limit, where desired and appropriate, the executor's power and authority (for instance, the client may not want the executor to make certain investments), and
3. provide authority to continue a business (or handle other property with special management or investment problems) and the special flexibility necessary to accomplish that objective, and
4. protect the executor against suit by other beneficiaries by specifying the powers necessary to accomplish the executor's role.

An (abbreviated) example of a powers clause is:

"I authorize my executor (as well as any substitute executor) in his, her, or its discretion, with respect to all property, real and personal, in addition to the powers conferred by law, to:

1. *retain assets*
2. *purchase investments*

3. *hold cash*
4. *vote and grant proxies*
5. *sell, exchange, or dispose of*
6. *distribute in cash or in kind*
7. *delegate to agents*
8. *assign or compromise claims*
9. *borrow funds*
10. *lease, manage, develop real estate*
11. *abandon property*
12. *make certain tax elections*
13. *receive and use employee benefits."*

Planners should check:

1. Are there any assets or problems in this case which require special powers to fulfill the desires of the client or provide the executor with sufficient flexibility? (Beware of "boilerplate" clauses). Are there powers that should be added? Are there "standard" powers that should be removed or modified?
2. Will any power adversely affect the estate tax marital deduction? For instance, a marital deduction trust, under IRC Sections 2056(b)(5) or 2056(b)(7), must provide that the surviving spouse receive all income at least annually. Consider the impact of a power allowing the trustee under a testamentary trust to retain nonincome producing property. Unless the will/trust also contains a provision allowing the surviving spouse to demand that the trust assets be sold or made income producing, the marital deduction may be lost. Will such a power thwart other objectives of the testator? For instance, what if the unproductive property was stock in a family corporation? A sale of such stock would raise income but could cause the loss of family control of the corporation. The draftsman might consider including a "savings clause" that would nullify any power, duty, or discretionary authority that might jeopardize the marital deduction.

3. Will any of the powers granted cause a conflict of interest? For instance, if the executor is a bank, discretionary authority to invest in its own securities or common trust funds will cause a conflict that must be specifically "forgiven" by the will (assuming the client wants to do so). Is the executor a business partner or co-shareholder of the insured? What problems might they create?
4. Is there specific authority for the executor to make distribution "in kind" (as opposed to selling estate assets and making the distribution in cash)? In some states absent specified power to do so, the executor may have no choice: the distribution must be made in cash.

Appointment of Fiduciaries Clause

The appointment of the executor, trustee of any testamentary trust, and guardian of any minor child, often comes toward the end of the will.

The purposes of the fiduciary appointment clause are:

1. to name the individual(s) or corporate fiduciary or combinations of individual(s) and fiduciaries who will administer the testator's estate and any trust that the will creates;
2. to give the executor the appropriate power to act on behalf of the estate and carry out the terms of the will;
3. to specify if and how the executor is to be compensated;
4. state whether or not the executor is to post bond;
5. to specify the authority of and decision making process for co-executors; and
6. to name guardian(s) and successor guardian(s) of any minor child of the testator.

An example of the appointment clause is:

"I appoint my nephew, Farnsworth Dowlrimple III, as the executor under this will. If for any reason he fails to qualify or ceases to act, I appoint the Left Bank and Trust of Overflow, Pa. as my executor. I confer upon my executor all the powers enumerated in clause above. No executor shall be required to furnish any bond or other security in any jurisdiction. I direct

that my nephew, Farnsworth, shall receive no compensation for his services as Executor and that the Left Bank and Trust of Overflow, Pa. be entitled to be compensated for its services as executor in accordance with its regularly adopted schedule of compensation in effect and applicable at the time of the performance of such services."

Planners should check:

1. Does the client trust the individual who is currently named as executor and backup executor? Is that individual or corporate fiduciary legally qualified to act as executor? (Has the attorney who drew the will been named as executor? Typically, absent special circumstances, this raises a number of ethical questions and raises the spectre of a conflict of interest.)
2. Should the executor's bond be waived?
3. Is the executor named willing to serve? (How recently has the client checked?)
4. Is the guardian for minors willing to act? Is he able to act? Is that person suitable?
5. Is a prolonged estate (or trust) administration anticipated? If so, consider giving executors (trustees) the power to appoint successors by filing an instrument with the probate or other appropriate court.

Testator's Signing Clause

The next to the last clause in a will is typically the testator's signing or "testimonium" provision. The purposes of the testimonium clause are

1. to establish that the document is intended to be the testator's last will,
2. to meet statutory requirements that require the testator's signature at the logical conclusion of the will, and
3. to state the date on which the will was signed.

An example of a testimonium clause is:

"In witness of the above, I subscribe my name, this 11th day of October 2004 at Bryn Mawr, Pennsylvania to this, my last will, which consists of 13 pages (each of which I have initialed at the bottom)."

Planners should check:

1. Is the will signed by the testator at its logical end? Is each page numbered? Is the page count correct?
2. Are there duplicate or triplicate signed wills in existence? If the testator was given a signed duplicate which is not found at his death, it is possible that a presumption will arise that the testator destroyed it with the intention of revoking it. The potential for litigation is therefore increased significantly. The better practice is for only one original to be executed.

Attestation Clause

The final clause in a will is the "attestation" provision. The purposes of the attestation (often called the witness) clause are to:

1. witness the testator's signing,
2. comply with statutory requirements,
3. underline the testamentary character of the document, and
4. comply with state law requirements in cases where the testator signed by a mark (such as an "X") or where, at the testator's direction and on his behalf, the will was signed by someone else (as would be the case where the testator was physically incapable of signing but mentally competent).

An example of an attestation clause is:

"This will was signed by Edward Grieg, the testator, and declared to be his last will in our presence. We, at his request and in his presence and in the presence of each other, state that we witnessed his signing and declaration and at his request we have signed our names as witnesses this 11th day of October 2004."

Planners should check:

1. Are there three witnesses to the testator's signing? Although most states require less, three witnesses will comply with the most stringent probate requirements of any state and as a practical matter provide stronger evidence of the competence and testamentary intent of the testator.
2. Were any of the witnesses beneficiaries under the will? This is inadvisable for at least two reasons: First, the witnesses may become incompetent to testify as to the execution or validity of the will. Second, witnesses who are also beneficiaries may be prevented from receiving bequests under the will.
3. Are the addresses of the witnesses stated? Although addresses may not be legally required, they make it easier to locate and identify witnesses when needed.
4. Is the will "self proving"? I.e., in some states a notarized affidavit attached to the will signed by the witnesses (and in some states, the testator, also) that describes the circumstances of the execution of the will may permit the will to be admitted to probate without the requirement that the witnesses be found or appear before the court in the probate proceeding.

Other Clauses

There are, of course, many other clauses that should be considered in reviewing a will.

Some additional points for the planner to check are:

1. Is the federal estate tax marital deduction important? If so, consider that the Uniform Simultaneous Death Act, which applies in most states, presumes that the testator survives in the event of a simultaneous death involving the testator and a beneficiary. This would cause a loss of the estate tax marital deduction unless the will superseded state law by providing a "common disaster" clause. This provision makes the presumption that the testator's spouse is deemed to have survived.

2. Does the will consider the possibility that one or more beneficiaries will disclaim? The will should state who would receive property if the named beneficiary renounces his interest. The transfer is then treated as if the decedent had left property directly to the ultimate recipient.
3. Have the provisions in the will been coordinated with other dispositive instruments? For instance, is the will coordinated with all trusts, with employee benefit plans, buy-sell agreements, and life insurance beneficiary designations?
4. Are the problems of minors, incompetents, and other beneficiaries with special needs o circumstances properly addressed in the will? In other words, is the right asset going to the right person at the right time and in the right manner? Has the client considered the financial burden that may be placed on the guardians of minor children, and have appropriate financial provisions been made so that they can afford to raise both the client's children and their own? (Some may want to set up a special life insurance funded trust that, if necessary, can provide to the guardians needed dollars, but, if not, will go to the client's children later in life.)
5. Is the client's spouse's will coordinated with the client's will?
6. Is there a "spendthrift clause" to provide protection against the claims of creditors?

Summary

Although only an attorney should draft a will, every member of the estate planning team should make it a practice to review a client's will on a regular basis. The non-attorney's role in the will review process should be thought of not as a replacement for or as a means of "second guessing" the attorney, but rather as a source of additional strength in the planning process. The estate planner can provide in that regard a valuable resource to ascertain how the client's total dispositive plan can most effectively and efficiently meet the current needs, circumstances, and goals of both the client and the client's beneficiaries.

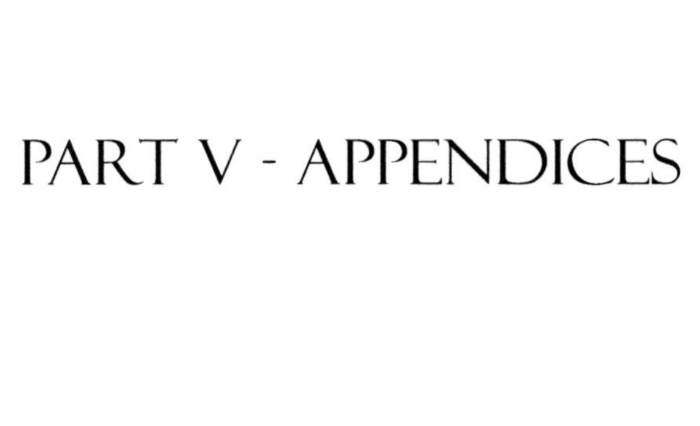

PART V - APPENDICES

Appendix 1-A

Provided Courtesy of the Probate Courts of Connecticut

Understanding Trusts: A Look at Living Trusts and Other Trusts

UNDERSTANDING TRUSTS

INTRODUCTION

In recent years the public has been bombarded with a barrage of advertisements, brochures, and articles about trusts of all kinds, especially so-called living trusts. Some of the information offered for public consumption is misleading and some of it is simply false.

This brochure is offered as a public service to give the average person an elementary understanding of the subject of trusts and to point out the dangers and pitfalls of false advertising. Many authors have written volumes on the subject without answering every question that could be raised. Therefore, of necessity, this brochure is a very modest attempt to answer some of the most basic questions about trusts and thereby give the reader enough information to ask more detailed and probing questions of professionals who promote and prepare trusts.

Consumers should be leery of marketers who offer truly incredible claims about what a trust can do, and they should be doubly leery when a hefty price is attached to the product the marketer is trying to sell. When in doubt, the age-old advice of getting a second opinion from someone who has no ax to grind and no profit to make from your business is more apt today than ever before.

BASIC TERMS

Trust: Generally, a legal device designed to provide financial assistance to someone without giving that person total control over the trust assets. A trust may be revocable or irrevocable, express or implied. This brochure will deal only with express, written documents that become irrevocable upon the death of the person who created the trust.

Testamentary Trust: A trust created within and as part of a person's will.

Living (Inter Vivos) Trust: A trust created and activated while the person who drafted it (settlor) is still living. It should not be confused with a living will, which is another legal device incorporating the drafter's wishes concerning the removal of life support systems under certain circumstances.

Settlor: The person who creates a living trust, frequently the one funding it. This person may also be referred to as a grantor or donor.

Testator: The person executing a will, with or without a testamentary trust.

Trustee: The person or institution entrusted with administering the trust. The term should be distinguished from an executor or administrator, who is responsible for settling a decedent's estate regardless of whether a trust is involved or not. The common characteristic that trustees, executors, and administrators share is that they are all fiduciaries, meaning that they have been entrusted with other people's property, and they are legally responsible to manage it properly.

Beneficiary: A person or institution for whose benefit the trust was created. A beneficiary is frequently a close relative of the settlor but need not be. Other typical beneficiaries include charities, friends of the settlor, and others whom the settlor wishes to benefit in some way.

Term: A trust may last for a short, fixed period of time or, if properly planned, for a longer period, even spanning generations. The most common type of trust is one designed to last during the life of the settlor's surviving spouse and beyond, usually until the settlor's children or other descendants reach a certain age of maturity. Charitable trusts often last indefinitely — for as long as there are assets to manage and distribute.

Spendthrift Trust: A trust designed to be immune from the claims of the beneficiaries' creditors, often including the state or federal government.

Medicaid: A federally-created program, which is administered by each state, that provides long-term nursing care and other benefits to those qualified to receive it. Medicaid is commonly referred to as "Title XIX."

Accounting: A report of the trustee's financial transactions, including a list of receipts, disbursements, sales, and purchases of assets and distributions to beneficiaries.

WHY TRUSTS MAY BE of VALUE

Trusts have generally been used to help people who fall into two basic categories: people who need financial assistance and people who are unable to manage their own money properly. Hence, trusts have been used to benefit children, those over the age of majority who are immature and otherwise unable to manage large sums of money, those with disabilities who aren't able to manage their own affairs, and those with substantial creditors.

In addition, trusts are commonly employed as devices to shield a person's assets from unnecessary taxation or court supervision. The trustee is normally directed to pay income to one or more beneficiaries and is given discretion to distribute principal, usually subject to certain stated standards. The payment of income may also be discretionary. The trust, therefore, allows the settlor (even after his or her death) to distribute assets to favored parties and to control those assets "from the grave" through the trustee whom he or she has appointed. For example, an individual who has children from a prior marriage might establish a trust for his or her spouse to ensure that the individual's children receive the trust property after the spouse's death. If properly created, a "spendthrift trust" (see definition above) may be crafted to shelter assets from the reach of the beneficiaries' creditors, including the government.

Tax Benefits

One of the greatest advantages of the trust is its ability to shelter certain assets from taxation at the time of the settlor's death. The Internal Revenue Service taxes both lifetime gifts and property passing after death, if certain exemptions are exceeded. The subject is a complicated one, but the reader should be aware of the fact that gifts or bequests between spouses are normally exempt. As long as both spouses are still living and competent, the proper utilization of a trust may shelter additional assets from taxation if the trust is drafted properly. It does not matter whether the trust is a testamentary or living trust. Contrary to the suggestions of some living trust marketers, the tax benefits are identical.

The use of an irrevocable life insurance trust or a charitable remainder trust may also offer potentially attractive tax benefits.

THE PROS and CONS of TESTAMENTARY and LIVING TRUSTS

Both testamentary and living trusts can play a viable role in professional estate planning. Each device should be analyzed on the basis of fact, not fiction. If scare tactics are employed in promoting one over the other, that is a fairly reliable clue that the entire truth is not being told, and the listener should beware. What follows is a summary of the most common benefits and detriments mentioned by objective practitioners in the field.

May a testamentary or living trust be modified or revoked?

A testamentary trust is always revocable and modifiable as long as the testator is living and competent. Naturally, it becomes irrevocable when the testator dies. A living trust, as the term is commonly used, is ordinarily revocable, although certain types of trusts established during the settlor's life may be irrevocable, usually for tax reasons. For example, a typical life insurance trust (and often a charitable remainder trust) is irrevocable upon formation.

Does the person creating the trust lose control of his assets?

Since a testamentary trust does not spring into use until the testator's death, the testator retains full control and use of his assets in his own name, without transferring them to the trust. In a revocable living trust, the settlor (who normally appoints himself as the first in a series of trustees) usually remains in control of his assets as long as he is alive and competent. He normally must transfer all of his assets to the trust and thereafter controls their use as his own self-appointed trustee. Therefore, all those holding his assets (banks, brokerage houses, etc.) must be notified of the transfers, and the correct forms must be completed to transfer the assets properly. Without completing these transfers, the living trust may be of virtually no value, since the trustee of a living trust cannot control assets that have not been properly transferred to the trust. It is somewhat cumbersome to transfer assets in and out of a living trust, and sometimes the result is that assets that were intended to be made part of the trust fall outside of the trust because they were not properly transferred to it.

How is real estate transferred to a living trust?

If real estate is part of a living trust, a proper deed must be drafted, executed, and placed on the public land records to properly transfer the real estate to the trust. If the settlor subsequently wants the real estate back in his or her name, another deed will have to be employed to reverse the process. The transfer may also necessitate notifying the mortgage holder and obtaining its approval. In addition, the homeowner's insurance company should be notified. An attorney should always be consulted before making real estate transfers, since important tax and other implications are involved. Property tax ramifications should also be carefully weighed and considered before making such a transfer, because the transfer may invalidate an existing tax exemption. With a testamentary trust, the settlor retains direct ownership of the real estate, so deeding it to the trust is not necessary.

What do attorneys charge for testamentary and living trusts?

There is no fixed rule about what attorneys may charge for either kind of trust. It is normally part of an overall estate plan. Traditionally, fees will depend on the complexity of the estate, the complexity of the legal document, and the amount of time expended. Some attorneys charge substantially more to draft a living trust than a testamentary trust, even though the legal work may be very similar. It is always a good idea to obtain a fee quotation in advance for both kinds of trusts and to weigh the pros and cons of the work performed against the fees charged. When in doubt, get a second opinion.

What about the confidentiality of the trust?

A testamentary trust remains confidential until the settlor dies, and the will is submitted to the probate court. At that time, the entire will, including the trust, becomes a matter of public record, although few people bother to look at other people's wills. A living trust may remain confidential as to uninterested parties. Probate courts and the taxing authorities may, under certain circumstances, require a copy of the trust instrument. Interested parties may have a right to know the contents of the trust instrument, but the intervention of a Court may be required if the trustee fails to provide it. Contrary to the public statements of some promoters of living trusts, it is not proper to prevent a beneficiary with a legitimate interest in the trust from receiving a copy of at least the portion of the trust applicable to that beneficiary. In addition, a beneficiary has the right to petition the probate court for a copy of the instrument as part of his request for an accounting from the trustee.

Can a testamentary or living trust protect trust assets from creditors?

The promoters of living trusts often boast that the assets in a living trust can be insulated from the claims of the settlor's creditors. What they do not always say is that there are important exceptions. For example, the creditors of a settlor who has created a revocable, funded living trust (the most common of all) and named himself as trustee can and do reach the settlor's assets. That applies also to a settlor or his spouse who needs long term care (whether at home or in a nursing home) and submits an application for Title XIX Medicaid assistance. Under current federal and state law, the revocable trust assets will be deemed available to the settlor or his spouse and could result in denial of Title XIX benefits. On the other hand, properly drafted testamentary spendthrift trusts can shield trust assets from the creditors of beneficiaries. For example, the beneficiary of a properly drafted spendthrift testamentary trust would be eligible for Title XIX assistance, since the assets within such a trust would not be deemed available to the beneficiary. This area of the law is extremely technical and fraught with potential pitfalls. An attorney with expertise in Title XIX law should always be consulted beforehand.

What about legal and other fees in administering a trust?

The legal and other professional fees in administering (as opposed to creating) either kind of trust may vary, but it is becoming more common in the legal community for attorneys to charge their clients on the basis of time and effort expended and not on the size of the estate. Ordinarily, accountants do the same. In that regard, there should be little difference between the legal or accounting fees incurred in handling one trust over another. The work is virtually identical:

(1) a list of the assets of the trust must be compiled, together with date of death values (and alternate valuation dates with larger estates);
(2) creditors' claims must be reviewed;
(3) appropriate tax returns must be filed with virtually identical tax results;
(4) information should be provided to interested beneficiaries as reasonably requested, and finally,
(5) some kind of an overall account should be provided to the beneficiaries.

Any suggestion that the administration of a living trust does not entail this work, especially in larger estates, is irresponsible and misleading. The trustee of a living trust who did not perform this elementary work would violate his fiduciary duty to the beneficiaries.

Some states have statutory schedules for the payment of testamentary trustees, executors, and administrators. In fact, some Connecticut promoters of living trusts use those fees as examples of the kinds of fees charged in Connecticut probate courts. Connecticut has no such law, and all fees are subject to probate review for reasonableness. Any party may challenge the fees charged by a trustee or any other fiduciary, and the fiduciary, under Connecticut law, has the burden of proving their reasonableness. If the Court considers the fees unjustifiable and excessive, the Court can and will reduce them.

The fees charged by the trustee of a living trust are not screened by anyone but the parties themselves. Even if they are excessive, the parties may not be aware of that fact and may be reluctant to question or object to them. If a disgruntled beneficiary gets up the courage to challenge the fees officially, he could invoke the jurisdiction of the probate court (at least in Connecticut) or bring a more costly action in the superior court.

What delays are involved in trust administration?

Promoters of living trusts frequently cite undocumented delays in the probate process as reasons for using a living trust. Delays in administering testamentary or living trusts are virtually always related to the actions of the trustee, not the document itself. Common causes of delays include time needed for federal or state tax audits, litigation involving the estate or trust, or simply the reluctance or inability of the trustee to perform the necessary duties in a timely fashion. It is almost never the probate court itself that causes a delay in the administration or distribution of trust assets. On the contrary, it is often the prodding of the probate court that prompts the trustee to complete his duties more expeditiously. With a living trust, there is no apparatus to "move the trustee along," except for the informal prodding of other family members. The problem is often compounded when the trustee and the beneficiaries do not enjoy a close personal relationship or worse, fight like cats and dogs.

What is the truth about "avoiding probate"?

Perhaps the most advertised "benefit" of the living trust is that it "avoids probate." What that often-misunderstood phrase means is that it avoids the supervision of the probate court. Avoiding probate does not avoid estate or inheritance taxes. Those taxes apply equally to assets held in a living trust or a testamentary trust, and the opportunity of minimizing those taxes applies equally to both kinds of trusts. Unbeknown to most lay people, a living trust does not avoid the statutory fees charged by the probate court. These fees, which are established by the state legislature, are a matter of public record, and they may be found in the Probate Court brochure entitled The Probate Court and You. For example, a $250,000 estate passing to a non-spouse would result in a $990 probate fee, while the fee to a surviving spouse would be $552.50, since there is a special exemption for spouses. Many experienced probate practitioners do not find these fees excessive, and most lay people, when they discover what they are, find them reasonable as well.

Living trust marketers usually fail to advise their clients that these probate fees are charged on the basis of the gross taxable estate as shown on the state estate tax return (or sometimes the federal estate tax return), which must be filed in the probate court even if all the decedent's property is passing through a living trust. Therefore, the same fees will generally be charged whether or not a living trust is used.

What are the advantages of probate court supervision?

If the beneficiary of a testamentary trust is not sure what the trustee is doing, and the trustee will not respond to legitimate requests for information, the beneficiary may ask the Court to hold an informal conference, and one will generally be held within 30 days. These informal conferences frequently resolve problems before they are formally litigated, thereby saving the parties a great deal of time and money. This is just one reason why many people consider the supervision of the probate court to be a positive, not a negative, feature. The role of the Court is not to interfere in the management of the estate, but to expedite it. Here are two other examples:

(1) When executors, administrators, or trustees are not acting properly or promptly, the Court can and will spur them on to complete their duties.

(2) Probate proceedings can be very simple and informal. Approximately 50% of Connecticut estates are administered by family members without the assistance of an attorney. These family members often forego

the payment of a fiduciary's fee or charge less than a professional.

Finally, experience has shown that some fiduciaries act dishonestly. While the vast majority of trustees perform their duties with integrity, one cannot ignore those incidents in which funds have been misappropriated, sometimes for years, without anyone being aware of it. The supervision of the probate court can be an excellent deterrent to such problems, and, in the event that a problem arises, it can be an effective and inexpensive mechanism to effect a remedy.

What can happen when the settlor of a living trust becomes incapable?

A currently-funded living trust provides a seamless mechanism for meeting the needs of a settlor who becomes incapacitated after creating the trust. What typically happens is this: the settlor, in the living trust instrument, provides that if he or she becomes incapacitated, a new trustee (named by the settlor) will take over management of the trust assets and provide for the settlor's care for the remainder of his or her life. Then, upon the settlor's death, the trustee would continue to manage the trust assets for the benefit of the settlor's beneficiaries. Advocates of this arrangement argue that this procedure avoids the appointment of a conservator for the incapacitated individual by the probate court, and they are right. It does. But whether or not that is a good thing is something for the settlor to consider carefully.

First of all, the trust normally provides that someone other than the settlor will determine whether the settlor has become incapacitated. If that determination is made, the settlor will be stripped of all rights over his own property without any impartial Court determination whatsoever. It is possible that a family member who would personally benefit from administering the trust could wrest control of the trust from an ailing but competent settlor.

Secondly, the trustee will be managing the trust assets for the incapacitated settlor without anyone checking to see whether he is treating the settlor fairly or not. Since a power of attorney for health care decisions is normally given to the trustee at the same time the trust is executed, the new trustee could sell the settlor's home, admit the settlor to a convalescent home of his own choice, and do a host of other things without any Court oversight at all.

Conversely, if the living trust did not provide this kind of power, the trustee or other family member would probably need to seek the appointment of a conservator through the probate court. Once an application is filed, certain important due process rights are guaranteed to the alleged incapable person:

(1) a copy of the application is given to the person so that he or she knows exactly what is being alleged and can challenge those allegations if he or she disagrees with them;
(2) an attorney must be appointed for the person if he or she cannot request one, so that his or her legal interests are adequately protected;
(3) a hearing is held before the judge in an informal atmosphere, which may occur within the person's own home or hospital room if he or she cannot attend the hearing in court;
(4) the person is invited to participate fully in the process, and his or her wishes are carefully considered by the Court, including the identity of the person who might become the conservator;
(5) the conservator's actions can be controlled by the Court, so that an inappropriate admission to a nursing home or the premature sale of the person's home can be avoided;
(6) the conservator must account to the Court for the actions taken, so as to avoid self-dealing, improper use of assets, and the taking of excessive fees;
(7) if any interested party is dissatisfied with the actions taken by the probate court, an appeal can be made to a higher court.

None of these fundamental rights are automatically afforded to a settlor in a living trust. The legal remedies available to such a settlor are cumbersome and very costly. Whether or not incapacity provisions should be included in a living trust is a very personal matter and should never be glossed over by the person preparing the instrument. As you can see, the settlor's most basic rights are at stake.

Can a dissatisfied family member attack a trust?

Some argue that it is easier for dissatisfied heirs to attack a person's will rather than a living trust. The fact is that either device may be challenged in court by a person with proper standing. Any competent attorney will take the necessary precautions to buttress the relevant instrument against attack, whether it be a will or a living trust. That is why great care should be exercised in selecting the proper attorney to advise about the appropriateness of each device.

If I have a living trust, do I still need a will?

Most lawyers will recommend to their clients who choose to have a living trust that they also execute what is called a "pour-over" will, simply because a living trust is ineffective as to any asset not transferred to the trust. For example, if the settlor neglects to transfer his house to the trust, that asset must pass through the probate process. If the settlor didn't execute a will leaving his assets to the trust or some other person, those assets may pass by law to persons the settlor never wanted to inherit from him. Hence, it is always a good idea to execute a will in addition to a living trust.

Do I need a living trust or not?

As the reader can readily see, there is no automatic answer to the question, "Should I have a living trust?" Living trusts, wills (with or without testamentary trusts), the utilization of jointly held assets, and other devices are all potentially useful and desirable estate planning tools to consider with proper legal advice. Embarking upon a sophisticated estate plan without proper professional guidance is like walking through a minefield without a map. The results can be catastrophic. Similarly, small estates with typical family beneficiaries do not usually warrant the cost or complexity of a living trust. For example, in general, a married couple with combined assets (including potential life insurance proceeds) below the federal estate tax exemption will not need a trust to save taxes. Also, those with modest estates consisting of a jointly held home and cash or securities under a few hundred thousand dollars may find little benefit in using a living trust. A cost/benefit analysis should be undertaken to determine if the added costs warrant such a device.

Therefore, great care should be exercised in locating a competent estate attorney to discuss the pros and cons of a living trust and any other estate planning device. If assistance is needed, contact your local or state bar association or obtain a referral from some other knowledgeable authority.

YOUR RIGHTS as the BENEFICIARY of a TESTAMENTARY or LIVING TRUST

The right to information and an accounting

The trustee of either a testamentary or living trust should communicate periodically and regularly with the trust beneficiaries as the trust or circumstances dictate. Beneficiaries should normally be kept abreast of major decisions affecting the trust: for example, the sale or exchange of a major asset of the trust, a major expense, the fees of the trustee and any other professional hired by the trustee, amounts distributed to beneficiaries, and other matters of direct concern. If the trustee does not so communicate, or if any beneficiary believes he or she is being kept "in the dark" by the trustee, the beneficiary has the right to petition the appropriate probate court for relief.

Section 45a-175(c) of the Connecticut General Statutes permits the probate court to order an accounting from the trustee of a living trust, if the Court finds:

(1) the beneficiary has a sufficient interest in the trust,
(2) cause has been shown that an accounting is necessary, and
(3) the request for an accounting is not for the purpose of harassment.

The location and identity of the specific probate court is determined by Section 45a-175(c)(2), which allows the matter to be brought to that probate court:

(1) which is the residence of the trustee, or if a corporate trustee, in which it has an office, or
(2) in which the trust assets are maintained, or
(3) in which the settlor presently resides or resided immediately prior to his death.

The beneficiary of a testamentary trust may ask the Court for an accounting at any time upon a proper showing of cause. In addition, the trustee of such a trust must render a written accounting to the Court at least every three years, unless the filing is excused by the will itself and the Court.

The right to a copy of the trust instrument

Any person may obtain copies of any non-confidential file in the probate court upon the payment of a reasonable copy charge. Testamentary trusts and wills so filed are not considered confidential and are therefore available for copying.

If the beneficiary or other interested party of a living trust requested the trustee to supply a copy of the trust but was refused, that person may apply to either the probate court or the appropriate superior court for an order compelling that disclosure as part of an action for an accounting. It is within the discretion of either Court to grant the request or not. Normally, the Court would be inclined to do so if the party could prove sufficient economic interest in the trust, which might be jeopardized without direct knowledge of the terms of the trust.

The right to compel the distribution of income or principal from the trust

Whether the beneficiary of either a living or testamentary trust has the right to compel the trustee to make a distribution of principal and/or income to him or any other beneficiary depends on the circumstances of each case. The answer depends on a number of factors, most importantly the provisions of the trust itself and, secondly, the finding by the Court that the failure to make such a distribution would be a violation of the trustee's fiduciary responsibility. For example, it is common for family trusts to provide for the mandatory payment of income only to a surviving spouse and such amounts of principal as the trustee determines are appropriate and reasonable. A surviving spouse who did not receive the mandatory payments of income would have a right to seek a court order compelling those income payments. However, whether or not the trustee's refusal to pay principal to the spouse amounted to a violation of fiduciary duty would be for the Court to determine after hearing all of the relevant facts of the case. It is always a good idea to consult with a knowledgeable attorney before attempting to file an application with the court to compel such a payment.

CONCLUSION

As the reader can see, it is not easy to decide whether or not to have a testamentary or living trust. The final decision depends upon the needs of the settlor and those of the family or others the settlor wants to benefit. The use of "one size fits all" trusts is almost always a bad idea — not because they cost so little, but because they can do so much damage to the unsuspecting consumer. Tax considerations, potential Title XIX issues, and a host of other critical factors must be carefully weighed in making the final decision. Both testamentary and living trusts can play a legitimate role in proper estate planning. Ask your attorney what makes the most sense for you.

Appendix 1-B

Provided Courtesy of the Probate Courts of Connecticut

Guidelines for Administration of Decedents' Estates

INTRODUCTION

The responsibility for settling the affairs of a decedent often falls upon a family member or friend. We have prepared this booklet to answer some questions about probate court procedures that are often asked during the settlement of a decedent's estate.

Since many of the estates handled in the probate courts deal with complex statutes and tax laws, it is important for each person to seek competent professional advice when faced with these problems. This booklet should not be considered as a substitute for that advice but rather as a guide to the fiduciary's responsibilities.

WHY DO PROBATE COURTS BECOME INVOLVED IN THE SETTLING OF DECEDENTS' ESTATES?

When a person who owns property dies, the Probate Court becomes involved to oversee the division of his property among those legally entitled to it. This division of property will be carried out according to the person's wishes if he had made them known by executing a will. If the person, referred to as a "decedent," left no will, the property will be divided according to certain laws known as the laws of "intestacy." In addition to overseeing the distribution of the estate, the Probate Court will ensure that any debts of the decedent, funeral expenses, and taxes are paid prior to distributing the remaining assets of the estate.

HOW DO PROBATE COURTS BECOME INVOLVED IN THE SETTLING OF DECEDENTS' ESTATES?

A decedent who left a will is known as a "testator." Within 30 days of the testator's death, the will must be brought to the probate court in the district in which he or she had last permanently resided. This is usually the responsibility of the "executor," a person named in the testator's will to carry out the terms of the will. Any other person who has knowledge of, or possession of, a will for the testator must deliver the will either to the executor or to the probate court within 30 days of the testator's death. There is a criminal penalty for failure to do so.

In addition to a will, there may be additions or amendments to the will that are known as "codicils." A codicil is the only legal document that can add to, delete, or modify provisions of a will. Any codicils must also be delivered to the probate court within 30 days of the testator's death. Before the provisions of a will are carried out, the will must be "probated" or "proved" in the probate court in a proceeding to determine the will's validity as a legal document. The Court approves the appointment of the executor named in the will as part of this process.

In the case of a person who dies "intestate," having left no will, an application for appointment of an administrator to handle the decedent's affairs and property must be filed in the probate court in the district in which the decedent had her permanent residence at the time of death. This is usually done by the decedent's surviving spouse, an adult child, or other relative. The Court will appoint an administrator who will have the same duties as an executor named in a will. The law favors the appointment of close relatives, such as the spouse or a child. Both the administrator and the executor are referred to as the "fiduciary," a term used to denote a person (or persons) who holds a position of trust involving the handling of the property of another.

WHAT ARE THE RESPONSIBILITIES OF A FIDUCIARY IN THE HANDLING OF A DECEDENT'S ESTATE?

The fiduciary's responsibilities in the handling of a decedent's estate include managing all transactions in a careful manner, ensuring the preservation of the estate's assets, and expediting the formal settlement of the estate. The fiduciary is expected to be fair and impartial in all dealings with creditors and beneficiaries. The fiduciary has the responsibility for filing all necessary documents in connection with the administration of the estate in the probate court. A step-by-step list of responsibilities is contained within this pamphlet.

WHEN SHOULD A FIDUCIARY SEEK PROFESSIONAL ASSISTANCE?

While the Probate Court may assist a fiduciary in administering an estate, it is often advisable for the fiduciary to engage professional assistance. For example, professional assistance may be necessary when the estate to be managed involves substantial or unusual assets or if the estate is large enough to involve the filing of a Federal Estate Tax Return. Forms that need to be filed in the probate court are available from the court, and instructions for their completion are often included on the forms.

IS THERE A SIMPLIFIED PROCEDURE FOR SETTLING SMALL ESTATES WITH LIMITED TYPES OF ASSETS?

A simplified procedure for settling the estate may be available if the total value of the estate assets does not exceed $20,000. In addition, at the time of death the decedent must not own any real estate other than survivorship property, and the estate assets must consist only of personal property and/or an unreleased interest in a mortgage with or without value. This simplified procedure may be used even though survivorship property passed to a survivor as a result of the death of the decedent.

In such a case it is not usually necessary to apply for the appointment of an administrator or admission of the will for probate. If the claims against the estate equal or exceed the assets, no distribution will be necessary. In the event that there are excess assets after the payment of debts and expenses, and either no will is found or the will's terms are not inconsistent with the laws of intestate succession, then the Court shall order distribution in accordance with the laws of intestacy without admitting the will to probate.

If, however, there is a will that provides for a distribution that is not consistent with the laws of intestate succession, then the Court shall order a distribution in accordance with the terms of the will only if the decedent's heirs-at-law sign a written waiver of their right to contest the will. In the alternative, the Court will order a distribution in accordance with the laws of intestacy if the beneficiaries named in the will consent in writing to such a distribution. If neither the heirs sign a waiver of their rights, nor the beneficiaries consent to an intestate distribution, the small estates procedure will not be available to settle the estate, and the will must be offered for probate.

When the small estates procedure is appropriate, the decedent's spouse, if any, or if none, any of the decedent's next of kin, or if there is no next of kin or if the surviving spouse or next of kin refuses, then any suitable person whom the Court deems to have sufficient interest may file an affidavit with the probate court certifying to the payment of all the decedent's debts, at least to the extent of the fair market value of all of the assets, and submit the will for filing only. The affidavit must also state whether or not the decedent had been receiving aid or care from the state. In addition to the affidavit, form CT-706 NT, Connecticut Estate Tax Return, must be filed. Please see Step 7.

The steps given below in bold print outline the major responsibilities of the fiduciary in settling a decedent's estate and include time limitations in which to carry out the function. The narrative following each step provides a more comprehensive description of the process, including the responsibilities of all parties involved. It should be noted that this outline of steps is not designed to be all-inclusive for every situation. There may be additional responsibilities for fiduciaries of certain estates, depending on individual circumstances.

STEP 1: FILE WILL AND APPLICATION FOR PROBATE OF WILL OR APPOINTMENT OF ADMINISTRATOR, PC-200, WITHIN THIRTY DAYS OF DECEDENT'S DEATH.

An application for administration or probate of will and the will (if there is one) are submitted to the probate court within 30 days of the decedent's death. The application must contain the names and addresses of all heirs (the decedent's closest relatives) and beneficiaries (those parties who would inherit under the will). A copy of the decedent's death certificate may be required by the Court. There are two options for the probate court hearing:

1. If all those entitled to notice waive their right to notice or do not request a formal hearing, and the Court does not believe a hearing is necessary, then the Court will enter a decree on the decree entry date without a formal hearing and without the parties being present.
2. If the matter is contested, if any interested party requests a formal hearing, or if the Court determines that a formal hearing is necessary, the Court will schedule a formal hearing. All parties will receive notice of the hearing.

If the will is determined to be valid, the executor named therein is normally appointed. In an intestate estate, an administrator is appointed. Any executor or administrator may be removed from this position by the Court for cause shown. The Court will appoint a guardian ad litem to protect the interest of any heir or beneficiary who is a minor or incompetent. If the will excuses bond, no bond will be required of the executor unless the Probate Court decides that there is sufficient reason to require one. All administrators must be bonded, with the amount being established by the Court. Please note the following exception to these bonding requirements. A probate judge may waive the requirement of a probate bond in a testate or intestate estate if the assets of the estate are less than $20,000, or if the amount of the estate that is not restricted by Probate Court order is less than $10,000.

STEP 2: TAKE POSSESSION OF DECEDENT'S PROPERTY.

The first responsibility of the fiduciary, following appointment by the Court, is to gather together the assets of the estate and place them under his control. For example, a bank account should be transferred from the decedent's name into an estate account. Stock certificates need not be registered in the name of the estate, although the transfer agents should be notified to send dividends in care of the fiduciary. Utility companies that have billed the decedent need to be notified of the decedent's death, and accounts to remain open should be transferred to the estate's account. The fiduciary must take care to keep the estate's income and expenses separate from his own. Any dwellings, seasonal homes, etc. should be secured and protected from the elements.

STEP 3: IF DECEDENT OWNED REAL ESTATE, FILE NOTICE FOR LAND RECORDS/APPOINTMENT OF FIDUCIARY, PC-251, WITHIN TWO MONTHS OF APPOINTMENT OF FIDUCIARY.

A Notice for Land Records/Appointment of Fiduciary must be filed with the town clerk in each town in Connecticut where real estate belonging to the decedent is located.

STEP 4: FILE INVENTORY, PC-440, WITHIN TWO MONTHS OF APPOINTMENT AS FIDUCIARY.

The fiduciary must file an inventory of the estate with the probate court within two months of appointment as fiduciary. In general, the inventory should list only property the decedent owned in her own name. However, it should also list life insurance policies payable to the decedent's estate, any partnership property, and any property owned with other persons not in survivorship. All property must be valued on the inventory at its fair market value at the time of death. It is the responsibility of the fiduciary to determine these values through inquiry and her own experience. Real estate should be described as it appears in the most recent deed, and a copy of the deed may be attached to the inventory. The amount of any mortgage(s) owed on real estate and the name of the person or corporation to whom the debt is owed must be included. Itemized lists of valuable personal property such as jewelry and antiques should also be included. Ordinarily, household effects and personal items need not be itemized, unless of particular value. They can be grouped together in categories unless an article is specifically bequeathed in the will.

STEP 5: OBTAIN CASH AS NEEDED FOR ESTATE ADMINISTRATION.

The fiduciary should anticipate the cash needs of the estate to pay for administration expenses, taxes, claims, and bequests. He or she has the authority to convert into cash any personal property not specifically bequeathed but must obtain permission from the Probate Court to sell, mortgage, or otherwise convey real estate, unless specifically authorized to do so under the terms of the will. When personal property is to be sold, the fiduciary (if the fiduciary is not named in the will as executor or is not a family member) must send a copy of the inventory to all interested parties, with a notice of intent to sell. They then have the right to object to the sale within five (5) days of the receipt of the notice. (The Court may waive this requirement if an expeditious sale is necessary.) A hearing will be held to determine the advisability of the requested sale. If parties interested in the estate do not want certain assets sold, cash may be advanced to the estate to pay estate obligations.

The surviving spouse or other dependent family members may apply to the Probate Court for a support allowance from the estate funds during the period of settlement of the estate. The fiduciary must sign the Application and Decree for Support Allowance, PC-202, indicating that she has no objection.

The surviving spouse or family of the decedent may be allowed to use the decedent's automobile while the estate is being settled, provided the decedent maintained the automobile as a family car. Permission to use the vehicle can generally be obtained from the Court by simply writing or calling the Court. The fiduciary need not register the automobile until the expiration of the registration that was in force at the time of the decedent's death. (Note: Under the provisions of C.G.S.§14-16, the owner of a motor vehicle can designate a beneficiary on the registration certificate in writing. In order to obtain ownership of the vehicle after the owner's death, the beneficiary must make application to the Department of Motor Vehicles within 60 days of the date of death.)

STEP 6: FOLLOW STATUTORY PROCEDURES FOR THE PAYMENT OF CLAIMS AGAINST THE ESTATE, AND FILE RETURN OF CLAIMS AND LIST OF NOTIFIED CREDITORS, PC-237, AT REQUIRED TIME.

The statutes relating to payment of claims against estates of decedents dying are summarized in this section.

Within 14 days after the first fiduciary's appointment, a newspaper notice will be placed by the Probate Court notifying the estate's creditors of the decedent's death, the creditor's obligation to present claims promptly, the fiduciary's name, and the address where claims are to be presented. "Claims" include all debts incurred by the decedent prior to his death. The statutes provide that the fiduciary may send certified mail notice to creditors informing them that claims must be presented to the fiduciary within 90 days of the date of the notice, but the fiduciary is under no obligation to send notice to creditors. Creditors who do not receive certified notice have 150 days to present their claims to the fiduciary. The statutes permit creditors to ask the Probate Court for an extension of time to present claims in appropriate circumstances.

It is the responsibility of the fiduciary to determine the validity of any claim and notify the creditor of any claims he feels are not proper, in whole or in part. If there is doubt regarding the validity of a claim, Court assistance should be sought. One hundred and fifty days after the appointment of the fiduciary, a good faith fiduciary who has distributed estate assets will not be liable to the creditors of the estate. Beneficiaries may be liable for legitimate claims properly brought after final distribution of all those assets known to the fiduciary. Within 60 days after the 150-day period, the fiduciary must file with the Court a Return of Claims and List of Notified Creditors, PC-237, sworn to by the fiduciary.

Any expenses related to the decedent's death and the settlement of the estate are known as "administration expenses." They include the funeral expenses, statutory probate court charges, legal fees, the fiduciary's fees, the cost of legal notices, and any expenses related to maintenance of the decedent's property incurred after the decedent's death. Certain expenses may take precedence over the claims of general creditors incurred before the decedent's death. Therefore, no claims from any creditor may be paid until it is determined that the assets of the estate are sufficient to cover the preferred expenses (taxes, funeral bills, expenses of last illness, etc.) and all claims of creditors. If the assets of the estate are not sufficient to cover the funeral expenses and expenses of the last illness of a married person, his spouse may be responsible for the payment of these expenses.

If the assets of the estate are not adequate to pay the debts, the estate may be settled as insolvent. The determination of whether an estate is insolvent will be made at a hearing held by the Probate Court following notice arranged by the fiduciary at the Court's direction. The procedure for settling an insolvent estate is substantially different from that for a solvent estate, and competent legal advice should be obtained.

STEP 7: FILE TAX RETURNS AND PAY TAXES DUE WITHIN NINE MONTHS OF DECEDENT'S DEATH.

Effective as of June 30, 2005, the Connecticut Succession Tax* does not apply to decedents dying on or after January 1, 2005. Public Act 05-251 accelerated the phase-out of the succession tax, replacing it with a unified Connecticut Estate and Gift Tax. The Connecticut Estate and Gift Tax are applicable to Connecticut taxable estates of more than two million dollars and includes Connecticut taxable gifts made on or after January 1, 2005.

As of the effective date of the act, (June 30, 2005), no Connecticut Succession Tax Returns will be required with reference to deaths occurring on or after January 1, 2005. However, estate tax returns will be required for each estate. For Connecticut taxable estates of more than two million dollars, the fiduciary must file an original Connecticut Estate and Gift Tax Return, Form CT-706/709, with the commissioner and a copy with the probate court for the district where the decedent resided at his or her date of death or, if the decedent died a nonresident of this state, the probate court for the district where real property or tangible personal property was located within Connecticut. The filing deadline is nine months from the date of death, and interest and penalties will accrue from that date.

The fiduciary must send any tax due directly to the Department of Revenue Services with a cover letter referencing the name of the estate. The Department of Revenue Services will review the Form CT-706/709 and issue its tax assessment accordingly. Forms CT-706/709 and CT-706 NT (explained below) are available each of Connecticut's probate courts. Any inquiries about the Connecticut Estate and Gift Tax should be directed to the Department of Revenue Services, 25 Sigourney St., Hartford, CT 06106.

The procedure is different for Connecticut taxable estates of two million dollars or less. The fiduciary must file Form CT-706 NT, Connecticut Estate Tax Return (For Nontaxable Estates), only with the probate court. On the basis of this return, if the judge of probate believes that the estate is not subject to tax, the judge shall issue a written opinion setting forth the reasons for such judge's opinion. The filing deadline is nine months from the date of death.

The filing of a U.S. Treasury Department Federal Estate Tax Return (Form 706) may be required if the total value of the estate's assets exceeds a certain amount, as specified in the Internal Revenue Code. To obtain the most current information concerning the Federal Estate Tax, the fiduciary should contact the Internal Revenue Service.

It is the fiduciary's responsibility to file both a federal and Connecticut Individual Income Tax Return (federal form 1040 and CT-1040) for the decedent for the tax year in which the decedent died, and to pay any state income tax that may be due. The fiduciary should determine whether a federal tax identification number is required for the estate. The fiduciary may also be required to file a Fiduciary Income Tax form (federal form 1041). If form 1041 must be filed, the fiduciary may be required to file form CT-1041, Connecticut Income Tax Return for Trusts and Estates. Please contact the Department of Revenue Services for further information.

**For those decedents who died before January 1, 2005, the prior laws and forms concerning the Connecticut Succession Tax and the Connecticut Estate Tax still apply. Please contact the Department of Revenue Services for further information at (860) 297-5737.*

STEP 8: FILE FINAL ACCOUNT, USUALLY WITHIN TWELVE MONTHS OF DEATH OF DECEDENT.

Except under certain circumstances described in the next paragraph, the fiduciary must file a final account, called an Administration Account, PC-241 or PC-242, or other form acceptable to the Court, when all debts, expenses, and taxes have been paid. Usually this is done within 12 months of the death of the decedent. This account informs the Court and the beneficiaries of all property and income received and all expenses paid during the settlement of the estate. The balance of receipts over expenses will be the amount remaining for distribution. The Probate Court will hold a hearing on the account to allow the beneficiaries or any other interested party to ask questions about or object to the proposed distribution or the manner in which estate funds were used. If all parties interested in the estate sign an Acceptance and Waiver Re: Final Account, PC-245, indicating that they have received and reviewed a copy of the final account and waive their right to a hearing, the Court may waive the formal hearing and act on the account without the parties having to appear.

The filing of an administration account may not be necessary if: a) no beneficiary is a trustee of a testamentary or intervivos trust, b) the fiduciary or fiduciaries are the sole beneficiary(ies) of the residue of the estate, and c) if all other dispositions to other beneficiaries are specific bequests or devises. The fiduciary may then file a Statement in Lieu of Account, PC-243, in which the fiduciary does the following: a) states under oath that all debts, funeral expenses, taxes, and expenses of administration have been paid; b) lists the total of any amount reported on the return of claims filed; c) lists the total amount inventoried in the estate; d) indicates that specific bequests have been or will be paid in full; e) states that all distributees have received a copy of the statement in lieu of account; and t) itemizes all funeral expenses, taxes, and expenses of administration. If all parties interested in the estate sign an Acceptance and Waiver Re: Statement in Lieu of Account, PC-244, indicating that they have received and reviewed a copy of the Statement in Lieu of Account and waive their right to a hearing, this statement may be sufficient for the Court to discharge the fiduciary from further responsibility and notify the surety company to terminate the probate bond. The Court may then waive a formal hearing and act on the account without the parties having to appear.

STEP 9: DISTRIBUTE ASSETS TO BENEFICIARIES.

When the final account has been approved, the Court will order the fiduciary to distribute the assets of the estate. The fiduciary then distributes the property to the beneficiaries according to the approved distribution.

STEP 10: FILE CLOSING STATEMENT, PC-213.

For all practical purposes, the fiduciary's final act as fiduciary is the filing of an affidavit of closing with the Court. If a probate bond has been required, the Court will send the surety company a certificate stating that the fiduciary has complied with all orders of the Court relating to the settlement of the estate and terminating the probate bond.

APPEALS FROM PROBATE — C.G.S.§§45a -186 — 193

Any person aggrieved by an order, denial, or decree of the Probate Court may appeal to the Superior Court. In general, appeals must be taken within 30 days of the date of the order, denial, or decree.

Appendix 1-C

Provided Courtesy of the Probate Courts of Connecticut

The Probate Court and You

Contents:

11. How Do You Make Application for the Probate of a Decedent's Will?
12. How Old Can a Will Be and Still Be Good?
13. What Can Be Done if a Person Dies and Has a Safe Deposit Box, and a Will May Be in the Box?
14. When A Person Dies, Are His Assets All "Frozen" and Unavailable to the Family?
15. What if a Person Dies Leaving No Will? What Happens to the Property?
16. How Is the Property Distributed When There Is No Will?
17. Does Death Relieve a Family from Making Payment of Monies Owed by a Decedent?
18. What Are the Various Costs Involved in Settling a Decedent's Affairs?
19. What Is the Basis for Computing Probate Charges?
20. How Are Probate Charges Used by the Probate Court?
21. What Is a Probate Court Hearing?
22. Probate Appeals
23. Information and Documents You May Need to Provide to the Probate Court:
24. Does a Probate Court Handle Matters Other Than Matters Associated with Decedents' Estates?

INTRODUCTION

Connecticut is divided into 123 probate districts, each of which is presided over by a Judge of Probate who is elected to office for a four-year term. Probate Courts have jurisdiction over many matters:

1) Probating wills and the administration of estates;
2) Overseeing testamentary and living trusts;
3) Determining title to real and personal property;
4) Construing the meaning of wills and trusts;
5) Appointing guardians for the mentally retarded;
6) Appointing conservators of the person and the estate of incapable individuals;
7) Committing those suffering from mental illness, alcoholism, or drug addiction to an appropriate facility;

8) Removing unfit parents as guardians of their children;
9) Terminating the parental rights of parents who cannot fulfill their parental responsibilities;
10) Granting adoptions;
11) Granting name changes;
12) Other matters.

Sometimes the issues presented to the Probate Courts are complex and difficult. Therefore, it is important that you seek competent professional advice, so that your legal rights are fully protected. Although this pamphlet is not a substitute for such assistance, it has been designed to give you an overview of probate court operations, with specific emphasis on the procedures that are to be followed in probating a will or administering an estate. The probate judge and staff will be happy to answer your procedural questions, but they are not allowed to give you specific legal advice.

Questions...and Answers

1. Why Do Probate Courts Become Involved in the Settling of Decedents' Estates?

When a person who owns property dies, the Probate Court becomes involved to oversee the division of property among those persons legally entitled to it. If the person, referred to as the "decedent," left a will, the division of property will be carried out according to the wishes of the decedent as set forth in the will. (The process of proving that a will is genuine and distributing the property in it is known as "probating" a will.) If the decedent did not leave a will, his or her property will be divided according to Connecticut's laws of "intestacy." (See the answer to question number 15.) In addition to overseeing the distribution of the estate, the Probate Court will insure that any debts of the decedent, funeral expenses, and taxes are paid before distributing the remaining assets of the estate.

2. When Is It Necessary to Open an Estate?

An estate must be opened if a decedent owned properties at the time of her death in her name alone or together with others, but not in survivorship. A court order is required to transfer this type of property to the proper party.

3. What Does "In Survivorship" Mean, and Must Survivorship Property Be Reported to the Probate Court?

The placing of a savings account, shares of corporate stock, bonds or real estate "in survivorship" with another means that each of the named parties has an undivided equal interest in the monies, stocks, bonds, or real estate during their joint lives. This form of ownership grants to the joint owner(s) who survives ownership of all of the monies, stocks, bonds, or real estate immediately upon the death of the joint owner. Survivorship property must be reported to the Probate Court on the Connecticut estate tax return required to be filed with the Court.

4. What Taxes Might Be Due at the Time of Death?

Taxes payable as a result of death include one to the federal government called the Federal Estate Tax, which is reported on federal form 706 and another to the State of Connecticut known as the Connecticut Estate and Gift Tax, which is reported on form CT 706/709. There may also be taxes payable to other states in which the decedent owned property. In addition, there may be income taxes, property taxes, and other taxes due from a decedent if these taxes accrued prior to death. It is the fiduciary's responsibility to ascertain and pay such taxes. Fiduciaries are also responsible for reporting income received during estate administration.

5. How Does the Connecticut Estate and Gift Tax Operate?

Effective as of June 30, 2005, the Connecticut Succession Tax does not apply to decedents dying on or after January 1, 2005. Public Act 05-251 accelerated the phase-out of the Connecticut Succession Tax, replacing it with a unified Connecticut Estate and Gift Tax. The Connecticut Estate and Gift Tax is applicable to Connecticut taxable estates of more than two million dollars and includes Connecticut taxable gifts made on or after January 1, 2005.

As of the effective date of the act (June 30, 2005), no Connecticut Succession Tax Returns will be required with reference to deaths occurring on or after January 1, 2005*. However, estate tax returns will be required in each estate. For Connecticut taxable estates of more than two million dollars, the fiduciary must file an original Connecticut Estate

* For those decedents who died before January 1, 2005, the prior laws and forms concerning the Connecticut Succession Tax and the Connecticut Estate Tax still apply. Please contact the Department of Revenue Services at (860) 297-5737 for further information.

and Gift Tax Return, Form CT-706/709 with the commissioner and a copy with the probate court for the district in which the decedent resided on the date of death. If the decedent was a nonresident of Connecticut at the time of death, the original form must be filed in the probate district where the decedent's real property or tangible personal property was located within Connecticut. The filing deadline is nine months from the date of death, and interest and penalties will accrue from that date.

The fiduciary must send any tax due directly to the Department of Revenue Services with a cover letter referencing the name of the estate. The Department of Revenue Services will review the Form CT-706/709 and issue its tax assessment accordingly. Forms CT-706/709 and CT-706 NT are available at each of Connecticut's probate courts. Any further inquiries about the Connecticut Estate and Gift Tax should be directed to the Department of Revenue Services, 25 Sigourney St., Hartford, CT 06106.

The procedure is different for Connecticut taxable estates of two million dollars or less. The fiduciary must file Form CT-706NT, Connecticut Estate Tax Return (For Nontaxable Estates), only with the probate court. If the judge of probate believes that the estate is not subject to tax on the basis of this return, the judge shall issue a written opinion setting forth the reasons for such judge's opinion. The filing deadline is nine months from the date of death.

6. *Is the Connecticut Estate and Gift Tax Determined in the Same Manner as the Federal Estate Tax?*

No. Although the Connecticut Estate and Gift Tax, like the federal estate and gift tax, is a unified system of taxing gifts and estates, there is no longer any direct connection between the state and federal taxes. With respect to individuals dying on or after January 1, 2005, the Connecticut Estate and Gift Tax will be determined with reference to the tax table set forth in C.G.S. § 12-391(g), as amended by Public Act 05-251, §69. The tax applies to Connecticut taxable estates of more than two million dollars, including Connecticut taxable gifts made on or after January 1, 2005. "Connecticut taxable estate" means (A) the gross estate less allowable deductions, as determined under Chapter 11 of the Internal Revenue Code, plus (B) the aggregate amount of all Connecticut taxable gifts, as defined in section 12-643, made by the decedent for all calendar years beginning on or after January 1, 2005. "Connecticut taxable gifts" mean taxable gifts made during a calendar year commencing on or after January 1, 2005, that are: (1) for residents of this state, taxable gifts wherever located, but excepting gifts of real estate or tangible personal property located outside this state, and (2) for nonresidents of this state, gifts of real estate or tangible personal property located within this state. More information is available on the website for the Department of Revenue Services at www.drs.state.ct.us.

7. What Is the Effect of Having Savings or Securities "In Trust For" Another Person? How Do Such Bank Accounts Differ from a Custodial Bank Account for a Minor?

Monies on deposit in a bank account standing in the name of a depositor "in trust for" another become the monies of the named beneficiary immediately upon the death of the depositor.

In 1997, the State Legislature changed the law to permit securities to be similarly owned by one individual "in trust for" another. Like the bank accounts, those securities remain the exclusive property of the owner until death, when they are transferred immediately to the survivor. These bank accounts or securities must be reported on a Connecticut estate tax return.

An alternative way of providing money in an account for the benefit of a minor child is by opening a custodial account under the Uniform Transfers to Minors Act. The depositor could act as a custodian of such monies. However, the monies in a custodial account belong to the minor at all times and can only be used for the minor's benefit. When the minor attains the age of 21, he or she is entitled to receive those monies and may ask the custodian for an accounting of how they were managed. The death of the custodian prior to the beneficiary's reaching the age of 21 may require the probate court to appoint a successor custodian.

8. Is There a Simple Method to Probate a Small Estate?

Yes, if the total assets left by a decedent in his name alone consist of personal property and do not exceed $20,000. The decedent may own survivorship real estate or other survivorship assets exceeding $20,000 in value and still[6] qualify for this simple procedure. In such an event, the transfer of both tangible and intangible personal property such as bank accounts, shares of corporate stock, bonds, unpaid wages, death benefits, insurance proceeds, or motor vehicles[*] can be passed simply to the surviving spouse or next of kin.

The only requirement is that the surviving spouse or next of kin or some suitable person file an affidavit in the Probate Court stating that the decedent's funeral expenses and other debts have been paid at least to the value of such assets or that such assets are necessary to pay funeral and physicians' expenses. Thereafter, the Judge will confirm that no other probate proceedings have been started and will authorize by a decree the transfer of the personal property to the surviving spouse, next of kin, some suitable person, the funeral director, or physician to the extent needed to pay such bills. A Connecticut estate tax return is also required for a small estate.

9. Who Can Serve as an Executor or Administrator of an Estate? What Duties Does One Have?

An executor or administrator can be anyone: a member of the decedent's family, an attorney, a bank, or a beneficiary of a will. An executor is named in the will and chosen by the person making the will. If that person is capable, the Court must appoint that individual as executor. If there is no will, the selection of an administrator is made by the Court. The law requires that a family member or designee of the family member be chosen, unless it appears to the Court that it would not be in the best interests of the parties concerned, in which case the Court will usually appoint an impartial person or a bank.

10. Is It Necessary to Have a Lawyer or Other Professional Help Probate an Estate or File the Required Tax Returns?

It is often advisable for the fiduciary to obtain professional assistance in connection with the administration of an estate. The Clerk of the Court or the Judge of Probate may provide limited assistance by helping an individual to complete required forms and reports. The Judge will be careful in the type of assistance given, since he or she may be called upon at a later time to adjudicate matters relating to the tax return, an account, or intermediate petitions. It is the fiduciary, however, who is

---

* Note: Under the provisions of C.G.S.§14-16, the owner of a motor vehicle can designate a beneficiary on the registration certificate in writing. In order to obtain ownership of the vehicle after the owner's death, the beneficiary must make application to the Department of Motor Vehicles within 60 days of the date of death.

primarily responsible for completing these forms and reports and for taking all of the other steps necessary to settle the estate. A booklet entitled "Guidelines for Administration of Decedents' Estates" is available from the Court of Probate to assist fiduciaries. Responsibilities such as preparation of tax returns and protecting unusual assets frequently require professional help.

11. How Do You Make Application for the Probate of a Decedent's Will?

Any person in possession of any will must deliver such will to the probate court in the town where the decedent had his or domicile within 30 days after the decedent's death. Ordinarily, at the time the will is brought to the probate court, an application for probate of the will is filed with the court, and after a hearing, an executor is named. However, if the decedent left no assets in his or her name that would pass under the will, the will is simply placed on file and not admitted to probate.

12. How Old Can a Will Be and Still Be Good?

A will can be legally binding no matter how old it is. However, certain subsequent events may cause a change in the will's formula of distribution. For example, the subsequent birth or adoption of a child, marriage, divorce, or annulment may alter the will's stated disposition. Therefore, it is extremely important for everyone to review the contents of their wills periodically, especially if such a major life event has occurred.

13. What Can Be Done if a Person Dies and Has a Safe Deposit Box, and a Will May Be in the Box?

If a decedent had a safe deposit box and it is suspected that a will or other important documents are in the safe deposit box, it is possible for a Probate Court to immediately issue an order authorizing a family member or other suitable person to gain access to the safe deposit box. The box will be opened in the presence of a bank officer and the contents cataloged. If a will is discovered, it will then have to be filed in the probate court.

A similar situation might involve a decedent who lived alone in a house or apartment, and no relative can be found to take proper action. The Court has the ability to appoint a temporary administrator immediately in order to safeguard the decedent's belongings and to take other action to protect the estate.

14. When A Person Dies, Are His Assets All "Frozen" and Unavailable to the Family?

In the overwhelming number of cases involving joint and survivorship assets between the decedent and family members, funds are immediately available to the survivors without Court approval. However, assets in the name of the decedent alone may not be used until an executor or administrator is appointed, which, in most cases, takes only one to two weeks. (In an emergency, the Court can provide immediate relief.) Thereafter, such assets may be used to pay proper debts and expenses. A family car may be used immediately with permission of the Court. In addition, if all the heirs consent, an estate can be opened in a single day so that the estate's funds can be accessed without delay.

Even though these assets may be available immediately to the family, with or without Court action, they still must be properly accounted for so that the claims of creditors and the State Tax Department are properly handled.

15. *What if a Person Dies Leaving No Will? What Happens to the Property?*

If the decedent left property in his own name, then it is necessary for an appropriate person (usually a family member) to make application to the Probate Court for administration of the decedent's estate. Since there is no will, the property is distributed in accordance with the Connecticut laws of descent and distribution. The estate is called "intestate" because there is no will.

16. How Is the Property Distributed When There Is No Will?

If the decedent is survived by:

- Spouse, and children* of both decedent and spouse: Spouse takes first $100,000, + ½ of the remainder. Children* take the other ½.
- Spouse, and children* of decedent, one or more of whom is not the child of the spouse: Spouse takes ½. All the children* share in the other ½ equally.
- Spouse and parent or parents (no children**): Spouse takes first $100,000 + ¾ of the remainder. Parent(s) take the other ¼.
- Spouse only (no children**, no parents): Spouse takes all.
- Children* only (no spouse): All goes to the children*.

- Parent(s) (no spouse, no children**): All goes to the parents(s).
- Brothers* and sisters* (no spouse, no parents, no children**): All goes to the brothers* and sisters*.
- Next of kin (no spouse, no children**, no parents, no brothers** or sisters**): All goes to the next of kin.
- If there is no next of kin, but there is a step-child*, he or she will be next in line to take.
- If there is no step-child**, all goes to the State of Connecticut.

17. Does Death Relieve a Family from Making Payment of Monies Owed by a Decedent?

A creditor has a right to look for payment of any outstanding obligation incurred in the decedent's lifetime from those properties owned by the decedent in her name alone. In most cases, creditors and family members agree on the amount that the decedent owed, and payment is made voluntarily by the executor or administrator. However, a creditor may want to protect himself by filing a written claim of the debt with the executor or administrator and, if he has been given a specific written notice by the executor or administrator inviting such a written claim, the creditor must file that claim within the time limited by that notice. The failure of the creditor to file such a claim as requested may very well bar that creditor's right of recovery.

In many instances, properties in the name of the decedent and another or others in survivorship will not be subject to the claims of all creditors against the decedent. However, there are exceptions to this rule that should be carefully considered. For example, if the decedent's estate is not sufficient to pay funeral expenses, debts due for the last illness of the deceased and expenses for settling the estate, and debts due to the State for aid or care to the deceased, the decedent's proportional share of the monies on deposit in a survivorship joint bank or savings account may be subject to payment of those expenses.

---

*If this person(s) has died before the decedent, his or her descendants may take instead.

** or descendants.

18. What Are the Various Costs Involved in Settling a Decedent's Affairs?

Upon the death of any person, some or all of the following costs may be payable to settle the decedent's affairs: (a) probate fees; (b) fees of an executor or administrator; (c) attorneys' fees; and (d) taxes, state or federal.

Probate fees and taxes due are fixed by law. The fees of an executor or administrator and of an attorney are based upon the work efforts of each and are subject to the approval of the Probate Court. Often, members of the family are willing to serve for little or no compensation.

19. What Is the Basis for Computing Probate Charges?

Charges made by the Probate Courts are strictly regulated by statute. They are based on the size of the estate in the decedent's name alone and on the amount that may have been owned with others, such as survivorship property and other taxable transfers. The following is the section that is used to compute probate charges for estates in which proceedings commence on or after April 1, 1998*:

- Basis for Computation of Costs: $0 to $500 Total Costs: $25
- Basis for Computation of Costs: $501 to $1,000 Total Costs: $50
- Basis for Computation of Costs: $1,000 to $10,000 Total Costs: $50 plus 1% of all in excess of $1,000
- Basis for Computation of Costs: $10,000 to $500,000 Total Costs: $150 plus 0.0035 of all in excess of $10,000
- Basis for Computation of Costs: $500,000 to $4,754,000 Total Costs: $1,865 plus 0.0025 of all in excess of $500,000
- Basis for Computation of Costs: $4,754,000 and over Total Costs: $12,500

Notes: 1) Any portion of the basis for costs that is determined by property passing to the surviving spouse shall be reduced by 50%. 2) If the basis for costs is less than $10,000 and a full estate is opened, the

---

*Please consult the statutes to compute charges for estates where proceedings commenced before April 1, 1998.

minimum cost is $150.00. 3) In estates where the gross taxable estate is less than $600,000 in which no succession tax return is required to be filed, a probate fee of .1% shall be charged against non-solely owned real estate, in addition to any other fees.

20 How Are Probate Charges Used by the Probate Court?

Statutory charges paid to the Probate Court are used to pay the salaries of the court staff and certain operational expenses. After payment of such costs, the net sum is retained by the Judge as his or her only compensation, subject to an assessment levied by the State of Connecticut. The statute strictly limits the amount a Judge may retain as compensation, and it now permits a Court with insufficient income to meet its reasonable and necessary operating expenses by requesting a subsidy from the Probate Court Administrator.

21. What Is a Probate Court Hearing?

A hearing at the probate court is an opportunity for all family members and other parties in interest to appear at the court to ask questions or to make certain that their views are known. The notice of a hearing should not be ignored if there are any questions on, or objections to, matters being heard.

The law presently mandates at least one hearing on all probated estates. That hearing is usually held at the closing or acceptance of the final accounting by the executor or administrator, unless all parties sign and file with the Court a written waiver acknowledging that they have reviewed the final account and have given it their approval.

Unless all interested parties voluntarily sign a waiver, notice of the hearing is required at the time each estate is opened to pass upon the admission of a will to probate or for the appointment of an administrator.

Other hearings may be necessary at intermediary stages of the proceedings, such as upon a request for an allowance for support of the surviving spouse or children or for the settlement of a doubtful or disputed claim or for the sale of real property.

Probate hearings are normally informal proceedings; however, unresolved or contested matters may require the taking of evidence at a hearing so that the Judge can make a proper determination of facts or law.

22. Probate Appeals

Any person aggrieved by an order, denial, or decree of the Probate Court may appeal to the Superior Court. In general, appeals must be taken within 30 days of the date of the order, denial, or decree.

23. Information and Documents You May Need to Provide to the Probate Court:

- Certified copy of Certificate of Death. Original will and codicil, if any.
- A list of names by which the deceased owned real or personal property that will be reported to the Court, either in the inventory or in the Connecticut estate tax return (first, middle, last name).
- You will have to indicate whether the decedent or any beneficiary received public assistance or was in a state hospital, including the receipt of benefits under the convalescent care program known as Title 19.
- A list of all names and addresses of the decedent's heirs. (Go on to next letter listing if no relatives in the previous class):
    a) Surviving husband or wife and children and, if any, children of a deceased child. (If there is a surviving spouse and no children, the parents of the deceased must be listed);
    b) Parents;
    c) Brothers and sisters and children of deceased brothers and sisters;
    d) Uncles and aunts;
    e) First cousins; if none, then second cousins; and so on.
- Names and addresses of those who receive anything under the will or codicil, if additional to those mentioned above.
- Listing of all assets left by decedent whether or not in survivorship, including:
    a) Checking or savings accounts (name of bank, account number, name or names on book, balance on date of death including interest);
    b) U.S. War or Savings Bonds (name or names on bonds, series number, number on bonds, face value of bonds, value at date of death);

c) Corporate Stock (name of corporation, certificate number, common or preferred, number of shares, name or names on certificate, value at date of death);
d) Real estate (copy of deed; assessed value of real estate, which can be found on real estate tax bill; market value at death);
e) Automobile (copy of title and/or registration; value at date of death);
f) Name and fair market value of any business that the deceased owned either totally or in part;
g) Valuable personal property (such as coin or stamp collections; jewelry, antiques, or art collections);
h) Policies of insurance not payable to a named beneficiary or any pension or profit-sharing plan for which a death benefit is payable;
i) Social Security or veterans' benefits to which the deceased was entitled;

- List of outstanding bills or debts of deceased, such as:
  a) Medical or hospital expenses and other monies owing for last illness;
  b) Mortgages due (lender's name, location of property, date of mortgage, amount due at date of death);
  c) Loans due (name of lender, amount owed at death);
  d) Unpaid taxes; income, personal property, or real estate;
  e) General obligations (name of creditor, amount due at date of death);
  f) Funeral charges and monument expense.

24. Does a Probate Court Handle Matters Other Than Matters Associated with Decedents' Estates?

Although a Probate Court is commonly thought of as dealing with the distribution of a person's property after death, there are many functions of the Court that assist the living. The Court may be called upon to terminate parental rights when parents are not carrying out parental responsibilities and, in a related matter, hear claims of paternity of unwed fathers. The Court also considers and approves adoptions.

In other cases, a child may need a guardian of his or her estate or person. The guardian of an estate of a minor is appointed by the Judge to oversee monies or properties belonging to a child, while a guardian of the person is appointed to approve the proper care of a child. The appointment of guardians for persons with mental retardation, as well as sterilizations and placements of mentally retarded persons, are also within the jurisdiction of the Courts.

The Court also aids mentally and/or physically incapable persons who are unable to manage or administer their own affairs. In such cases, the Court, after a hearing, appoints a conservator to act on behalf of the incapable person. In addition, the Court is empowered to commit a person suffering from severe mental illness to an appropriate hospital.

The Court also receives and passes on various fiduciaries' accounts, including accounts of conservators, guardians, testamentary trustees, and in some cases, trustees under an inter vivos trust.

Another responsibility of a Probate Judge is to approve or disapprove the marriage of a youth under the age of 16 years. The Court also has jurisdiction to grant a change of name. In addition, as a courtesy to the public, a large number of Courts will assist persons in obtaining passports.

For more specific information on the other areas of probate court jurisdiction, you may wish to consult the other pamphlets published by the Probate Court Administrator:

- Termination of Parental Rights and Adoption Procedures
- Guidelines for Guardianships of Minors
- Probate Court Proceedings Involving Persons with Mental Retardation
- Guidelines for Conservators
- Guidelines for Administration of Decedents' Estates
- Understanding Trusts: A Look at Living Trusts and Other Trusts

Glossary

PROBATE Broadly, a characterization of the functions of the Probate Court, whether it be the probate of a will, the approval of the accounts of an administrator of a decedent's estate, or any other judicial act within the province of the Court, including guardianships, conservatorships, and the like.

WILL A written declaration of a person's wishes concerning the distribution of property standing in his or her name after death, executed in accordance with specific legal procedures.

CODICIL An amendment or addition to a will.

TESTATE Referring to the estate of a deceased person who leaves a will at death.

INTESTATE Referring to the estate of a deceased person who dies without leaving a will.

FIDUCIARY One who holds property in a position of trust for another, such as an executor, administrator, trustee, guardian, or conservator.

EXECUTOR A person named in a will to manage and settle an estate and to carry out the directions and mandates of the decedent.

ADMINISTRATOR A person who has been named by the Probate Court to administer and settle the estate of a decedent who dies without leaving a will. The estate will be settled in accordance with the laws of descent and distribution, which are also known as the laws of intestacy.

TRUST Property, real or personal, held by one party for the benefit of another.

GUARDIAN A person given the power and duty by a Probate Court to manage the property or provide for the care of the person of a minor child or mentally retarded person.

CONSERVATOR A person named by the Probate Court to supervise the affairs of another person who is incapable or who needs assistance in managing his or her affairs or caring for himself or herself.

PROBATE BOND A promise by a fiduciary, usually guaranteed by a third party known as a surety, to replace any funds up to the amount of the bond to fulfill the faithful performance of his or her duties. Often, the surety is an insurance company.

REAL PROPERTY Real estate such as a home, land, or farm, including the ownership of a condominium unit.

PERSONAL PROPERTY Property not classified as real property, such as bank accounts, shares of corporate stock, bonds, automobiles, household furnishings and personal effects.

Appendix 3-A

Provided Courtesy of the Probate Courts of Connecticut

Connecticut Probate Court Fees and Costs

Decedent's Estate

Upon the death of any person, some or all of the following costs may be payable to settle the decedent's affairs: (a) probate fees and taxes that are fixed by law; (b) fees of an executor or administrator that are subject to the approval of the Probate Court; and (c) attorney's fees that are also subject to the approval of the Probate Court.

Decedent's Estate Fees: (for estates in which proceedings commence on or after 4/1/98) The minimum fee is $150.00 for a full probate estate with a gross taxable value of less than $10,000.

In estates where the gross taxable estate is less than $600,000 and no succession tax return is required to be filed, a probate fee of .1% shall be charged against non-solely owned real estate, in addition to any other fees.

The fee is based on the greater of: 1) the gross taxable estate for succession tax purposes (Sec. 12-349), OR the inventory (probatable estate) OR the Connecticut taxable estate as defined in C.G.S. 12-391, as amended, OR the gross estate for estate tax purposes (Ch. 217 and

218 of the Connecticut General Statutes), PLUS all damages recovered for injuries resulting in death, LESS hospital and medical expenses and attorney's fees and costs, LESS 50% of any portion of the property passing to the surviving spouse.

VALUE OF ESTATE	FEE
$0 to $500	$25.00
$500 to $1,000	$50.00
$1,000 to $10,000	$50.00 plus .01 of all in excess of $1,000
$10,000 to $500,000	$150.00 plus .0035 of all in excess of $10,000
$500,000 to $4,754,000	$1,865.00 plus .0025 of all in excess of $500,000
Over $4,754,000	$12,500.00

Conservatorships, Guardianships and Trusts: (Effective July 1, 1993)	
FILING	FEE
Account with no hearing	$25.00
Account requiring a hearing	Based on the greater of the book value, market value, or receipts. If more than one account is the subject of the hearing, the most recent account is used to determine the fee.
Of less than $25,000	$50.00
Of $25,000 to $375,000	.0020 of value
Over $375,000	$750.00

Other Fees and Costs: (As of January 1, 1998)	
Application fee (other than decedents' estates and fiduciary accountings)	$150.00
Each additional hearing on any matter	$25.00
Hearings that exceed one hour	$25.00/hour, after first hour (Not to exceed $300.00)
Application by creditor for the court consideration of disallowed claims	$50.00 (payable by creditor; if allowed, may order the fiduciary to reimburse from the estate)
Motion for appeal	$50.00
Continued hearing, either upon request of party or due to party's failure to appear which necessitates continuance. [Note: No charge if waived for cause shown.]	$50.00 (plus actual cost of mailing)
Each hearing notice in excess of two	$2.00 each
Fiduciary Certificates (first certificate) Additional certificates (up to 5) Each additional certificate (after 5)	No Charge $5.00 $1.00
Copies (up to 5 pages) Additional pages	$5.00 $1.00 per page
Certified Copies (for first two pages) (for each page thereafter)	$5.00 $2.00
Document recording (after first 5 pages)	$3.00 per page
Will for filing only	$5.00
Other documents for filing only	$25.00
Marriage waivers	$25.00

How Are Probate Charges Used by the Probate Court?

Statutory charges paid to the Probate Court are used to pay the salaries of the court staff and certain operational expenses. After payment of such costs, the net sum is retained by the judge as his or her only compensation, subject to an assessment levied by the State of Connecticut. The statute strictly limits the amount a judge may retain as compensation, and it now permits a court with insufficient income to meet its reasonable and necessary operating expenses by requesting a subsidy from the Probate Court Administrator.

Appendix 3-B

Provided Courtesy of FindLaw, a Thompson Corporation Service

Attorney Fee Agreements

In your initial meeting with your lawyer you should discuss the lawyer's fees and the fee arrangement. Your fee agreement should set out the services the lawyer will perform for you, the type of fees, and the amount you will be expected to pay. The agreement should also identify how other costs will be handled and explain the lawyer's billing practices.

Types of Legal Fees

The type of fee arrangement that you make with your lawyer will have a significant impact on how much you will pay for the services. Legal fees depend on several factors, including the amount of time spent on your problem; the lawyer's ability, experience, and reputation; the novelty and difficulty of the case; the results obtained; and costs involved. There will be other factors such as the lawyer's overhead expenses (rent, utilities, office equipment, computers, etc.) that may affect the fee charged.

There are several common types of fee arrangements used by lawyers:

- Consultation Fee: The lawyer may charge a fixed or hourly fee for your first meeting where you both determine whether the lawyer can assist you. Be sure to check whether you will be charged for this initial meeting.

- Contingency Fees: The lawyer's fee is based on a percentage of the amount awarded in the case. If you lose the case, the lawyer does not get a fee, but you will still have to pay expenses. Contingency fee percentages vary. A one-third fee is common. Some lawyers offer a sliding scale based on how far along the case has progressed before it is settled. Courts may set a limit on the amount of a contingency fee a lawyer can receive. This type of fee arrangement may be charged in personal injury cases, property damage cases, or other cases where a large amount of money is involved. Lawyers may also be prohibited from making contingency fee arrangements in certain kinds of cases such as criminal and child custody matters. Contingency fee arrangements are typically not available for divorce matters, if you are being sued, or if you are seeking general legal advice such as the purchase or sale of a business.
- Flat Fees: A lawyer charges a specific, total fee. A flat fee is usually offered only if your case is relatively simple or routine such as a will or an uncontested divorce.
- Hourly Rate: The lawyer will charge you for each hour (or portion of an hour) that the lawyer works on your case. Thus, for example, if the lawyer's fee is $100 per hour and the lawyer works 5 hours, the fee will be $500. This is the most typical fee arrangement. Some lawyers charge different fees for different types of work (legal research versus a court appearance). In addition, lawyers working in large firms typically have different fee scales with more senior members charging higher fees than young associates or paralegals.
- Referral Fee: A lawyer who refers you to another lawyer may ask for a portion of the total fee you pay for the case. Referral fees may be prohibited under applicable state codes of professional responsibility unless certain criteria are met. Just like other fees, the total fee must be reasonable and you must agree to the arrangement.

Your state or local bar association may have additional information about the appropriateness of a referral fee.

- Retainer Fees: The lawyer is paid a set fee, perhaps based on the lawyer's hourly rate. You can think of a retainer as a "down payment" against which future costs are billed. The retainer is usually placed in a special account and the cost of services is deducted from that account as they accrue. Many retainer fees are non-refundable unless the fee is deemed unreasonable by a court. A retainer fee can also mean that the lawyer is "on call" to handle your legal problems over a period of time. Since this type of fee arrangement can mean several different things, be sure to have the lawyer explain the retainer fee arrangement in detail.
- Statutory Fee: The fees in some cases may be set by statute or a court may set and approve a fee that you pay. These types of fees may appear in probate, bankruptcy, or other proceedings.

Types of Legal Costs

The amount a lawyer charges you for legal services may include the lawyer's fees plus additional expenses and costs. If the lawyer will represent you in a court proceeding, you may have to pay a filing fee or other court costs as well.

There area number of costs that may appear on your lawyer's bill. Some lawyers may charge for these costs separately. Other lawyers may lump the expenses together as a separate item on your bill, while others may include some of these costs in their fee. Be sure to find out before you hire your lawyer if these types of costs are included and whether they will be itemized on your bill. Costs in addition to the lawyer's time may include:

- Filing Fees and Court Costs
- Photocopying
- Telephone and Postage Charges
- Paralegal Time
- Messengers
- Computer or Research Related Costs

- Secretarial and Staff Time
- Deposition and Court Reporter Costs
- Facsimiles (faxes)
- Experts, Consultants, and Witness Fees
- Investigators
- Process Servers (delivery of legal documents relating to case)
- Travel Expenses

There may be other charges not listed above. It is a good idea to ask the lawyer for a written estimate of anticipated costs to make sure you understand all the different costs that you will have to pay. For example, you will want to find out if there is a set rate for some costs (e.g., $0.15 per page for copying costs). If you are concerned about the costs building up, you can also tell your lawyer that any costs over a certain amount have to be approved by you in advance. You also may be able to negotiate in advance the amount charged for many of these costs.

With all types of fee arrangements you should ask what costs and other expenses are covered in the fee. Does the fee include the lawyer's overhead and costs or are those charged separately? How will the costs for staff, such as secretaries, messengers, or paralegals be charged. In contingency fee arrangements, make sure to find out whether the lawyer calculates the fee before or after expenses.

Your discussions with your lawyer about fees and costs might cover the following topics:

- Type of Fee Arrangement: How will the lawyer bill?
  Will the lawyer bill on an hourly basis, is it a contingency fee arrangement, or will you pay a retainer fee?
- Type of Permissible Costs: Which costs are properly passed on to you?
  Will you have to pay for copying costs? How much per page?
  Will you be responsible for electronic research charges?
  Make sure you and the lawyer agree which costs you will pay and at what rate you will pay them.
- Estimated Fees and Costs: What will the case cost?
  The lawyer may not be able to determine the exact amount of time and effort required to handle your case, but should

be in a position to give you an estimate of both fees and costs based upon past experience.

- Frequency and Detail: You should find out how often you will be billed and whether interest or other charges will be added to unpaid amounts. The lawyer's bills should include details of the services provided along with an itemization of costs. If the lawyer is working on a contingency arrangement, find out how often you will be billed for costs and when you will receive payment if the cases is resolved favorably.
- Basic Charges: If the lawyer charges by the hour, you should find out the minimum billing segment. Is it one-quarter or one-tenth of an hour or some other figure? For example, a lawyer may bill you for a tenth of an hour (six minutes) for a simple three minute telephone call. You should also find out whether you will be billed for work by others — associates, legal assistants, or paralegals.
- Control: How much control will you have over fees and expenses? Do you want to be notified after fees and expenses reach a certain amount? Do you want to be notified before the lawyer incurs an expense over a certain amount?

You might want to take notes during your discussions so you can know what terms you and the lawyer agreed upon. Based on your discussions, you should have the fee arrangement put in writing.

The lawyer may have a pre-printed fee agreement for you to sign. If the agreement does not include the terms you discussed with the lawyer, ask the lawyer to change the language. The agreement should state clearly what you and the lawyer agreed to do.

Appendix 4-A

Estate Tax Case Study

The following example is from IRS Publication 559 (2006 edition).

On April 9, 2005, your father, John R. Smith, died at the age of 62. He had not resided in a community property state. His will named you to serve as his executor (personal representative). Except for specific bequests to your mother, Mary, of your parents' home and your father's automobile and a bequest of $5,000 to his church, your father's will named your mother and his brother as beneficiaries.

After the court has approved your appointment as the executor, you should obtain an employer identification number for the estate. Next, you use Form 56 to notify the Internal Revenue Service that you have been appointed executor of your father's estate.

Assets of the estate. Your father had the following assets when he died.

His checking account balance was $2,550 and his savings account balance was $53,650.

Your father inherited your parents' home from his parents on March 5, 1979. At that time it was worth $42,000, but was appraised at the time of your father's death at $150,000. The home was free of existing debts (or mortgages) at the time of his death.

Your father owned 500 shares of ABC Company stock that had cost him $10.20 a share in 1983. The stock had a mean selling price (midpoint between highest and lowest selling price) of $25 a share on the day he died. He also owned 500 shares of XYZ Company stock that had cost him $30 a share in 1988. The stock had a mean selling price on the date of death of $22.

The appraiser valued your father's automobile at $6,300 and the household effects at $18,500.

Your father owned a coin collection and a stamp collection. The face value of the coins in the collection was only $600, but the appraiser valued it at $2,800. The stamp collection was valued at $3,500.

Your father's employer sent a check to your mother for $11,082 ($12,000 - $918 for social security and Medicare taxes), representing unpaid salary and payment for accrued vacation time. The statement that came with the check indicated that no amount was withheld for income tax. The check was made out to the estate, so your mother gave you the check.

The Easy Life Insurance Company gave your mother a check for $275,000 because she was the beneficiary of his life insurance policy.

Your father was the owner of several series EE U.S. savings bonds on which he named your mother as co-owner. Your father purchased the bonds during the past several years. The cost of these bonds totaled $2,500. After referring to the appropriate table of redemption values (see U.S. savings bonds acquired from decedent, earlier), you determine that interest of $840 had accrued on the bonds at the date of your father's death. You must include the redemption value of these bonds at date of death, $3,340, in your father's gross estate.

On July 1, 1993, your parents purchased a house for $90,000. They have held the property for rental purposes continuously since its purchase. Your mother paid one-third of the purchase price, or $30,000, and your father paid $60,000. They owned the property, however, as joint tenants with right of survivorship. An appraiser valued the property at $120,000. You include $60,000, one-half of the value, in your father's gross estate because your parents owned the property as joint tenants with right of survivorship and they were the only joint tenants.

Your mother also gave you a Form W-2, Wage and Tax Statement, that your father's employer had sent. In examining it, you discover that your father had been paid $11,000 in salary between January 1, 2005, and April 9, 2005 (the date he died). The Form W-2 showed $11,000 in box 1 and $23,000 ($11,000 + $12,000) in boxes 3 and 5. The Form

W-2 indicated $805 as federal income tax withheld in box 2. The estate received a Form 1099-MISC from the employer showing $12,000 in box 3. The estate received a Form 1099-INT for your father showing he was paid $1,900 interest on his savings account at the First S&L of Juneville, in 2005, before he died.

Final Return for Decedent

From the papers in your father's files, you determine that the $11,000 paid to him by his employer (as shown on the Form W-2), rental income, and interest are the only items of income he received between January 1 and the date of his death. You will have to file an income tax return for him for the period during which he lived. (You determine that he timely filed his 2004 income tax return before he died.) The final return is not due until April 17, 2006, the same date it would have been due had your father lived during all of 2005.

The check representing unpaid salary and earned but unused vacation time was not paid to your father before he died, so the $12,000 is not reported as income on his final return. It is reported on the income tax return for the estate (Form 1041) for 2005. The only taxable income to be reported for your father will be the $11,000 salary (as shown on the Form W-2), the $1,900 interest, and his portion of the rental income that he received in 2005.

Your father was a cash basis taxpayer and did not report the interest accrued on the series EE U.S. savings bonds on prior tax returns that he filed jointly with your mother. As the personal representative of your father's estate, you choose to report the interest earned on these bonds before your father's death ($840) on the final income tax return.

The rental property was leased the entire year of 2005 for $1,000 per month. Under local law, your parents (as joint tenants) each had a half interest in the income from the property. Your father's will, however, stipulates that the entire rental income is to be paid directly to your mother. None of the rental income will be reported on the income tax return for the estate. Instead, your mother will report all the rental income and expenses on Form 1040. Checking the records and prior tax returns of your parents, you find that they previously elected to use the alternative depreciation system (ADS) with the mid-month convention. Under ADS, the rental house is depreciated using the straight-line method over a 40-year recovery period. They allocated $15,000 of the cost to the land (which is never depreciable) and $75,000 to the rental house. Salvage value was disregarded for the depreciation computation. Before 2005, $21,485 had been allowed as depreciation. (For information on ADS, see Publication 946.)

Deductions. During the year, you received a bill from the hospital for $615 and bills from your father's doctors totaling $475. You paid these bills as they were presented. In addition, you find other bills from his doctors totaling $185 that your father paid in 2005 and receipts for prescribed drugs he purchased totaling $536. The funeral home presented you a bill for $6,890 for the expenses of your father's funeral, which you paid.

The medical expenses you paid from the estate's funds ($615 and $475) were for your father's care and were paid within 1 year after his death. They will not be used to figure the taxable estate so you can treat them as having been paid by your father when he received the medical services. See Medical Expenses under Final Return for Decedent, earlier. However, you cannot deduct the funeral expenses either on your father's final return or on the estate's income tax return. They are deductible only on the federal estate tax return (Form 706).

In addition, after going over other receipts and canceled checks for the tax year with your mother, you determine that the following items are deductible on your parents' 2005 income tax return.

Health insurance	$4,250
State income tax paid	$891
Real estate tax on home	$1,100
Contributions to church	$3,800

Rental expenses included real estate taxes of $700 and mortgage interest of $410. In addition, insurance premiums of $260 and painting and repair expenses for $350 were paid. These rental expenses totaled $1,720.

Your mother and father owned the property as joint tenants with right of survivorship and they were the only joint tenants, so her basis in this property upon your father's death is $95,859. This is found by adding the $60,000 value of the half interest included in your father's gross estate to your mother's $45,000 share of the cost basis and subtracting your mother's $9,141 share of depreciation (including 2005 depreciation for the period before your father's death), as explained next.

For 2005, you must make the following computations to figure the depreciation deduction.

For the period before your father's death, depreciate the property using the same method, basis, and life used by your parents in previous years. They used the mid-month convention, so the amount deductible for three and a half months is $547. (This brings the total depreciation to $22,032 ($21,485 + $547) at the time of your father's death.)

For the period after your father's death, you must make two computations.

Your mother's cost basis ($45,000) minus one-half of the amount allocated to the land ($7,500) is her depreciable basis ($37,500) for half of the property. She continues to use the same life and depreciation method as was originally used for the property. The amount deductible for the remaining eight and a half months is $664.

The other half of the property must be depreciated using a depreciation method that is acceptable for property placed in service in 2005. You chose to use ADS with the mid-month convention. The value included in the estate ($60,000) less the value allocable to the land ($10,000) is the depreciable basis ($50,000) for this half of the property. The amount deductible for this half of the property is $886 ($50,000 × .01771). See chapter 4 and Table A-13 in Publication 946.

Show the total of the amounts in (1) and (2)(a), above, on line 17 of Form 4562, Depreciation and Amortization. Show the amount in (2)(b) on line 20c. The total depreciation deduction allowed for the year is $2,097.

Filing status. After December 31, 2005, when your mother determines the amount of her income, you and your mother must decide whether you will file a joint return or separate returns for your parents for 2005. Your mother has rental income and $400 of interest income from her savings account at the Mayflower Bank of Juneville, so it appears to be to her advantage to file a joint return.

Tax computation. The tax refund is $232. The computation is as follows:

Income:	
Salary (per Form W-2)	$11,000
Interest income	$3,140
Net rental income	$8,183
Adjusted gross income	$22,323
Minus: Itemized deductions	$10,178
Balance	$12,145
Minus: Exemptions (2)	$6,400
Taxable Income	$5,745
Income tax from tax table	$573
Minus: Tax withheld	$805
Refund of taxes	$232

Income Tax Return of an Estate—Form 1041

2005 income tax return. Having determined the tax liability for your father's final return, you now figure the estate's taxable income. You decide to use the calendar year and the cash method of accounting to report the estate's income. This return also is due by April 17, 2006.

In addition to the amount you received from your father's employer for unpaid salary and for vacation pay ($12,000) entered on line 8 (Form 1041), you received a dividend check from the XYZ Company on June 17, 2005. The check was for $750 and you enter it on line 2a (Form 1041). The amount is a qualified dividend and you show the allocation to the beneficiaries and the estate on line 2b. The amount allocated to the beneficiary ($121) is based on the distributable dividend income before any deductions. The estate received a Form 1099-INT showing $2,250 interest paid by the bank on the savings account in 2005 after your father died. Show this amount on line 1 (Form 1041).

In September, a local coin collector offered you $3,000 for your father's coin collection. Your mother was not interested in keeping the collection, so you accepted the offer and sold him the collection on September 23, 2005.

You will have to report the sale on Schedule D (Form 1041) when you file the income tax return of the estate. The estate has a capital gain of $200 from the sale of the coins. The gain is the excess of the sale price, $3,000, over the value of the collection at the date of your father's death, $2,800. See Gain (or loss) from sale of property under Income Tax Return of an Estate—Form 1041 and its discussion, Income To Include, earlier.

Deductions. In November 2005, you received a bill for the real estate taxes on your parents' home. The bill was for $2,250, which you paid. Include real estate taxes on line 11 (Form 1041). Real estate tax on the rental property was $700; this amount, however, is reflected on Schedule E (Form 1040).

You paid $325 for attorney's fees in connection with administration of the estate. This is an expense of administration and is deducted on line 14 (Form 1041). You must, however, file with the return a statement in duplicate that such expense has not been claimed as a deduction from the gross estate for figuring the federal estate tax on Form 706, and that all rights to claim that deduction on Form 706 are waived.

Distributions. You made a distribution of $2,000 to your father's brother, James. The distribution was made from current income of the estate under the terms of the will.

The income distribution deduction ($2,000) is figured on Schedule B of Form 1041 and deducted on line 18 (Form 1041).

You characterized the $2,000 that is included in income and reported it on Schedule K-1 (Form 1041) as follows:

Step 1 Allocation of Income & Deductions

Type of Income	Amount	Deductions	Distributable Net Income
Interest (15%)	$ 2,250	$(386)	$ 1,864
Dividends (5%)	$750	$(129)	$621

Other Income (80%)	$12,000	$(2,060)	$9,940
Total	$15,000	$(2,575)	$12,425

Step 2 Allocation of Distribution (Report on the Schedule K-1 for James)

Line 1 – Interest $2,000 × (1,864 ÷ 12,425)	$300
Line 2b – Total Dividends $2,000 × (621 ÷ 12,425)	$100
Line 5 a – Other Income $2,000 × (9,940 ÷12,425)	$1,600
Total Distribution	$2,000

The estate took an income distribution deduction, so you must prepare Schedule I (Form 1041), Alternative Minimum Tax, regardless of whether the estate is liable for the alternative minimum tax.

The other distribution you made out of the assets of the estate in 2005 was the transfer of the automobile to your mother on July 1. This is included in the bequest of property, so it is not taken into account in computing the distributions of income to the beneficiary. The life insurance proceeds of $275,000 paid directly to your mother by the insurance company are not an asset of the estate.

Tax computation. The taxable income of the estate for 2005 is $10,025, figured as follows:

Gross income:	
Income in respect of a decedent	*$12,000*
Dividends	$750
Interest	$2,250
Capital gain	$200

Total Gross Income	*$15,200*
Minus: Deductions and income distribution	
Real estate taxes	$2,250
Attorney's fee	$325
Exemption	$600
Distribution 2,000	$2,000
Total: Deductions and income distribution	$5,175
Taxable income	*$10,025*

The estate had a net capital gain and taxable income, so you use the Schedule D Tax Worksheet to figure the tax, $2,486, for 2005.

2006 income tax return for estate. On January 7, 2006, you receive a dividend check from the XYZ Company for $500. You also have interest posted to the savings account in January totaling $350. On January 28, 2006, you make a final accounting to the court and obtain permission to close the estate. In the accounting, you list $1,650 as the balance of the expense of administering the estate.

You advise the court that you plan to pay $5,000 to Hometown Church under the provisions of the will, and that you will distribute the balance of the property to your mother, the remaining beneficiary.

Gross income. After making the distributions already described, you can wind up the affairs of the estate. The gross income of the estate for 2006 is more than $600, so you must file a final income tax return, Form 1041, for 2006 (not shown). The estate's gross income for 2006 is $850 (dividends $500 and interest $350).

Deductions. After making the following computations, you determine that none of the distributions made to your mother must be included in her taxable income for 2006.

Gross income for 2006:	
Dividends	$500
Interest	$350
Total Gross Income	$850

Less deductions:	
Administration expense	$1,650
Loss	($800)

Note that because the contribution of $5,000 to Hometown Church was not required under the terms of the will to be paid out of the gross income of the estate, it is not deductible and was not included in the computation.

The estate had no distributable net income in 2006, so none of the distributions made to your mother have to be included in her gross income. Furthermore, because the estate in the year of termination had deductions in excess of its gross income, the excess of $800 will be allowed as a miscellaneous itemized deduction subject to the 2%-of-adjusted-gross-income limit to your mother on her individual return for the year 2006, if she itemizes deductions.

Termination of estate. You have made the final distribution of the assets of the estate and you are now ready to terminate the estate. You must notify the IRS, in writing, that the estate has been terminated and that all of the assets have been distributed to the beneficiaries. Form 56 can be used for this purpose. Be sure to report the termination to the IRS office where you filed Form 56 and to include the employer identification number on this notification.

Appendix 6-A

Provided Courtesy of the Probate Courts of Connecticut

Guidelines for Guardianships of Minors

INTRODUCTION

Under certain circumstances, it becomes necessary to appoint or remove a guardian of the person or estate of the minor. The Probate Courts of Connecticut are given the responsibility for such appointments and removals. Court-appointed guardians are responsible to the Court for protecting the interests of such minors.

This booklet has been prepared to answer some of the questions you may have regarding the procedures, roles, and responsibilities of the Probate Court and the guardian whom the Court appoints. It should be considered only as a guide in connection with the guardianship process and not as a substitute for competent professional advice.

WHAT IS GUARDIANSHIP?

In Connecticut, a person under the age of 18 is considered to be a minor. A guardian is a person who has the legal right and duty to take care of a minor or a minor's property. Guardianship results either by virtue of the role as parent of the minor or appointment by a Probate

Court or other Court of competent jurisdiction. This right and duty includes the obligation of care and control of that minor and/or his property and the authority to make major decisions affecting the minor's welfare. In some states, guardianship also refers to persons who manage the estate or person of an adult, but guardianship in Connecticut refers only to minors, except in the case of mentally retarded persons.

TYPES OF GUARDIANSHIP FOR MINORS

There are two types of guardianship for minors: guardianship of the person of a minor and guardianship of the estate of a minor. A guardian of the person has the responsibility to care for the person of the minor. A guardian of the estate is required to manage the property of the minor. The following is a description of the duties and responsibilities of guardians for minors.

A. Guardian of the Person of a Minor

The guardian of the person of a minor is an adult authorized by law to take physical control of and provide care for the minor. That broad authority includes making medical and personal decisions concerning the welfare of the minor. By law, the birth parents of a child born in wedlock are entitled to and expected to exercise the care of, and the control over, the minor on a daily basis. For this reason, they are automatically the guardians of the person of the minor. They are also "joint guardians" of their minor, which means that their powers, rights, and responsibilities with respect to their minor are equal, unless altered by a Court.

The father and mother of a child born out of wedlock are also joint guardians, provided the father's paternity has been determined under the laws of Connecticut. In cases where this has not occurred, the mother is the sole guardian of the person of a minor.

B. Temporary Guardian of the Person of a Minor

If a parent or guardian of the person of a minor is unable to care for the minor for a period of time due to illness or absence from the area or for some other reason, the parent or guardian may file an application for appointment of a temporary guardian of the person of a minor in the Probate Court for the district in which the minor resides.

The temporary guardian serves with, but does not replace, the parent as natural guardian, so that either the parent or the temporary guardian may make important decisions affecting the child. The temporary guardianship will immediately terminate whenever the parent notifies the Probate Court and the temporary guardian to that effect. Unless revoked, the appointment may not last for more than one year, unless the Court grants a reappointment.

C. Standby Guardian

C.G.S. §45a-624 allows a parent or guardian to designate a standby guardian. The standby guardianship will take effect upon the occurrence of a specified contingency, including, but not limited to, the mental incapacity, physical debilitation, or death of the parent or guardian. The designation must be in writing, it must be signed by the parent or guardian, and it must be witnessed by at least two witnesses. The standby guardianship may be revoked at any time. The revocation must be made in writing, and the standby guardian must be notified.

In order for the guardianship to take effect, the standby guardian must complete an affidavit indicating that the contingency upon which the guardianship is based has occurred. The affidavit must be signed, witnessed, and sworn to under oath. The standby guardianship will cease when the specified contingency no longer exists or at the end of one year, whichever is sooner. If the parent or guardian dies while the guardianship is in effect, the guardianship will cease 90 days after such death, unless the standby guardian files an application for guardianship with the probate court in the district in which the minor resides, and temporary custody of the minor is granted to the standby guardian or the Court appoints the standby guardian as guardian of the person of the minor.

Like the temporary guardian, the standby guardian does not replace the parent, unless the parent is no longer physically or mentally able to carry out his or her responsibilities as parent.

D. Co-Guardians

Pursuant to the provisions of C.G.S.§45a-616, a parent or guardian who is the sole guardian of the person of a minor child may apply to the probate court in the district in which the child resides for the appointment of one or more persons to serve as co-guardian(s). The Commissioner of Children and Families may also make such application with regard to a child in the department's care, providing the child's parent/guardian consents to the application. Upon receipt of an application for the appointment of a co-guardian(s), the Court will, in most cases, order an investigation and report to be completed by the Department of Children and Families as required by C.G.S. §45a-619. The hearing will be held within 30 days of receipt of the results of the investigation. If the Court waives the investigation requirement for cause shown, the hearing will be held within 30 days of the receipt of the application. If the minor child is over 12 years of age, the Court will order notice to him or her by certified mail, return receipt requested, deliverable to the addressee only, at least 10 days prior to the date of the hearing. The Court will notify the petitioner and all other interested parties by regular mail.

Whenever the Court appoints a guardian or co-guardian, it must take into consideration the following factors:

(1) The ability of the prospective co-guardian(s) to meet the physical, emotional, moral, and educational needs of the minor on a continuing day-to-day basis;
(2) The minor's wishes if he or she is over the age of 12 OR is of sufficient maturity and capable of forming an intelligent preference;
(3) The existence or nonexistence of an established relationship between the minor and the prospective co-guardian(s); and
(4) The best interests of the child.

When the appointment takes effect, the co-guardian(s) have the obligation of care and control and the authority to make major decisions affecting the minor's welfare, including, but not limited to, consent determinations regarding marriage, enlistment in the armed forces and major medical, psychiatric, or surgical treatment. These rights and obligations are to be shared with the parent or the previously-appointed guardian of the person of the minor, and they may be exercised independently by the parent/guardian or the co-guardian(s). In the event of a dispute between a parent/guardian and the co-guardian(s), the matter may be submitted to the probate court that appointed the co-guardian(s).

The appointment of the co-guardian(s) may take effect immediately after the hearing or, if requested by the parent/guardian, it may take effect upon the occurrence of a specified contingency. The specified contingency may include, but is not limited to, the mental incapacity, physical debilitation, or death of the parent or guardian. When the contingency occurs, the prospective co-guardian(s) must notify the Court by written affidavit. The Court may hold a hearing to verify the occurrence of the contingency. Upon verification, the appointment will take effect and will continue until further order of the Court. The co-guardian(s) must accept the appointment in writing. If the Court deems it necessary, a probate bond may be required.

Upon the death of the parent/guardian, any appointed co-guardian(s) of the person of a minor child shall become the sole guardian(s) of the person of the minor child.

E. Guardian of the Estate of a Minor

The guardian of the estate of a minor provides the legal care of, and control over, the financial affairs of a minor. However, the minor, not the guardian, has legal title to the property.

F. Guardian Ad Litem

A guardian ad litem of a minor is a person appointed by a Court to represent the minor's interests in a particular court proceeding. The guardian ad litem does not act as a guardian of the person or estate of the minor. A parent or attorney will often be appointed guardian ad litem.

G. Testamentary Guardian

A surviving parent has the right to appoint a guardian of the person and/or estate of the minor in her will. A guardian appointed in this manner is called a testamentary guardian. If the custody of a minor has been given to either parent by the Superior Court, that parent alone has the power of appointing a guardian by will.

Even though a testamentary guardian is appointed by will rather than by the Probate Court, the guardianship is under the supervision of the Court. An application must be made to the probate court for confirmation of the guardianship. Probate bond will be required of a guardian of the estate and may be required of a guardian of the person. Please note the following exception to these bonding requirements. A probate judge may waive the requirement of a bond if the assets of the estate are less than $20,000. The duties and powers of a testamentary guardian are the same as guardians appointed by the Probate Court.

REMOVAL OF PARENT OR OTHER GUARDIAN OF THE PERSON OF THE MINOR

One or both parents of a minor may have their rights as guardian of the person removed by a Probate Court if the Court finds certain conditions to be present or if the parent consents to be removed as guardian. Any adult relative of the minor or an attorney representing the minor may file an application for the removal of one or both parents as guardian in the probate court for the district in which the minor resides. Under certain circumstances, the Court may also initiate such an action on its own motion.

Upon receipt of an application for removal of guardian, the Court will set a time and place for a hearing on the application and notify all interested parties. Both parents of the minor and the minor, if 12 years of age or over, will be personally notified of the hearing. If a parent resides in another state or is absent from the state, he or she may be notified by registered or certified mail. If the whereabouts of a parent are unknown, the Court may order notice to be given by publication in a newspaper that has a circulation at the parent's last known place of residence.

Any parent who is the subject of such an application has the right to be represented by an attorney and may request the Court to appoint an attorney if he cannot obtain or pay for one. The Court will appoint a guardian ad litem to protect the rights of any minor or incompetent parent. In all cases involving abuse or neglect, the Court must appoint counsel to represent the minor child. The Court may also appoint counsel to represent the child in other types of proceedings. Federal law requires the appointment of a guardian ad litem to represent the best interests of the child in all cases involving child abuse or neglect. Under state law, the Court must also appoint a guardian ad litem in all other matters where the Court deems it appropriate.

Please see the sections entitled "Transfer to Another Probate Judge" and "Transfer of Contested Matters to Superior Court" later in this booklet for information about transferring removal and custody matters.

When an application for removal of a guardian has been filed in a probate court, the Court will, in most cases, order an investigation and report to be completed by the Department of Children and Families. An investigation is required in cases where the applicant has alleged abuse or neglect or in cases where the probate judge has reason to believe the minor child has been abused or neglected. The Department of Children and Families investigates and reports to the Probate Court any facts that may be relevant in assisting the Court with its decision.

Pursuant to C.G.S. §45a-609, the Court may order the examination of the child by a physician, psychiatrist, or licensed clinical psychologist. The Court may also order the examination of a parent or custodian whose competency or ability to care for the child is at issue. The expenses of any examination ordered by the Court on its own motion will be paid by the applicant; the expenses of any examination requested by another party shall be paid by the party requesting the examination. If such applicant or the party requesting the examination is unable to pay for the examination, payment will be made by the Probate Court Administration Fund. If the matter has been transferred to superior court, payment will be made from funds appropriated to the judicial department.

After a hearing, the Court may remove a parent or other Court-appointed guardian as guardian if it finds by clear and convincing evidence that one or more of the following conditions are present:

(1) The parent consents to removal as guardian.
(2) The minor child has been abandoned by the parent in the sense that the parent has failed to maintain a reasonable degree of interest, concern, or responsibility for the minor's welfare.
(3) The minor child has been denied the care, guidance, or control necessary for her physical, educational, moral, or emotional well-being as a result of acts of parental commission or omission, whether the acts are the result of the physical or mental incapability of the parent or conditions attributable to parental habits, misconduct, or neglect, and the parental acts or deficiencies support

the conclusion that the parent cannot exercise, or should not in the best interest of the minor child be permitted to exercise, parental rights and duties at this time.

(4) The minor child has had physical injury or injuries inflicted upon him by a person responsible for such child's health, welfare, or care or by a person given access to such child by such responsible person, other than by accidental means, or has injuries which are at variance with the history given of them or is in a condition which is the result of maltreatment such as, but not limited to, malnutrition, sexual molestation, deprivation of necessities, emotional maltreatment, or cruel punishment. The minor child has been found to be neglected or uncared for, as defined in C.G.S. §46b-120.

(5) Due to the serious consequences resulting from filing an application for removal of a parent or other person as guardian and the complex nature of the legal grounds for the removal, anyone considering such action should seek legal advice prior to filing such an application. There are legal penalties for willfully filing a false application, conspiring with another to file a false application, or testifying falsely in any removal proceeding.

Temporary Custody or Immediate Temporary Custody of the Minor Pending Removal of Guardian

After holding a hearing on the matter, the Court may award temporary custody of the minor to an appropriate custodian pending the removal hearing if:

(1) the Court determines that the parent has either abandoned the minor in the sense that the parent has failed to maintain a reasonable degree of interest, concern, or responsibility for the minor's welfare, OR

(2) the Court determines that the minor has been denied the care, guidance, or control necessary for his physical, educational, moral, or emotional well-being, OR

(3) the Court determines that the minor has had physical injury or injuries inflicted upon her by a person responsible

for such child's health, welfare, or care, or by a person given access to such child by such responsible person, other than by accidental means or has injuries which are at variance with the history given of them or is in a condition which is the result of maltreatment, AND THAT

(4) these acts place the health or welfare of the minor in danger.

Under certain stringent conditions, the Court may order immediate temporary custody without a hearing if the Court finds that:

(1) the child was not taken or kept from the custodial parents, AND
(2) there is a substantial likelihood that the child will be removed from the probate court district prior to a hearing, OR
(3) to return the child to the parent would place the child in circumstances which would result in serious physical illness or injury, or the threat thereof, or imminent physical danger prior to a hearing for temporary custody.

If the child is hospitalized as a result of a serious physical illness or injury, even if the child is in the custody of the parent, the Court may grant an application for immediate temporary custody if a certificate signed by two Connecticut doctors is filed with the Court stating that (1) the child is in need of immediate medical or surgical treatment, the delay of which would be life-threatening, (2) the parent refuses or is unable to consent to such treatment, and (3) determination of the need for temporary custody cannot await a formal hearing.

If the Court orders immediate temporary custody without prior notice to the parents, a hearing must be held within five business days after the date of the order to determine whether the statutory requirements exist to continue temporary custody.

The rights and duties of the temporary custodian are: the obligation of care and control, the authority to make decisions regarding routine medical treatment or school counseling and psychological, emergency medical, psychiatric, or surgical treatment, and any other rights and duties that the Probate Court may order.

An order for temporary custody is not permanent, and the order will be in effect only until a determination can be made on the application for removal of the guardian.

Child Support Orders in Removal and Custody Matters

If a minor child is the subject of a pre-existing child support order issued by the Superior Court, certain procedures must be followed when the Court removes a parent as guardian or transfers custody or guardianship of the child. The Support Enforcement Services Unit at the Department of Social Services must be notified when:

(1) the custody of the child is returned to the parent ordered to pay child support, in which case the child support order will be suspended,
OR
(2) the Court grants guardianship or custody to a new guardian.

The telephone number of the Support Enforcement Unit is 1-800-228-5437.

Transfer to Another Probate Judge

On its own motion or that of any interested party, the Probate Court may transfer any guardianship or custody matter under C.G.S. §45a-603 to 622 to another probate judge. This includes cases involving removal of guardianship, immediate temporary custody, temporary custody, temporary guardianship, and co-guardianship. The judge shall be appointed by the Probate Court Administrator from a panel of qualified probate judges who specialize in children's matters. If the case is transferred, the clerk will transfer the original files and papers in the case to the probate court that will hear the matter.

Transfer of Contested Matters to Superior Court

Before a hearing is held on the merits of a contested removal or guardianship matter under C.G.S. §45a-603 to 622, either the Probate Court or any legal party (except the petitioner) may request the transfer of the case to Superior Court. If the matter is heard by the Probate

Court, any party may appeal to the Superior Court, where a new trial will be held without regard to the findings of the Probate Court.

Visitation Rights of Parent Removed as Guardian

A Probate Court may grant visitation rights to any person who has been removed as guardian of any minor child or children, any relative of any minor child or children, or any parent who has been denied temporary custody of any minor child or children pending a removal or termination of parental rights hearing. An order to this effect must be made by the Court after the hearing. The Court must be guided by the best interest of the minor, giving consideration to the minor's wishes if he or she is of sufficient age and is capable of forming an intelligent opinion.

Reinstatement of Guardianship Rights

Any parent or other guardian of the person of a minor who has been removed as guardian may apply to the Probate Court that removed her for reinstatement if, in her opinion, the factors that resulted in the removal have been resolved satisfactorily.

After the hearing, if the Court determines that the factors that resulted in the removal of the parent have been resolved satisfactorily, the Court may reinstate the parent as guardian of the person of the minor.

APPOINTMENT OF GUARDIAN OF THE PERSON OF THE MINOR

In the case of a minor who has no guardian of the person due to the death of his parents, the probate court for the district in which the minor resides may appoint a guardian for the minor on its own initiative. When the Court has removed both parents as guardians of the minor's person, it must appoint a successor guardian. If the Court removes only one parent as guardian, or if one parent dies, the remaining parent is the sole guardian of the person of the minor.

If the minor is age 12 or over, the Court shall take into consideration the minor's wishes in appointing a guardian of the person. Factors the Court will consider when selecting an appropriate person to be guardian are the ability of the prospective guardian to meet, on a continuing day-to-day basis, the physical, emotional, moral, and educational needs of the minor and the existence or nonexistence of an established relationship between the minor and the prospective guardian.

The guardian of the person of a minor must present an annual report about the minor's condition to the Probate Court that appointed the guardian. The report form, PC-570, will be given to the guardian at the time of appointment, with instructions to submit the report to the Court one year from the date of appointment.

Guardianship of the person will terminate when the minor reaches the age of 18, dies, or if the guardian is removed by a Court.

REVIEW OF CASES INVOLVING CHILDREN WITH MENTAL ILLNESS OR EMOTIONAL DISTURBANCES

C.G.S.§17a-11 provides for the review of those mentally ill or emotionally disturbed children who are at risk of being placed outside of their homes and are receiving voluntary services from the Department of Children and Families (DCF). The Commissioner of DCF may admit to the Department on a voluntary basis any child whom she believes would benefit from services offered by the Department. The application for voluntary admission may be made by the parent or guardian of the child, if the child is under the age of 14, or by the child himself or herself if he or she is 14 years old or older.

Not more than 120 days after admitting a child on a voluntary basis, the Department must petition the Probate Court for a determination as to whether continuation of care is in the child's best interests and, if so, whether there is an appropriate permanency plan. After giving notice to all interested parties of the hearing, the Court shall approve a permanency plan that is in the best interests of the child/youth and takes into consideration the child/youth's need for permanency. The health or safety of the child/youth shall be of paramount concern in formulating the plan.

As set forth in C.G.S. § 17a-11(d), the permanency plan may include the goal of: 1) placement of the child or youth with the parent or guardian, 2) transfer of guardianship, 3) long-term foster care with a relative licensed as a foster parent or certified as a relative caregiver, 4) termination of parental rights and adoption, or 5) such other planned permanent living arrangement* ordered by the Court, provided the Commissioner has documented a compelling reason why it would not be in the best interests of the child or youth for the permanency plan to include the goals stated above.

The Court must consider the following at the hearing:

(1) the appropriateness of the Department's plan for service to the child/youth and his family,

(2) the treatment and support services that have been offered and provided to the child/youth to strengthen and reunite the family,

(3) if return home is not likely, the efforts that have been made or should be made to evaluate and plan for other modes of care,

(4) any further efforts that have been or will be made to promote the best interests of the child/youth.

In addition, the Court shall review the status of the child and the progress being made to implement the permanency plan, determine a timetable for attaining the permanency prescribed by the plan, and determine whether the Commissioner has made reasonable efforts to achieve the permanency plan.

At the conclusion of the hearing, the Court may: 1) direct that the services being provided, or the placement of the child or youth and reunification efforts, be continued, if the Court determines that continuation of the child or youth in services or placement is in the child's or youth's best interests, OR 2) direct that the child's or youth's services or placement be modified to reflect the child's or youth's best interests.

After 10 months and every year thereafter, the Commissioner must file a motion with the Probate Court requesting a review of the permanency plan, based upon the same standards as set forth in the previous paragraph, and the Court shall enter an appropriate order based upon the child's best interests.

---

* Other planned permanent living arrangements may include, but not be limited to, placement of a child or youth with an independent living program or long-term foster care with an identified foster parent.

If you have a child with these special needs, you should call the Regional Office of the Department of Children and Families.

SUBSIDIZED GUARDIANSHIPS

C.G.S. § 17a-126 provides for the establishment of a program by the Department of Children and Families to subsidize certain guardianships for children in the care or custody of the Commissioner who have been living with and cared for by other relatives aside from the parents and who have been in foster care or certified relative care for not less than 18 months.

If the guardian qualifies for the program, the Commissioner may grant a special needs subsidy, consisting of a lump sum payment for one-time expenses involved in taking initial care of the child, as well as a medical subsidy and a monthly cash subsidy equal to the prevailing foster care rate. These subsidies shall continue until the child reaches the age of 18 or the age of 21 if the child is in full time attendance at a secondary school, technical school, or college or is in a state-accredited job training program. Each year, the subsidized guardian must submit a report to the Commissioner that would justify the continuation of the subsidy. For further information on this subsidy program, you should consult with your local office of the Department of Children and Families.

PROBATE COURT JURISDICTION OVER EMANCIPATION OF MINORS

C.G.S. §§46b-150 — 150c give the probate courts concurrent jurisdiction with the superior courts to emancipate a minor. Under the provisions of these sections, a minor is defined as a person who has reached his sixteenth birthday. Jurisdiction is in the district in which the minor or his parents or guardian reside, and the petition may be filed by a minor who has reached the age of 16 and is residing in this state or by any parent or guardian of such minor. The petition shall be verified and must plainly state: 1) the facts which bring the minor within the Court's jurisdiction; 2) the name, date of birth, sex, and residence of the minor, 3) the name and residence of the parent, 4) the name of the petitioner and his relationship to the minor.

The hearing must be held not later than 30 days after the filing of the petition, and the minor and his parent (if the parent is not the petitioner) must be notified by personal service at least seven days prior to the hearing. If the parent is the petitioner, notice must be given by certified mail. The Probate Court must give such notice as it directs to the Commissioner of the Department of Children and Families and other persons having an interest in the minor. In most cases, the Court will order the Department of Children and Families to investigate the matter and report to the Probate Court any facts that may be relevant in assisting the Court with its decision. The Court will also appoint counsel to represent the minor. The minor must pay the cost of counsel, unless he or she is unable to pay and files an affidavit to that effect with the Court, in which case the Probate Court Administration Fund will pay.

Pursuant to C.G.S. §46b-150a, the Court may make a finding at the hearing or at any time while the emancipation proceeding is pending that an examination is warranted. If this finding is made, the Court, on its own motion or on the motion of any party, may order the minor to be examined by a physician, psychiatrist, or licensed clinical psychologist appointed by the Court. The Court may also order the examination of a parent or custodian whose competency or ability to care for the minor is at issue. The expenses of any examination ordered by the Court on its own motion will be paid by the petitioner; the expenses of any examination requested by another party shall be paid by the party requesting the examination. If such petitioner or the party requesting the examination is unable to pay for the examination, payment will be made by the Probate Court Administration Fund. The Court may consider the results of the examination in ruling on the merits of the petition.

After the hearing, the Probate Court may enter an order of emancipation if the judge finds that:

(1) the minor has entered into a valid marriage; or
(2) the minor is on active duty with any of the armed forces; or
(3) the minor willingly lives separate and apart from his parents and is managing his own financial affairs, regardless of the source of lawful income; or
(4) for good cause shown, emancipation will be in the best interest of the minor, any child of the minor, or the parent or guardian of the minor.

APPOINTMENT OF GUARDIAN OF THE ESTATE OF A MINOR

A guardian of the estate of a minor is one who has legal control over the financial affairs of the minor. The parent or guardian of the person of a minor may give a valid release for and manage the property of the minor if the estate is $10,000 or less in value. If the minor's estate exceeds $10,000 in value, a guardian of the estate of the minor must be appointed by the Probate Court for the district in which the minor resides. A parent, guardian, or spouse may hold property for a minor under the Uniform Transfers to Minors Act without being appointed by the Court. If the minor is not a resident of Connecticut, the Probate Court for the district in which the minor owns property may, after a hearing, appoint a guardian of the estate who shall manage the minor's property.

Although the Probate Court can appoint any suitable person as the guardian of the estate of a minor, the Court will ordinarily look first to the parents or the guardian of the person of the minor. If that person is unwilling or unqualified for the appointment, the Probate Court will appoint some suitable person as guardian, and, if the minor is 12 years of age or over, she may propose a guardian to the Court.

A guardian of the estate may be referred to as a "fiduciary," a term used to describe a person who is responsible for administering the property of another. The Court will require the guardian of the estate to furnish a probate bond for the protection of the minor's property. The value of the probate bond is usually equal to the value of the assets of the minor's estate, excluding any real property. The appointment of a guardian of the estate is not effective until the probate bond is filed with the court, but a bond may not be required if a bank is the guardian of the estate. In addition, the judge may waive the requirement of a bond if the minor's assets are less than $20,000. Upon furnishing the probate bond, the guardian will be issued a Fiduciary's Probate Certificate that will allow the guardian to negotiate the assets of the minor within the limits imposed by law.

Duties of the Guardian of the Estate of the Minor

The guardian of the estate of a minor has control over all the minor's property, whether acquired before or after the guardian's appointment, except for property managed under the Uniform Transfers to Minors Act or bequests managed under a trust. Investments of a minor's property by a guardian are strictly limited by law. The minor's property may only be used for the benefit of the minor. It may not be used to pay the expenses that a parent or guardian of the person is legally responsible to provide.

The guardian of the estate should file copies of the Fiduciary's Probate Certificate with persons or agencies where the minor's ownership of property is a matter of record. The certificate provides notice that the minor's property has come under the jurisdiction of the Probate Court and that the guardian of the estate has been given custody of such property.

Within two months of appointment, the guardian must file an inventory with the Court listing all the minor's property at its fair market value as of the date of the appointment. If the guardian of the estate wishes to sell or mortgage any of the real property belonging to the minor, he must file an application in the probate court that made the appointment. The Court will hold a hearing on the application after publishing notice in the local newspaper and notifying interested parties. If the Court determines that the requested transaction is in the best interest of the minor, the application will be granted. A guardian of the estate may also arrange to lease the real property of the minor upon application to the Court, notice, a hearing, and the Court's approval.

The guardian must file periodic accounts with the probate court showing all financial transactions that occurred on the minor's behalf during the accounting period. Upon receipt of the periodic account, the Probate Court will notify interested parties of its availability for examination. A periodic account hearing must be held at least once in every three-year period. More frequent account hearings may be ordered by the Probate Court or requested by an interested party.

If a guardian of the estate becomes incapable, neglects to perform the required duties, or mishandles the minor's assets, the Court that granted the appointment may remove him as guardian. The Court will then appoint another guardian of the estate.

The guardianship of the estate will terminate when the minor reaches the age of 18, dies, or if the Court removes the guardian. The guardian should file the estate's final account in the probate court with a receipt and release signed by the minor. If the Court approves the account, the remaining assets must be delivered to the former minor. The probate bond will then be released.

APPEALS FROM PROBATE

Any person aggrieved by an order, denial, or decree of the probate court may appeal to the Superior Court. In general, appeals must be taken within 30 days from the date of the order, denial, or decree.

CONCLUSION

Guardianship has been described as a trust of the highest and most sacred character. The guardian is lawfully invested with the power and charged with the duty of taking care of a minor person and, in appropriate cases, the minor's property. The minor is a person under the age of full legal rights and, in many circumstances, is legally unable to act for herself. In view of these serious responsibilities, a person acting as guardian for a minor's person and/or estate should always seek competent professional advice when making decisions on behalf of the minor.

PROBATE COURT FORMS

Temporary Custody and Guardianship
Application/Removal of Guardian: PC-500*
Application/Immediate Temporary Custody: PC-501 *
Application/Temporary Custody: PC-502*
Application/Appointment of Guardian of the Estate: PC-503*
Application/Appointment of Temporary Guardian PC-504*
Custodian's Affidavit/Immediate Temporary Custody: PC-510
Guardian's Report/Guardianship of the Person of a Minor: PC-570
Application/Emancipation of Minor: PC-905

These forms are available at the probate court. Forms marked with an asterisk are also available on the Judicial Department website: www.jjud.state.ct.us. Forms for standby guardianship and co-guardianship must be reproduced from the Probate Clerk's Manual.

Appendix 6-B

Provided Courtesy of ACTEC

Wills: Why You Should Have One and the Lawyer's Role in Its Preparation

Q: What is a will?

A: A will is an instrument by which a person provides for the disposition of his or her property after death.

Q: Who may make a will?

A: Generally, every person of sound mind and memory, 18 years of age or over, may dispose of his or her property by will.

Q: May a person dispose of property by will in any way he or she wishes?

A: Generally speaking, yes, but with a few exceptions. For example, a surviving husband or wife may have the right to elect to take a fixed share of the estate regardless of the will. Children may be disinherited, although children born after a will is made generally will inherit as if there were no will unless the will shows an intent to disinherit children born after the will was drawn.

Q: What else can be done by a will?

A: By use of a will, an individual may designate as executor someone who is qualified and in whom he or she has confidence. An individual may establish a trust or trusts for the management of assets, the protection of family members, and for the savings of taxes in connection with an overall family estate plan. He or she may give discretionary powers to the executor and to a trustee to spend income or principal according to the changing needs of children or other relatives. An individual may select the persons to receive property and leave it to them in designated proportions. He or she may select a person to be guardian of his or her minor children

By supplementary documents, an individual may provide instructions regarding burial or cremation or anatomical gifts. Even in those cases where a testator desires to leave property to the same persons who would inherit it if he or she left no will, the testator may, by the use of a will, simplify the administration of the estate.

Q: Can a will be changed?

A: A will may be modified or added to or entirely revoked at any time before the maker's death as long as the maker is competent and able physically to change it. An amendment to a will is called a codicil. In some states, the will may refer to a memorandum disposing of tangible property (such as household items, jewelry, automobiles, etc.) which may be changed from time to time without the formalities of a will.

Q: What happens where there is no will?

A: If there is no will, the court will direct the distribution of the estate in accordance with state law. In general, this means to the immediate family—that is, the surviving husband or wife and children. Often the state law does not reflect commonly held attitudes regarding provisions for the spouse as primary and does not provide the spouse adequate means of support. If there is no surviving husband, wife, or children, other blood relatives become entitled to the property and in many cases the situation becomes very complicated. The law is rigid and gives no consideration to the needs or circumstances of the individual heirs. The law further designates who may administer the estate and may require a surety bond at the expense of the estate.

Q: Is the cost of administering an estate greater with or without a will?

A: A skillfully drawn will generally reduces expenses by giving the executor authority to act efficiently without unnecessary delay and expense. It may provide that there need be no surety bond and thus save the estate considerable expense and in many states it can direct that the intervention or involvement of the probate court can be kept to a minimum. If the will is "self-proved," court proceedings for its proof may be avoided.

Q: Is joint tenancy a substitute for a will?

A: Joint tenancy may be a useful method of transferring property, such as the family automobile and the family checking account, at death. In other situations, especially where tax considerations are involved, it can sometimes produce very unfortunate results. Even where joint tenancy is desirable, it does not take care of the situation on the death of the surviving joint tenant or a common disaster, so the necessity for a will is not eliminated. Because joint tenancy property passes outside the will, having too much property in joint tenancy may frustrate the basic family estate plan reflected in the will. Joint tenancy may also produce unexpected results when the "wrong" joint tenant dies first and has led to many disputes, including litigation, between the estate of the original owner and the surviving joint tenant as to whether the survivor's name was added as a matter of convenience or management or whether a gift was intended. A decision to put property in joint tenancy should never be made without consulting a lawyer.

Q: What is the effect of a will on life insurance?

A: If a life insurance policy is payable to an individual, then the will of the insured has no effect on the proceeds. If the life insurance policy is payable to the estate of a person, then the disposition of the proceeds can be directed by will in the same manner as any other kind of property.

Q: What is the effect of marriage or divorce on a will?

A: In many states a will is revoked by marriage unless the will expressly states that it was executed in contemplation of the particular marriage and that it shall not be revoked by such marriage. Divorce or dissolution of marriage either revokes the entire will or those provisions in favor of the former spouse. This depends on the details of your state's law.

Q: Can taxes be saved by a will?

A: Under certain conditions, definite savings can be made by the carefully planned disposition of a family estate in accordance with provisions of a skillfully drafted will. In this regard, the will may provide especially for the surviving spouse (by trust or otherwise) to minimize or eliminate taxes payable on the death of the survivor.

Q: When should a will be made?

A: A will should be made while the maker is in good health and free from emotional stress. A will that is hastily planned and drafted under pressure seldom does credit either to the maker or the drafter. The "deathbed" will is often the subject of long, expensive, and sometimes bitter litigation. Because of changing conditions in family, in size of estate, and in tax laws, a will should be reviewed periodically. A will should always be reviewed when there is a change in marital status.

Q: Who should prepare the will?

A: Generally, a will must be written and witnessed in a special manner provided by law. The drafting of a will requires learning, skill, and experience obtained only by study, training, and practice. Only a practicing lawyer can perform this service.

Appendix 7-A

Provided Courtesy of the Probate Courts of Connecticut

Guidelines for Conservators

INTRODUCTION

The Probate Courts of Connecticut become involved in the lives of individuals who are incapable of caring for themselves and/or their property. The Courts are entrusted with the responsibility of protecting the interests of these individuals. This trust is carried out by the appointment of a conservator, who is authorized by law to provide supervision and who is, in many respects, an agent of the Court.

This booklet has been prepared to answer some of the questions you may have regarding the procedures, roles, and responsibilities of the Probate Court and the conservator whom the court appoints. It should be considered only as a guide in connection with the conservatorship process and not as a substitute for competent professional advice.

Notes: 1) As used in this booklet, words referring to the masculine gender may be applied to females, and words referring to the feminine gender may be applied to males. 2) Applications for conservatorship are available at the probate court or online at the Judicial Branch's web site: www.jud.state.ct.us. (Click on "Court Forms" under "Quick Links.")

WHAT IS A CONSERVATOR?

A conservator is a person appointed by the Probate Court to oversee the financial and/or personal affairs of an adult person who is determined by the Probate Court to be incapable of managing his or her affairs or unable to care for himself or herself. A conservator may also be appointed for the same purpose for a capable person who requests such assistance.

There are two basic types of conservatorships to accommodate the different needs of individuals. A "conservator of the person" is appointed to supervise an individual's personal affairs, including arranging for medical needs and seeing to it that he has proper and adequate food, clothing, personal hygiene, and housing and is protected from physical abuse. A "conservator of the estate" is appointed to supervise the financial affairs of an individual who is found by the Court to be incapable of doing so himself to the extent that property will be wasted unless management is provided.

A person may be in need of one or both types of conservators. Two separate individuals may perform these two roles, or one person may serve in both capacities. A conservator of the estate or person may be an individual, a legally authorized municipal or state official, or a private or nonprofit corporation. However, hospitals and nursing homes cannot be appointed conservators of either the person or the estate, and banks cannot be appointed conservators of the person.

A mentally retarded adult may be in need of a conservator of the estate to manage his financial affairs, while a guardian of the mentally retarded person is appropriate to oversee his or her personal affairs.

MAY A PERSON NAME A CONSERVATOR IN ADVANCE OF INCAPACITY?

Yes. Prior to becoming incapable, a person may name a future conservator by executing a document with the same formality and requirements necessary for executing a will.

WHAT IS TEMPORARY CONSERVATORSHIP?

The laws of Connecticut provide for the possibility that an individual may be in need of a conservator on a temporary basis. Any person deemed by the Court to have sufficient interest in the welfare of the alleged incapable person (referred to as "the respondent") may petition for appointment of a temporary conservator. The necessary forms may be obtained from the probate court. In addition to the application, the Court is required to receive a physician's report on the respondent's condition. This report may be waived in certain circumstances, however.

The Court will hold a hearing on the application following the appointment of an attorney and notice to the respondent, the respondent's next of kin, and the respondent's attorney. The hearing must be held within 72 hours of the filing of the application (excluding Saturdays, Sundays, and holidays), unless it is continued by the Court.

In order to appoint a temporary conservator, the Court must find that the respondent is incapable of managing his affairs or of caring for himself *and that* immediate and irreparable personal, financial, or legal damage will result if a temporary conservator is not appointed. In making the appointment, the Court must limit the temporary conservator's duties, responsibilities, and powers to the conditions that gave rise to the application. The judge must consider the respondent's wishes, his abilities, any prior appointment of a health care agent or other person legally acting on his behalf, available support services, and any other relevant evidence.

A temporary conservator may be appointed on an emergency basis if the judge determines that the delay caused by giving notice and appointing an attorney would cause immediate and irreparable injury to the respondent's mental or physical health or financial and legal affairs. In the decree, the judge must specifically state why the emergency appointment was necessary. Immediately following the emergency appointment, the Court must schedule a hearing to be held within 72 hours (excluding Saturdays, Sundays, and holidays), appoint an attorney for the respondent (who is referred to as "the ward" after the conservator is appointed), and give formal notice of the hearing to the ward, the ward's next of kin, and the ward's attorney. At the hearing, the Court shall confirm or revoke the temporary conservatorship, or the judge may modify the duties, responsibilities, or powers assigned under the emergency appointment.

Temporary conservatorship may last no longer than 30 days, unless an application for involuntary conservatorship is filed while the temporary conservatorship is in effect. If such an application is filed, the Court may extend the appointment of the temporary conservator until disposition of the application for involuntary conservatorship or for an additional 30 days, whichever occurs first. The Court may also terminate the appointment of a temporary conservator if the conditions that led to the application for temporary conservatorship no longer exist. Upon termination of the temporary conservatorship, the temporary conservator must file a Conservator's Report, PC-371.

Change of Residence

A temporary conservator may not change the ward's residence without a hearing and approval by the Court, except under certain circumstances, as explained below.

Placement in an Institution for Long-Term Care/Reporting Requirements

If the temporary conservator determines that the ward needs to be placed in an institution for long-term care*, he must first file a report (PC-371A) with the probate court that made the appointment. However, if the placement will be made because of the ward's discharge from a hospital or if irreparable injury to the ward's mental or physical health or financial or legal affairs would result from filing the report before making the placement, the temporary conservator must make the placement before filing the report. Under these circumstances, the temporary conservator must file the report within five days of making the placement, and he must include a statement in the report about the hospital discharge or a description of the "irreparable injury" that the placement averted.

The report must state the basis for the conservator's decision about the placement, the community resources that were considered to avoid the placement, and the reasons why the ward's physical, mental, and psychosocial needs cannot be met in a less restrictive and more integrated setting. Community resources to be considered include area agencies on aging, the Department of Social Services, the Office of Protection and Advocacy for Persons with Disabilities, the Department of Mental Health and Addiction Services, the Department of Mental Retardation, independent living centers, residential care homes, and congregate or subsidized housing. The temporary conservator must give notice of the placement and a copy of the report to the ward and any other interested parties as determined by the Court.

**An "institution for long-term care" is defined as a facility that has been "federally certified as a skilled nursing facility or intermediate care facility."*

Hearing on the Report and Placement

The Court is required to hold a hearing on the report and placement upon the request of the ward or an interested party. The hearing must be held within 30 days of the request. The Court also has the authority to hold a hearing on its own motion. If a hearing is held and the Court determines that the ward's physical, mental, and psychosocial needs can be met in a less restrictive and more integrated setting within the limits of his financial resources or through private or public assistance, the Court must order that the ward be placed in that type of setting.

WHAT IS VOLUNTARY REPRESENTATION (CONSERVATORSHIP)?

The supervisory relationship of the Court over the appointed conservator has given rise to another type of conservatorship. This is termed "voluntary representation" or voluntary conservatorship and is used when a person who is not legally incapable would like another person to manage her affairs, subject to oversight by the Court. In most cases, voluntary representation results in appointment of a conservator of the estate, but it could also involve appointment of a conservator of the person.

Prior to appointing a conservator in voluntary proceedings, the Probate Court in the district in which the individual resides or is domiciled will hold a hearing on the Application for Voluntary Representation. The person requesting the voluntary conservatorship must be present at the hearing, or, if attendance at the hearing is not possible, the judge must visit him. After hearing the reasons for the individual's request for a conservator, the Court may grant voluntary representation for the individual without making a finding of incapacity. A conservator, usually of the respondent's choice, is then appointed. Since this relationship is voluntary, the ward may terminate the conservatorship with 30 days' notice to the Court. A conservator appointed under the voluntary process has the same powers and duties as a conservator appointed in involuntary proceedings. Appointment of a conservator of the estate in voluntary proceedings has the effect of nullifying any power of attorney previously granted by the ward.

HOW IS A CONSERVATOR APPOINTED IN INVOLUNTARY PROCEEDINGS?

"Involuntary representation" usually involves a long-term appointment. Any person alleging that a person is incapable of caring for himself or herself may file an Application for Appointment of Conservator in the probate court in the district in which the alleged incapable person (the "respondent") resides or is domiciled. There is a criminal penalty for filing a fraudulent or malicious application or for testifying fraudulently as to a person's incapacity, temporary or otherwise.

The Probate Court will hold a hearing within 30 days of receipt of the application. The hearing may be continued to a later date if good cause is shown for postponing the hearing. Unless the Court finds that personal service would be detrimental to the respondent's health or welfare, a state marshal will make personal service of the notice of hearing on the respondent. The respondent's spouse will also receive personal service, if he or she is not the applicant, except as provided by statute (C.G.S. §45a-649). If the respondent is unable to request or obtain an attorney, the Court will appoint one. Compensation for the attorney's services will be paid by the Probate Court Administration Fund if the respondent cannot afford to pay for counsel. The respondent has a right to be present at the hearing, and it may be held at a place other than the probate court if that would facilitate his attendance. If this is not practical and the respondent is in Connecticut, the judge may visit the respondent before the hearing.

At the court hearing for involuntary representation, the petitioner is required to present medical evidence about the respondent's incapacity from one or more physicians who have examined the respondent within 30 days of the hearing. In certain circumstances, the Court may waive the requirement of medical evidence, but the judge must state the reason for doing so. The Court may also consider other relevant evidence, such as the physical and social functioning level or ability of the respondent and the availability of support services from the family and other appropriate sources. In addition to the medical evidence provided by the petitioner, the Court may, if it finds it necessary, order the examination of the respondent by another physician, a psychiatrist, or a psychologist. The fees for such an examination will be assessed against the petitioner, the respondent, or the party requesting the exam. If the party is unable to pay for the examination, payment will be made by the Probate Court Administration Fund.

If the Court finds by clear and convincing evidence that the respondent is incapable of managing his financial affairs, the Court shall appoint a conservator of the *estate,* UNLESS it appears to the Court that the respondent's financial affairs are being managed properly without the appointment of a conservator. Likewise, if the Court finds by clear and convincing evidence that the respondent is incapable of caring for himself, the Court shall appoint a conservator of the *person,* UNLESS it appears to the Court that the respondent is being cared for properly without the appointment of a conservator.

When determining whether a conservator should be appointed and in selecting a conservator, the Court must be guided by the best interests of the respondent. In making this determination, the Court must consider whether the respondent had made alternate arrangements for the management of his affairs or for the care of his person, such as the execution of a valid durable power of attorney, the appointment of a health care agent, or other similar document.

Appointment of a conservator of the estate in involuntary proceedings has the effect of nullifying any power of attorney previously granted by the respondent (who is referred to as the "ward" after a conservator is appointed) and any voluntary conservatorship previously established.

Placement in an Institution for Long-Term Care/Reporting Requirements

If the conservator determines that the ward needs to be placed in an institution for long-term care*, he must first file a report with the probate court that made the appointment. However, if the placement will be made because of the ward's discharge from a hospital <u>or</u> if irreparable injury to the ward's mental or physical health or financial or legal affairs would result from filing the report before making the placement, the conservator must make the placement before filing the report. Under these circumstances, the conservator must file the report within five days of making the placement, and he must include a statement in the report about the hospital discharge or a description of the "irreparable injury" that the placement averted.

The report must state the basis for the conservator's decision about the placement, the community resources that were considered to avoid the placement, and the reasons why the ward's physical, mental, and psychosocial needs cannot be met in a less restrictive and more integrated setting. Community resources to be considered include area agencies on aging, the Department of Social Services, the Office of Protection and Advocacy for Persons with Disabilities, the Department of Mental Health and Addiction Services, the Department of Mental Retardation, independent living centers, residential care homes, and congregate or subsidized housing. The conservator must give notice of the placement and a copy of the report to the ward and any other interested parties as determined by the Court.

**An "institution for long-term care" is defined as a facility that has been "federally certified as a skilled nursing facility or intermediate care facility."*

Hearing on the Report and Placement

The Court is required to hold a hearing on the report and placement upon the request of the ward or an interested party. The hearing must be held within 30 days of the request. The Court also has the authority to hold a hearing on its own motion. If a hearing is held and the Court determines that the ward's physical, mental, and psychosocial needs can be met in a less restrictive and more integrated setting within the limits of his financial resources or through private or public assistance, the Court must order that the ward be placed in that type of setting.

MAY THE PROBATE COURT'S DECISION BE APPEALED?

Any party involved in the conservatorship proceeding who is aggrieved by the Court's decision may appeal to the superior court within 30 days of the issuance of the decree.

WHAT ARE THE COSTS ASSOCIATED WITH APPOINTING A CONSERVATOR?

A court entry fee of $150.00 will be charged to the person applying to the probate court for voluntary, involuntary, or temporary conservatorship. The respondent must also pay for an attorney to represent her at the hearing. If the respondent is unable to pay for the services of an attorney, the cost of such services will be paid from the Probate Court Administration Fund. If a conservator is not appointed, the petitioner will also be required to pay the charges for the services listed below. If a conservator is appointed, the ward's assets will be used to pay for these charges, which are as follows:

1. the cost of personal service (involuntary proceedings)
2. the recording of any documents
3. notices in excess of two with respect to any hearing or continued hearing
4. certified or registered mailing of notices
5. making and certifying copies of documents

If it would cause undue delay or hardship on the petitioner's part, the Court may postpone, reduce, or waive payment of the entry fee and other charges incurred in connection with the conservatorship. If the Court finds that the petitioner is indigent, all fees and costs will be waived.

WHO MAY BE APPOINTED CONSERVATOR?

Although it is the petitioner's responsibility to suggest an appropriate person, the Court determines whom to appoint as conservator by considering the best interests of the respondent. The conservator will often be a relative or friend of the respondent who is willing and able to carry out the duties of a conservator. The Court will honor the respondent's preference in the matter, unless it determines that the choice is not in the respondent's best interests.

The Commissioner of Social Services may be appointed conservator of the estate and/or conservator of the person if no suitable conservator can be found, and the respondent meets certain guidelines. He must be 60 years of age or older, and his liquid assets, excluding burial insurance in an amount up to $1,500.00, cannot exceed $1,500.00 at the time of the Commissioner's appointment as conservator.

VISITATION

Any parent of a mentally disabled or mentally retarded adult person for whom a conservator of the person or a guardian has been appointed may file a motion for visitation with the Probate Court that has jurisdiction over the conservatorship or guardianship. After notice and hearing, the Court may grant an order of visitation pursuant to the provisions of C.G.S.§45a-598. The order must contain a schedule specifying the date(s), time(s) and place(s) of visits (including overnight visits, if permitted) and any other conditions that the judge believes to be in the best interest of the ward.

WHAT ARE THE DUTIES OF THE CONSERVATOR OF THE ESTATE?

The duties of the conservator of the estate involve management of the assets of the ward in order that the ward's rights and interests will be protected. The first duty of the conservator is to complete an inventory of the ward's property and assets. In preparing the inventory, the conservator must obtain an appraisal of the fair market value as of the date of appointment as conservator, of all property, both real and personal, in which the ward has a legal interest. Jointly owned property, such as a bank account, must also be appraised and its value stated on the inventory. The conservator must file the inventory in the probate court within two months of appointment.

The conservator must transfer any bank accounts in the ward's name to the name of the estate (i.e. Estate of Samuel E. Jones; John Doe, Conservator) and notify the bank of the appointment as conservator. If there are other assets in the ward's name, such as stocks and bonds, the financial institutions and/or corporations involved should be notified of the conservator's appointment and requested to direct income payments to the conservator of the estate. The conservator should obtain a Fiduciary's Probate Certificate from the Court for this purpose. In addition, the conservator is required to notify and make a return of personal property to the town assessor in any town where the ward owns taxable personal property. The conservator must also file a Certificate of Notice for Land Records in any town where the ward owns real estate. This certificate is also available from the Probate Court.

The ongoing responsibility of the conservator is to use the assets of the ward's estate to support the ward and any members of the ward's family whom the ward is legally liable to support. A hearing may be required to determine the amount of support. When an application for spousal support is filed, the person filing the application must certify to the Court that a copy of the application and accompanying attachments have been sent to the Commissioner of Social Services. The Court will provide notice to the Commissioner at least fifteen business days before the hearing, and the Commissioner (or his designee) has the right to appear at the hearing to present the Commissioner's position on the application. The conservator is responsible for paying the ward's bills and taxes and collecting debts owed to the ward.

The conservator must consult the Probate Court prior to the sale or mortgage of assets and before making any expenditures other than routine payments.

The law regulates the investments that the conservator is permitted to make on behalf of the ward. Investments received by the conservator at the time of appointment may be retained unless otherwise ordered by the Probate Court or unless retention is clearly imprudent. Questions regarding permissible investments should be directed to legal counsel and the Probate Court. A recently issued Certificate of Appointment is usually required in order to negotiate the transfer of any asset belonging to the ward. When negotiating the assets of the ward, the conservator signs his or her name as conservator of the estate of the ward. Under certain circumstances, conservators may be permitted to make gifts on behalf of the ward from estate funds, but the conservator must receive prior authorization from the Probate Court.

The conservator of the estate may be required by the Court to file a Periodic Account annually in the probate court. Although there are exceptions, the statute generally requires an accounting at least once in every three-year period and more often if the Court directs. The Court will notify interested parties and hold a hearing on the account. The Court will charge a fee based upon the size of the conservatorship estate.

WHAT ARE THE DUTIES OF THE CONSERVATOR OF THE PERSON?

The duties of the conservator of the person as specified by law include the responsibility for the general custody of the ward; providing for the ward's care, comfort, and maintenance; and caring for the ward's personal effects. The conservator also has authority to establish the ward's residence within the state, to apply for entitlement programs for which the ward may be eligible, and to file an application in the probate court to determine a ward's competency to vote in a primary, referendum, or election. In addition, a conservator may consent to the performance of medical treatment and procedures on the ward. When the medical procedure recommended is extraordinary, the conservator may wish to obtain authority from the Probate Court before making such a decision on behalf of the ward. All of these duties must be carried out within the limitations of the resources available to the ward, either through the ward's own estate or through private or public assistance.

In addition to his or her responsibilities relating to the care of the ward, the conservator of the person must report at least annually on the ward's condition by filing a Conservator's Report with the probate court.

ARE THERE ANY LIMITATIONS ON A CONSERVATOR'S AUTHORITY?

When issuing the decree appointing a conservator, the Court may limit the powers and duties of a conservator of the person or a conservator of the estate to include some, but not all, of the powers and duties explained above. In the decree, the judge must make specific findings to justify any limitations, and they must be made in the best interests of the ward. In determining whether or not any limitations should be imposed, the Court will consider the abilities of the ward; the prior appointment of any attorney-in-fact, health care agent, trustee or other fiduciary acting on behalf of the ward; any support services that are otherwise available to the ward; and any other relevant evidence. The Court may modify its decree upon any *change in* circumstances.

HOW IS A CONSERVATORSHIP TERMINATED?

Conservatorships are most commonly terminated due to the death of the ward or depletion of the estate's assets. If the estate's assets at the time of the ward's death are not sufficient to pay the debts incurred during the ward's lifetime, the funeral and burial expenses, and any probate or other administration expenses necessary to settlement of the estate, the conservator of the estate may pay these expenses and list them for credit on the conservator's Final Account. In other cases, the assets of the estate must be delivered to the executor or administrator of the ward's estate upon the ward's death.

Following notice and a hearing, the Probate Court may also terminate a conservatorship of the estate if it finds that the ward's assets do not exceed the asset limits allowed for the state supplement program. Currently, these asset limits are $1,600.00 for an individual and $2,400.00 for a married couple. In the event that the conservatorship is terminated, the conservator of the estate must distribute the ward's remaining assets to the conservator of the person or, if there is none, to another suitable person.

A conservatorship may also be terminated when an interested person feels that the ward has been restored to capacity and makes a request in writing to the Court to review the need for the conservatorship. The Court will set a time and place for a hearing and will issue notice to appropriate individuals. If the Court determines at the hearing that the ward is no longer in need of a conservator, the conservatorship will be terminated.

A ward may also ask the Court to review the conservatorship. The ward and his attorney will be notified annually of the ward's right to a hearing, and, if requested, a hearing will be held.

At least every three years, the Court must review each conservatorship to determine the appropriateness of continuing, modifying, or terminating the conservatorship. Within 45 days of a request from the Court, the conservator, attorney for the ward, and a physician licensed to practice medicine in this state must each submit a written report to the Court on the condition of the ward. The physician must examine the ward within the 45-day period preceding the date of the submission of the report.

If the Court determines that there has been no change in the status of the ward after a review of the three written reports, a hearing need not be held. However, the Court, in its discretion, may hold a hearing on the status of the ward. In addition, the Court must hold a hearing within 30 days if the ward's attorney, conservator, or physician requests a hearing. If the ward is unable to request or obtain an attorney, the Court will appoint one. Compensation for the attorney's services will be paid by the Probate Court Administration Fund if the ward cannot afford to pay for counsel.

After a conservatorship of the estate has been terminated, the conservator should file a final account in the probate court within two months of the termination. The Court will hold a hearing on the account, following notice to the ward and the ward's attorney.

IS A CONSERVATOR ELIGIBLE TO RECEIVE COMPENSATION FOR HIS OR HER SERVICES?

A conservator of either the person or estate is allowed to charge the estate a fee for the services rendered to the ward. The fee must be found to be reasonable by the Probate Court and is limited by statute in certain cases.

WHAT IS A PROBATE BOND AND WHEN IS IT REQUIRED FOR A CONSERVATOR?

A probate bond is a form of surety purchased by a conservator to guarantee protection of the ward's assets. A conservator of the estate is required to purchase a bond usually equal in value to the liquid assets of the ward's estate. (Please note the following exception to this bonding requirement. If the ward's assets are less than $20,000, or if the amount of the ward's estate not restricted by Probate Court order is less than $10,000, the judge may waive the bond.) The Court may accept a lower bond if a conservator is willing to accept a restriction on the control of assets. If the estate's assets change in value, or if the estate is a small one and the spouse or next of kin is the conservator, the value of the bond may be increased or decreased accordingly. A conservator of the person may also be required to purchase a probate bond. In all cases, the Probate Court sets the amount of the bond required in accordance with rules adopted by the Connecticut Supreme Court.

CONCLUSION

The relationship between conservator and ward is one characterized by trust. Essential elements in the relationship are confidence on one side and active good faith on the other. The law looks on a conservator as a trustee, and, as such, the conservator cannot neglect the ward's interests. As a general rule, any profit or advantage that arises from the conservator's management of the ward's estate accrues to the ward, not to the conservator.

The seriousness of the conservator's responsibility for the ward's person and/or property cannot be overstated. For this reason, the conservator should always consult with the Probate Court or legal counsel when making decisions that may have serious consequences for the ward.

RECORD OF IMPORTANT DATES

- Appointment as Conservator Inventory Due (two months from date of appointment)
- Periodic Account Due (at least once in every three year period; more often if ordered by the Court)
- Conservator's Report, PC-371 (Due annually)
- Conservator's Report/Placement or Request for Hearing on Placement, PC-371A
- Mandatory Review by Probate Court (At least every three years)
- Termination of Conservatorship
- Final Account Due (No later than two months from date of termination of conservatorship)

Appendix 7-B

Provided Courtesy of Cummings & Lockwood, LLC

Sample Connecticut Advanced Directive

(Rev. November 2006)

This document is intended to convey to you the principal characteristics involved with estate planning as they apply to common situations, and does not constitute an attorney-client engagement. Under no circumstances should you or your other advisors rely solely on the contents of this document for technical advice nor should you reach any decisions with respect to this topic without further discussion and consultation with a qualified estate planning attorney.

LIVING WILL AND APPOINTMENT OF HEALTH CARE AGENT AND HEALTH CARE ATTORNEY-IN-FACT

To any physician who is treating me: These are my health care instructions including those concerning the withholding or withdrawal of life support systems, together with the appointment of my health care agent and my attorney-in-fact for health care decisions. As my physician, you may rely on any decision made by my health care agent or attorney-in-fact for health care decisions, if I am unable to make a decision for myself.

I, AUTHOR, of [City, State], being of sound mind, make the following requests, appointments and designations, after careful reflection, as a testament of my wishes. Any party receiving a duly executed copy, photocopy or facsimile of this document may rely upon it unless such party has received actual notice of my revocation of it.

LIVING WILL:

If the time comes when I am incapacitated to the point when I can no longer actively take part in decisions for my own life, and am unable to direct my physician as to my own medical care, I wish this statement to stand as a testament of my wishes.

I request that, if my condition is deemed terminal or if I am determined to be permanently unconscious, I be allowed to die and not be kept alive through life support systems. By terminal condition, I mean that I have an incurable or irreversible medical condition which, without the administration of life support systems, will, in the opinion of my attending physician, result in death within a relatively short time. By permanently unconscious I mean that I am in a permanent coma or persistent vegetative state which is an irreversible condition in which I am at no time aware of myself or the environment and show no behavioral response to the environment.

The life support systems which I do not want include, but are not limited to:

- Artificial Respiration
- Cardiopulmonary Resuscitation
- Artificial Means of Providing Nutrition and Hydration

(Cross out and initial life support systems you want administered).

The foregoing provisions notwithstanding, I do want sufficient pain medication to maintain my physical comfort, including treatment to relieve pain that might occur by the withholding or withdrawing of life support systems. I do not intend any direct taking of my life, but only that my dying not be unreasonably prolonged.

Other specific requests:

____

____

____

____

APPOINTMENT OF HEALTH CARE AGENT AND ATTORNEY-IN-FACT:

I appoint my AGENT, to be my health care agent and my attorney-in-fact for health care decisions. If my attending physician determines that I am unable to understand and appreciate the nature and consequences of health care decisions and unable to reach and communicate an informed decision regarding treatment, my health care agent and attorney-in-fact for health care decisions is authorized to:

(1) Convey to my physician my wishes concerning the withholding or removal of life support systems;

(2) Take whatever actions are necessary to ensure that my wishes are given effect; and

(3) Consent, refuse or withdraw consent to any medical treatment including treatment designed solely for the purpose of maintaining physical comfort.

If AGENT is unwilling or unable to serve as my health care agent and my attorney-in-fact for health care decisions, I appoint ALTERNATE to be my alternative health care agent and my attorney-in-fact for health care decisions.

AUTHORIZATION TO RELEASE PROTECTED HEALTH INFORMATION:

I hereby designate my AGENT, as my personal representative within the meaning of, and having all of the same rights as I would have under, the Health Insurance Portability and Accountability Act of 1996, 42 U.S.C. § 1320(d) and 45 C.F.R. §§ 160-164. If AGENT is unwilling or unable to serve as my personal representative, I appoint ALTERNATE to be my personal representative. To that end I hereby authorize all health care providers, including physicians, nurses, hospitals, and all other persons (including entities) who may have provided, or be providing, me with any type of health care, to disclose to my said personal representative designated above all protected health information that relates directly or indirectly to my capacity to make rational and reasonable decisions regarding my health care when requested by my said personal representative. This authorization is intended to provide my health care providers with the authorization necessary to allow each of them to disclose protected health information regarding me to my said personal representative for the purpose of facilitating a determination regarding my capacity to make health care decisions.

Once such a determination that I am unable to understand and appreciate the nature and consequences of health care decisions and unable to reach and communicate an informed decision regarding treatment has been made, I further authorize all health care providers, including physicians, nurses, hospitals, and all other persons (including entities) who may have provided, or be providing, me with any type of health care, to disclose to my personal representative designated above all protected health information, including information that relates to my past, present or future physical or mental health or condition, the provision of health care, or the past, present or future payment for the provision of health care.

Notwithstanding any other provision of law to the contrary, my personal representative shall have the right to access, inspect and copy my protected health information held by hospitals, clinics, health plans and other covered entities, to request amendments to my protected health information, to request an accounting of disclosures that have been made without my authorization to anyone other than me for purposes other than treatment, payment and health care operations, to receive a Notice of Privacy Practices from any health care provider, health plan or others in the health care system, to request confidential communications of protected health information, to request restrictions on uses or disclosures of protected health information and to complain about privacy practices to any covered entity and the Secretary of Health and Human Services.

I recognize that information disclosed by a health care provider pursuant to this authorization is subject to redisclosure and may no longer be protected by the privacy rules of 45 C.F.R. § 164. This authorization may be revoked by a writing signed by me. This authorization shall expire five years following my death unless validly revoked prior to that date.

WAIVER AND INDEMNITY:

To the extent permitted by law, I, for myself and for my heirs, executors, legal representatives and assigns, hereby release and discharge and agree to indemnify and hold harmless my health care agent and attorney-in-fact for health care decisions from and against any claim or liability whatsoever resulting from or arising out of the reliance of my health care agent and attorney-in-fact for health care decisions on my wishes and directions as expressed herein and as otherwise known to him or her. To induce any third party to act hereunder, I hereby agree that any third party receiving a duly executed copy, photocopy or facsimile of this instrument may act hereunder, and that revocation or termination by me hereof shall be ineffective as to such third party unless and until actual notice or knowledge of such revocation shall have been received by such third party, and, to the extent permitted by law, I for myself and for my heirs, executors, legal representatives and assigns, hereby release and discharge and agree to indemnify and hold harmless any such third party from and against any claims or liability whatsoever that may arise against such third party by reason of such third party having relied on the provisions of this instrument.

SEVERABILITY:

If any portion of this instrument is invalid, ineffective or unenforceable, I direct that the balance of this instrument shall not be affected and shall continue in full force and effect.

Signed by ______________________________ AUTHOR

This document was signed and dated in our presence by AUTHOR, the Author of this document, who appeared to be eighteen years of age or older, of sound mind and able to understand the nature and consequences of health care decisions at the time this document was signed. The Author appeared to be under no improper influence. We have subscribed this document in the Author's presence and at the Author's request and in the presence of each other.

Insert Signature of Witnesses and their Addresses

On the ______ day of [Month], in the year 2005, before me, the undersigned, personally appeared AUTHOR, personally known to me or proved to me on the basis of a driver's license or other satisfactory evidence to be the individual whose name is subscribed to the within instrument and acknowledged before me that he/she executed the same as his/her free act and deed in his/her capacity therein stated, that by his/her signature on the instrument, the individual, or the person upon behalf of whom the individual acted, executed the instrument for the purposes therein contained, and that such individual made such appearance before the undersigned in ______________________________, ______________________________. Notarized and witnessed:

We, ______________________________ and ______________________________, the subscribing witnesses, being duly sworn, say that we witnessed the execution of the within LIVING WILL AND APPOINTMENT OF HEALTH CARE AGENT AND HEALTH CARE ATTORNEY-IN-FACT by AUTHOR, the Author; that the Author subscribed, published and declared the same to be the Author's LIVING WILL AND APPOINTMENT OF HEALTH CARE AGENT AND HEALTH CARE ATTORNEY-IN-FACT in our presence; that we thereafter subscribed the document as witnesses in the Author's presence, at the Author's request, and in the presence of each other; that at the time of the execution of said document the Author appeared to us to be eighteen years of age or older, of sound mind, able to understand the nature and consequences of said document, and under no improper influence, and we make this affidavit at the Author's request this ____ day of [Month], 2005. Signatures of Witnesses Notarized.

Appendix 7-C

Provided Courtesy of Internet Legal Research Group, by Maximilian Ventures, LLC

Connecticut General Durable Power of Attorney

THE POWERS YOU GRANT BELOW ARE EFFECTIVE ONLY IF YOU BECOME DISABLED OR INCOMPETENT

NOTICE: THE POWERS GRANTED BY THIS DOCUMENT ARE BROAD AND SWEEPING. THEY ARE EXPLAINED IN THE UNIFORM STATUTORY FORM POWER OF ATTORNEY ACT. IF YOU HAVE ANY QUESTIONS ABOUT THESE POWERS, OBTAIN COMPETENT LEGAL ADVICE. THIS DOCUMENT DOES NOT AUTHORIZE ANYONE TO MAKE MEDICAL AND OTHER HEALTH-CARE DECISIONS FOR YOU. YOU MAY REVOKE THIS POWER OF ATTORNEY IF YOU LATER WISH TO DO SO.

______________________________ insert your name and address] appoint _________________________ [insert the name and address of the person appointed] as my Agent (attorney-in-fact) to act for me in any lawful way with respect to the following initialed subjects:

TO GRANT ALL OF THE FOLLOWING POWERS, INITIAL THE LINE IN FRONT OF (N) AND IGNORE THE LINES IN FRONT OF THE OTHER POWERS. TO GRANT ONE OR MORE, BUT FEWER THAN ALL,

OF THE FOLLOWING POWERS, INITIAL THE LINE IN FRONT OF EACH POWER YOU ARE GRANTING. TO WITHHOLD A POWER, DO NOT INITIAL THE LINE IN FRONT OF IT. YOU MAY, BUT NEED NOT, CROSS OUT EACH POWER WITHHELD.

Note: If you initial Item A or Item B, which follow, a notarized signature will be required on behalf of the Principal.

INITIAL

____________ **(A) Real property transactions.** To lease, sell, mortgage, purchase, exchange, and acquire, and to agree, bargain, and contract for the lease, sale, purchase, exchange, and acquisition of, and to accept, take, receive, and possess any interest in real property whatsoever, on such terms and conditions, and under such covenants, as my Agent shall deem proper; and to maintain, repair, tear down, alter, rebuild, improve manage, insure, move, rent, lease, sell, convey, subject to liens, mortgages, and security deeds, and in any way or manner deal with all or any part of any interest in real property whatsoever, including specifically, but without limitation, real property lying and being situated in the State of Connecticut, under such terms and conditions, and under such covenants, as my Agent shall deem proper and may for all deferred payments accept purchase money notes payable to me and secured by mortgages or deeds to secure debt, and may from time to time collect and cancel any of said notes, mortgages, security interests, or deeds to secure debt.

____________ **(B) Tangible personal property transactions.** To lease, sell, mortgage, purchase, exchange, and acquire, and to agree, bargain, and contract for the lease, sale, purchase, exchange, and acquisition of, and to accept, take, receive, and possess any personal property whatsoever, tangible or intangible, or interest thereto, on such terms and conditions, and under such covenants, as my Agent shall deem proper; and to maintain, repair, improve, manage, insure, rent, lease, sell, convey, subject to liens or mortgages, or to take any other security interests in said property which are recognized under the Uniform Commercial Code as adopted at that time under the laws of the State of Connecticut or any applicable state, or otherwise hypothecate (pledge), and in any way or manner deal with all or any part of any real or personal

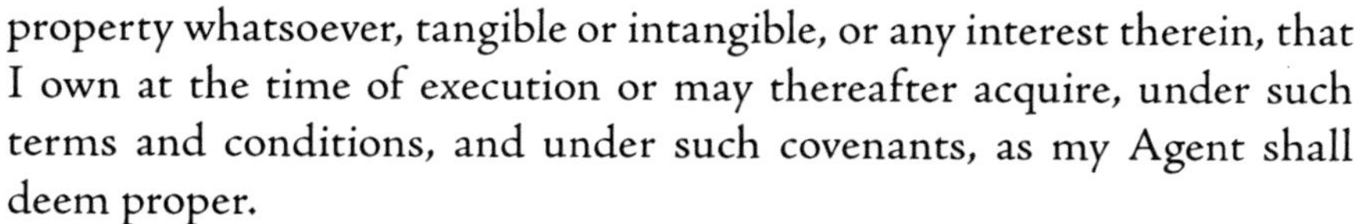

property whatsoever, tangible or intangible, or any interest therein, that I own at the time of execution or may thereafter acquire, under such terms and conditions, and under such covenants, as my Agent shall deem proper.

______________ (C) **Stock and bond transactions.** To purchase, sell, exchange, surrender, assign, redeem, vote at any meeting, or otherwise transfer any and all shares of stock, bonds, or other securities in any business, association, corporation, partnership, or other legal entity, whether private or public, now or hereafter belonging to me.

______________ (D) **Commodity and option transactions.** To buy, sell, exchange, assign, convey, settle and exercise commodities futures contracts and call and put options on stocks and stock indices traded on a regulated options exchange and collect and receipt for all proceeds of any such transactions; establish or continue option accounts for the principal with any securities or futures broker; and, in general, exercise all powers with respect to commodities and options which the principal could if present and under no disability.

______________ (E) **Banking and other financial institution transactions.** To make, receive, sign, endorse, execute, acknowledge, deliver and possess checks, drafts, bills of exchange, letters of credit, notes, stock certificates, withdrawal receipts and deposit instruments relating to accounts or deposits in, or certificates of deposit of banks, savings and loans, credit unions, or other institutions or associations. To pay all sums of money, at any time or times, that may hereafter be owing by me upon any account, bill of exchange, check, draft, purchase, contract, note, or trade acceptance made, executed, endorsed, accepted, and delivered by me or for me in my name, by my Agent. To borrow from time to time such sums of money as my Agent may deem proper and execute promissory notes, security deeds or agreements, financing statements, or other security instruments in such form as the lender may request and renew said notes and security instruments from time to time in whole or in part. To have free access at any time or times to any safe deposit box or vault to which I might have access.

______________ (F) **Business operating transactions.** To conduct, engage in, and otherwise transact the affairs of any and all lawful business ventures of whatever nature or kind that I may now or hereafter be involved in. To conduct, engage in, and otherwise transact the affairs of any and all lawful business ventures of whatever nature or kind that I may now or hereafter be involved in. To organize or continue and conduct any business which term includes, without limitation, any farming, manufacturing, service, mining, retailing or other type of business operation in any form, whether as a proprietorship, joint venture, partnership, corporation, trust or other legal entity; operate, buy, sell, expand, contract, terminate or liquidate any business; direct, control, supervise, manage or participate in the operation of any business and engage, compensate and discharge business managers, employees, agents, attorneys, accountants and consultants; and, in general, exercise all powers with respect to business interests and operations which the principal could if present and under no disability.

_____________ **(G) Insurance and annuity transactions.** To exercise or perform any act, power, duty, right, or obligation, in regard to any contract of life, accident, health, disability, liability, or other type of insurance or any combination of insurance; and to procure new or additional contracts of insurance for me and to designate the beneficiary of same; provided, however, that my Agent cannot designate himself or herself as beneficiary of any such insurance contracts.

_____________ **(H) Estate, trust, and other beneficiary transactions.** To accept, receipt for, exercise, release, reject, renounce, assign, disclaim, demand, sue for, claim and recover any legacy, bequest, devise, gift or other property interest or payment due or payable to or for the principal; assert any interest in and exercise any power over any trust, estate or property subject to fiduciary control; establish a revocable trust solely for the benefit of the principal that terminates at the death of the principal and is then distributable to the legal representative of the estate of the principal; and, in general, exercise all powers with respect to estates and trusts which the principal could exercise if present and under no disability; provided, however, that the Agent may not make or change a will and may not revoke or amend a trust revocable or amendable by the principal or require the trustee of any trust for the benefit of the principal to pay income or principal to the Agent unless specific authority to that end is given.

_____________ **(I) Claims and litigation.** To commence, prosecute, discontinue, or defend all actions or other legal proceedings touching my property, real or personal, or any part thereof, or touching any matter in which I or my property, real or personal, may be in any way concerned. To defend, settle, adjust, make allowances, compound, submit to arbitration, and compromise all accounts, reckonings, claims, and demands whatsoever that now are, or hereafter shall be, pending between me and any person, firm, corporation, or other legal entity, in such manner and in all respects as my Agent shall deem proper.

______________ (J) **Personal and family maintenance.** To hire accountants, attorneys at law, consultants, clerks, physicians, nurses, agents, servants, workmen, and others and to remove them, and to appoint others in their place, and to pay and allow the persons so employed such salaries, wages, or other remunerations, as my Agent shall deem proper.

______________ (K) **Benefits from Social Security, Medicare, Medicaid, or other governmental programs, or military service.** To prepare, sign and file any claim or application for Social Security, unemployment or military service benefits; sue for, settle or abandon any claims to any benefit or assistance under any federal, state, local or foreign statute or regulation; control, deposit to any account, collect, receipt for, and take title to and hold all benefits under any Social Security, unemployment, military service or other state, federal, local or foreign statute or regulation; and, in general, exercise all powers with respect to Social Security, unemployment, military service, and governmental benefits, including but not limited to Medicare and Medicaid, which the principal could exercise if present and under no disability.

______________ (L) **Retirement plan transactions.** To contribute to, withdraw from and deposit funds in any type of retirement plan (which term includes, without limitation, any tax qualified or nonqualified pension, profit sharing, stock bonus, employee savings and other retirement plan, individual retirement account, deferred compensation plan and any other type of employee benefit plan); select and change payment options for the principal under any retirement plan; make rollover contributions from any retirement plan to other retirement plans or individual retirement accounts; exercise all investment powers available under any type of self-directed retirement plan; and, in general, exercise all powers with respect to retirement plans and retirement plan account balances which the principal could if present and under no disability.

____________ (M) **Tax matters.** To prepare, to make elections, to execute and to file all tax, social security, unemployment insurance, and informational returns required by the laws of the United States, or of any state or subdivision thereof, or of any foreign government; to prepare, to execute, and to file all other papers and instruments which the Agent shall think to be desirable or necessary for safeguarding of me against excess or illegal taxation or against penalties imposed for claimed violation of any law or other governmental regulation; and to pay, to compromise, or to contest or to apply for refunds in connection with any taxes or assessments for which I am or may be liable.

____________ (N) **ALL OF THE POWERS LISTED ABOVE.** YOU NEED NOT INITIAL ANY OTHER LINES IF YOU INITIAL LINE (N).

SPECIAL INSTRUCTIONS:

ON THE FOLLOWING LINES YOU MAY GIVE SPECIAL INSTRUCTIONS LIMITING OR EXTENDING THE POWERS GRANTED TO YOUR AGENT.

____

THIS POWER OF ATTORNEY SHALL BE CONSTRUED AS A GENERAL DURABLE POWER OF ATTORNEY.

THIS POWER OF ATTORNEY BECOMES EFFECTIVE ONLY UPON MY DISABILITY OR INCAPACITY. I shall be considered disabled or incapacitated for purposes of this power of attorney if a physician certifies in writing at a date later than the date this power of attorney is executed that, based on the physician's medical examination of me, I am mentally incapable of managing my financial affairs. I authorize the physician who examines me for this purpose to disclose my physical or mental condition to another person for purposes of this power of attorney. A third party who accepts this power of attorney is fully protected from any action taken under this power of attorney that is based on the determination made by a physician of my disability or incapacity.

(YOUR AGENT WILL HAVE AUTHORITY TO EMPLOY OTHER PERSONS AS NECESSARY TO ENABLE THE AGENT TO PROPERLY EXERCISE THE POWERS GRANTED IN THIS FORM, BUT YOUR AGENT WILL HAVE TO MAKE ALL DISCRETIONARY DECISIONS. IF YOU WANT TO GIVE

YOUR AGENT THE RIGHT TO DELEGATE DISCRETIONARY DECISION-MAKING POWERS TO OTHERS, YOU SHOULD KEEP THE NEXT SENTENCE, OTHERWISE IT SHOULD BE STRICKEN.)

Authority to Delegate. My Agent shall have the right by written instrument to delegate any or all of the foregoing powers involving discretionary decision-making to any person or persons whom my Agent may select, but such delegation may be amended or revoked by any agent (including any successor) named by me who is acting under this power of attorney at the time of reference. (YOUR AGENT WILL BE ENTITLED TO REIMBURSEMENT FOR ALL REASONABLE EXPENSES INCURRED IN ACTING UNDER THIS POWER OF ATTORNEY. STRIKE OUT THE NEXT SENTENCE IF YOU DO NOT WANT YOUR AGENT TO ALSO BE ENTITLED TO REASONABLE COMPENSATION FOR SERVICES AS AGENT.) **Right to Compensation.** My Agent shall be entitled to reasonable compensation for services rendered as agent under this power of attorney. (IF YOU WISH TO NAME SUCCESSOR AGENTS, INSERT THE NAME(S) AND ADDRESS(ES) OF SUCH SUCCESSOR(S) IN THE FOLLOWING PARAGRAPH.) **Successor Agent.** If any Agent named by me shall die, become incompetent, resign or refuse to accept the office of Agent, I name the following (each to act alone and successively, in the order named) as successor(s) to such Agent:

____

____

Choice of Law. THIS POWER OF ATTORNEY WILL BE GOVERNED BY THE LAWS OF THE STATE OF CONNECTICUT WITHOUT REGARD FOR CONFLICTS OF LAWS PRINCIPLES. IT WAS EXECUTED IN THE STATE OF CONNECTICUT AND IS INTENDED TO BE VALID IN ALL JURISDICTIONS OF THE UNITED STATES OF AMERICA AND ALL FOREIGN NATIONS.

I am fully informed as to all the contents of this form and understand the full import of this grant of powers to my Agent.

I agree that any third party who receives a copy of this document may act under it. Revocation of the power of attorney is not effective as to a third party until the third party learns of the revocation. I agree to indemnify the third party for any claims that arise against the third party because of reliance on this power of attorney. Signed this ____________ day of ____________, 20____________

Statement of Witness

On the date written above, the principal declared to me in my presence that this instrument is his general durable power of attorney and that he or she had willingly signed or directed another to sign for him or her, and that he or she executed it as his or her free and voluntary act for the purposes therein expressed. (Signed and Notarized)

ACKNOWLEDGMENT OF AGENT

BY ACCEPTING OR ACTING UNDER THE APPOINTMENT, THE AGENT ASSUMES THE FIDUCIARY AND OTHER LEGAL RESPONSIBILITIES OF AN AGENT. (Signed and Notarized)

Appendix 11-A

IRS Publication 590
Appendix C. Uniform Lifetime Table

Table III (Uniform Lifetime)			
(For Use by: • Unmarried Owners, • Married Owners Whose Spouses Are Not More Than 10 Years Younger, and • Married Owners Whose Spouses Are Not the Sole Beneficiaries of their IRAs)			
Age	**Distribution Period**	**Age**	**Distribution Period**
70	27.4	93	9.6
71	26.5	94	9.1
72	25.6	95	8.6
73	24.7	96	8.1
74	23.8	97	7.6
75	22.9	98	7.1
76	22.0	99	6.7
77	21.2	100	6.3
78	20.3	101	5.9
79	19.5	102	5.5

Age	Distribution Period	Age	Distribution Period
80	18.7	103	5.2
81	17.9	104	4.9
82	17.1	105	4.5
83	16.3	106	4.2
84	15.5	107	3.9
85	14.8	108	3.7
86	14.1	109	3.4
87	13.4	110	3.1
88	12.7	111	2.9
89	12.0	112	2.6
90	11.4	113	2.4
91	10.8	114	2.1
92	10.2	115 and over	1.9

Appendix 11-B

IRS Publication 590
APPENDIX C. Life Expectancy Tables

Table I (Single Life Expectancy) **(For Use by Beneficiaries)**			
Age	**Life Expectancy**	**Age**	**Life Expectancy**
0	82.4	15	67.9
1	81.6	16	66.9
2	80.6	17	66.0
3	79.7	18	65.0
4	78.7	19	64.0
5	77.7	20	63.0
6	76.7	21	62.1
7	75.8	22	61.1
8	74.8	23	60.1
9	73.8	24	59.1
10	72.8	25	58.2
11	71.8	26	57.2
12	70.8	27	56.2
13	69.9	28	55.3
14	68.9	29	54.3

Age	Life Expectancy	Age	Life Expectancy
30	53.3	65	21.0
31	52.4	66	20.2
32	51.4	67	19.4
33	50.4	68	18.6
34	49.4	69	17.8
35	48.5	70	17.0
36	47.5	71	16.3
37	46.5	72	15.5
38	45.6	73	14.8
39	44.6	74	14.1
40	43.6	75	13.4
41	42.7	76	12.7
42	41.7	77	12.1
43	40.7	78	11.4
44	39.8	79	10.8
45	38.8	80	10.2
46	37.9	81	9.7
47	37.0	82	9.1
48	36.0	83	8.6
49	35.1	84	8.1
50	34.2	85	7.6
51	33.3	86	7.1
52	32.3	87	6.7
53	31.4	88	6.3
54	30.5	89	5.9
55	29.6	90	5.5
56	28.7	91	5.2
57	27.9	92	4.9
58	27.0	93	4.6
59	26.1	94	4.3
60	25.2	95	4.1
61	24.4	96	3.8
62	23.5	97	3.6
63	22.7	98	3.4
64	21.8	99	3.1

Age	Life Expectancy	Age	Life Expectancy
100	2.9	106	1.7
101	2.7	107	1.5
102	2.5	108	1.4
103	2.3	109	1.2
104	2.1	110	1.1
105	1.9	111 and over	1.0

Appendix 12-A

Internal Revenue Service Publication 950

(Rev. September 2004)

Introduction to Estate and Gift Taxes

Go to www.irs.gov. for up to date forms.

Introduction

If you give someone money or property during your life you may be subject to federal gift tax. The money and property you own when you die (your estate) may be subject to federal estate tax. The purpose of this publication is to give you a general understanding of when these taxes apply and when they do not. It explains how much money or property you can give way during your life time or leave to your heirs at your death before any tax will be owed.

No tax owed. Most gifts are not subject to the gift tax and most estates are not subject to the estate tax. For example, there is usually no tax if you make a gift to your spouse or if your estate goes to your spouse at your death. If you make a gift to someone else, the gift tax does not apply until the value of the gifts you give that person exceeds the annual exclusion for the year. See *Annual exclusion* under *Gift Tax.* Even if tax applies to your gifts or your estate, it may be eliminated by the unified credit, discussed later. No return needed. Gift tax returns are filed annually. However, you do not need to file a gift tax return unless you give someone, other than your spouse, money or property worth more than the annual exclusion (discussed on page 4) for that year. An estate tax return generally will not be needed unless the estate is worth more than the applicable exclusion amount for the year of death. This amount is shown in the table under *Unified Credit (Applicable Exclusion Amount)*.

No tax on the person receiving your gift or estate.

The person who receives your gift or your estate will not have to pay any federal gift tax or estate tax because of it. Also, that person will not have to pay income tax on the value of the gift or inheritance received.

No income tax deduction. Making a gift or leaving your estate to your heirs does not ordinarily affect your federal income tax. You cannot deduct the value of gifts you make (other than gifts that are deductible charitable contributions).

What this publication contains. If you are not sure whether the gift tax or the estate tax applies to your situation, the rest of this publication may help you. It explains in general terms:

- When tax is not owed because of the unified credit,
- When the gift tax does and does not apply,
- When the estate tax does and does not apply, and
- When to file a return for the gift tax or the estate tax.

This publication does not contain any information about state or local taxes. That information should be available from your local taxing authority.

Where to find out more. This publication does not contain all the rules and exceptions for federal estate and gift taxes. It does not contain the rules that apply to nonresident aliens. If you need more information, see the following forms and their instructions:

- Form 706, United States Estate (and Generation-Skipping Transfer) Tax Return, and
- Form 709, United States Gift (and Generation-Skipping Transfer) Tax Return.

To order these forms, call 1-800-TAX-FORMS (1-800-829-3676). If you have access to TTY/TDD equipment, you can call 1-800-829-4059. To get these forms with your personal computer or by fax, see the first page of this publication.

Unified Credit (Applicable Exclusion Amount) a credit is an amount that eliminates or educes tax. A unified credit applies to both the gift tax and the estate tax. You must subtract the unified credit from any gift tax that you owe. Any unified credit you use against your gift tax in one year reduces the amount of credit that you can use against your gift tax in a later year. The octal amount used during life against your gift tax reduces the credit available to use against your estate tax.

Under prior law, the same unified credit amount applied to both the gift tax and the estate tax. Under current law, however, the unified credit against taxable gifts will remain at $345,800 (exempting $1 million from tax) through 2009, while the unified credit against estate tax increases during the same period. The following table shows the unified credit and applicable exclusion amount for the calendar years in which a gift is made or a decedent dies after 2003. For Gift Tax For Estate Tax Purposes:

	For Gift Tax Purposes		For Estate Tax Purposes	
Year	Unified Credit	Applicable Exclusion Amount	Unified Credit	Applicable Exclusion Amount
2006,2007,2008	345,800	1,000,000	780,800	2,000,000
2009	345,800	1,000,000	1,455,800	3,500,000

For examples of how the credit works, see *Applying the Unified Credit to Gift Tax* and *Applying the Unified Credit to Estate Tax*, later.

Gift Tax

The gift tax applies to the transfer by gift of any property. You make a gift if you give property (including money), or the use of or income from property, without expecting to receive something of at least equal value in return. If you sell something at less than its full value or if you make an interest-free or reduced interest loan, you may be making a gift.

The general rule is that any gift is a taxable gift. However, there are many exceptions to this rule. Generally, the following gifts are not taxable gifts:

- Gifts that are not more than the annual exclusion for the calendar year,
- Tuition or medical expenses you pay directly to a medical or educational institution for someone,
- Gifts to your spouse,
- Gifts to a political organization for its use, and
- Gifts to charities.

Annual exclusion. A separate annual exclusion applies to each person to whom you make a gift. For 2004, the annual exclusion is $11,000. Therefore, you generally can give up to $11,000 each to any number of people in 2004 and none of the gifts will be taxable.

If you are married, both you and your spouse can separately give up to $11,000 to the same person in 2004 without making a taxable gift. If one of you gives more than $11,000 to a person in 2004, see *Gift Splitting*, later.

Inflation adjustment. After 2004, the $11,000 annual exclusion may be increased due to a cost-of-living adjustment. See the instructions for Form 709 for the amount of the annual exclusion for the year you make the gift.

Example 1. In 2004, you give your niece a cash gift of $8,000. It is your only gift to her this year. The gift is not a taxable gift because it is not more than the $11,000 annual exclusion.

Example 2. You pay the $15,000 college tuition of your friend. Because the payment qualifies for the educational exclusion, the gift is not a taxable gift.

Example 3. In 2004, you give $25,000 to your 25-year-old daughter. The first $11,000 of your gift is not subject to the gift tax because of the annual exclusion. The remaining $14,000 is a taxable gift. As explained later under *Applying the Unified Credit to Gift Tax,* you may not have to pay the gift tax on the remaining $14,000. However, you do have to file a gift tax return.

More information. See Form 709 and its instructions for more information about taxable gifts.

Gift Splitting

If you or your spouse make a gift to a third party, the gift can be considered as made one-half by you and one-half by your spouse. This is known as gift splitting. Both of you must consent (agree) to split the gift. If you do, you each can take the annual exclusion for your part of the gift.

In 2004, gift splitting allows married couples to give up to $22,000 to a person without making a taxable gift. If you split a gift you made, you must file a gift tax return to show that you and your spouse agree to use gift splitting. You must file a Form 709 even if half of the split gift is less than the annual exclusion.

Example. Harold and his wife, Helen, agree to split the gifts that they made during 2004. Harold gives his nephew, George, $21,000, and Helen gives her niece, Gina, $18,000. Although each gift is more than the annual exclusion ($11,000), by gift splitting they can make these gifts without making a taxable gift. Harold's gift to George is treated as one-half ($10,500) from Harold and one-half ($10,500) from Helen. Helen's gift to Gina is also treated as one-half ($9,000) from Helen and one-half ($9,000) from Harold.

In each case, because one-half of the split gift is not more than the annual exclusion, it is not a taxable gift. However, each of them must file a gift tax return.

Applying the Unified Credit to Gift Tax

After you determine which of your gifts are taxable, you figure the amount of gift tax on the total taxable gifts and apply your unified credit for the year.

Example. In 2004, you give your niece, Mary, a cash gift of $8,000. It is your only gift to her this year. You pay the $15,000 college tuition of your friend, David. You give your 25-year-old daughter, Lisa, $25,000. You also give your 27-year-old son, Ken, $25,000. Before 2004, you had never given a taxable gift. You apply the exceptions to the gift tax and the unified credit as follows:

1. Apply the educational exclusion. Payment of tuition expenses is not subject to the gift tax. Therefore, the gift to David is not a taxable gift.
2. Apply the annual exclusion. The first $11,000 you give someone during 2004 is not a taxable gift. Therefore, your $8,000 gift to Mary, the first $11,000 of your gift to Lisa,

and the first $11,000 of your gift to Ken are not taxable gifts.

3. Apply the unified credit. The gift tax on $28,000 ($14,000 remaining from your gift to Lisa plus $14,000 remaining from your gift to Ken) is $5,560.You subtract the $5,560 from your unified credit of $345,800 for 2004. The unified credit that you can use against the gift tax in a later year is $340,240. You do not have to pay any gift tax for 2004. However, you do have to file Form 709.

Filing a Gift Tax Return

Generally, you must file a gift tax return on Form 709 if any of the following apply.

- You gave gifts to at least one person (other than your spouse) that are more than the annual exclusion for the year.
- You and your spouse are splitting a gift.
- You gave someone (other than your spouse) a gift that he or she cannot actually possess, enjoy, or receive income from until some time in the future.
- You gave your spouse an interest in property that will be ended by some future event. You do not have to file a gift tax return to report gifts to (or for the use of) political organizations and gifts made by paying someone's tuition or medical expenses.

You also do not need to report the following deductible gifts made to charities:

- Your entire interest in property, if no other interest has been transferred for less than adequate consideration or for other than a charitable use; or
- A qualified conservation contribution that is a restriction (granted forever) on the use of real property.

More information. If you need to file a gift tax return, you should see Form 709 and its instructions.

Estate Tax

Estate tax may apply to your taxable estate at your death. Your taxable estate is your gross estate less allowable deductions.

Gross Estate

Your gross estate includes the value of all property in which you had an interest at the time of death. Your gross estate also will include the following:

- Life insurance proceeds payable to your estate or, if you owned the policy, to your heirs;
- The value of certain annuities payable to your estate or your heirs; and
- The value of certain property you transferred within 3 years before your death.

Taxable Estate

The allowable deductions used in determining your taxable estate include:

- Funeral expenses paid out of your estate,
- Debts you owed at the time of death, and
- The marital deduction (generally, the value of the property that passes from your estate to your surviving spouse).

More information.

For more information on what is included in your gross estate and the allowable deductions, see Form 706 and its instructions.

Applying the Unified Credit to Estate Tax

Basically, any unified credit not used to eliminate gift tax can be used to eliminate or reduce estate tax. However, to determine the unified credit used against the estate tax, you must complete Form 706.

Filing an Estate Tax Return

An estate tax return, Form 706, must be filed if the gross estate, plus any adjusted taxable gifts and specific gift tax exemption, is more than the filing requirement for the year of death. Adjusted taxable gifts is the total of the taxable gifts you made after 1976 that are not included in your gross estate. The specific gift tax exemption applies only to gifts made after September 8, 976, and before 1977.

Filing requirement. The following table lists the filing requirement for the estate of a decedent dying after 2003.

Filing

Year of Death: Requirement:
2004 and 2005 1,500,000
2006, 2007, and 2008 2,000,000
2009 3,500,000

More information. If you think you will have an estate on which tax must be paid, or if your estate will have to file an estate tax return even if no tax will be due, see Form 706 and its instructions for more information. You (or your estate) may want to get a qualified estate tax professional to help with estate tax questions.

Appendix 15-A

Connecticut's Civil Union Statute
An Act Concerning Civil Unions

Be it enacted by the Senate and House of Representatives in General Assembly convened:

Section 1. (NEW) (*Effective October 1, 2005*) For the purposes of sections 1 to 15, inclusive, of this act:

(1) "Civil union" means a union established pursuant to sections 1 to 15, inclusive, of this act between two eligible persons; and

(2) "Party to a civil union" means a person who has established a civil union pursuant to sections 1 to 15, inclusive, of this act.

Sec. 2. (NEW) (*Effective October 1, 2005*) A person is eligible to enter into a civil union if such person is:

(1) Not a party to another civil union or a marriage;

(2) Of the same sex as the other party to the civil union;

(3) Except as provided in section 10 of this act, at least eighteen years of age; and

(4) Not prohibited from entering into a civil union pursuant to section 3 of this act.

Sec. 3. (NEW) (*Effective October 1, 2005*)

(a) A woman shall not enter into a civil union with her mother, grandmother, daughter, granddaughter, sister, brother's daughter, sister's daughter, father's sister or mother's sister.

(b) A man shall not enter into a civil union with his father, grandfather, son, grandson, brother, brother's son, sister's son, father's brother or mother's brother.

(c) A civil union between persons prohibited from entering into a civil union pursuant to subsection (a) or (b) of this section is void.

Sec. 4. (NEW) (*Effective October 1, 2005*)

(a) All judges and retired judges, either elected or appointed, including federal judges and judges of other states who may legally join persons in marriage or a civil union, family support magistrates, state referees and justices of the peace may join persons in a civil union in any town in the state, and all ordained or licensed members of the clergy, belonging to this state or any other state, as long as they continue in the work of the ministry may join persons in a civil union. All civil unions solemnized according to the forms and usages of any religious denomination in this state are valid. All civil unions attempted to be celebrated by any other person are void.

(b) No public official legally authorized to issue civil union licenses may join persons in a civil union under authority of a license issued by such official, or such official's assistant or deputy; nor may any such assistant or deputy join persons in a civil union under authority of a license issued by such public official.

(c) Any person violating any provision of this section shall be fined not more than fifty dollars.

Sec. 5. (NEW) (*Effective October 1, 2005*) Any person who undertakes to join persons in a civil union, knowing that such person is not authorized to do so, shall be fined not more than five hundred dollars or imprisoned not more than one year or both.

Sec. 6. (NEW) (*Effective October 1, 2005*) Any person authorized to join persons in a civil union pursuant to section 4 of this act, who fails or refuses for any reason to join persons in a civil union shall not be subject to any fine or other penalty for such failure or refusal.

Sec. 7. (NEW) (*Effective October 1, 2005*)

(a) No persons may be joined in a civil union in this state until both have complied with the provisions of sections 8 to 10, inclusive, of this act and have been issued a license by the registrar of vital statistics for the town in which (1) the civil union is to be celebrated, or (2) either person to be joined in the civil union resides, which license shall bear the certification of the registrar that the persons named therein have complied with the provisions of sections 8 to 10, inclusive, of this act.

(b) Such license, when certified by the registrar, is sufficient authority for any person authorized to perform a civil union ceremony in this state to join such persons in a civil union, provided the ceremony is performed not more than sixty-five days after the date of application.

(c) Any person who joins any persons in a civil union without having received such license from them shall be fined not more than one hundred dollars.

Sec. 8. (NEW) (*Effective October 1, 2005*) No license for a civil union may be issued by the registrar of vital statistics until both persons have appeared before the registrar and made application for a license. The license shall be completed in its entirety, dated, signed and sworn to by each applicant and shall state each applicant's name, age, race, birthplace, residence, whether single, widowed or divorced and whether under the supervision or control of a conservator or guardian. The Social Security numbers of the two persons shall be recorded in the "administrative purposes" section of the license. If the license is signed and sworn to by the applicants on different dates, the earlier date shall be deemed the date of application. The registrar shall issue a copy of sections 1 to 15, inclusive, of this act to any person making application for a license.

Sec. 9. (NEW) (*Effective October 1, 2005*)

(a) No civil union license may be issued to any applicant under the supervision or control of a conservator, appointed in accordance with sections 45a-644 to 45a-662, inclusive, of the general statutes unless the written consent of the conservator, signed and acknowledged before a person authorized to take acknowledgments of conveyances under the provisions of section 47-5a of the general statutes or authorized to take acknowledgments in any other state or country, is filed with the registrar of vital statistics.

(b) Any person who enters into a civil union without the consent provided for in subsection (a) of this section shall acquire no rights by such civil union in the property of any person who was under such control or supervision at the time the civil union was entered into.

Sec. 10. (NEW) (*Effective October 1, 2005*) No civil union license may be issued to any applicant under eighteen years of age.

Sec. 11. (NEW) (*Effective October 1, 2005*)

(a) Each person who joins any person in a civil union shall certify upon the license certificate the fact, time and place of the civil union, and return it to the registrar of vital statistics of the town where it was issued, before or during the first week of the month following the celebration of the civil union. Any person who fails to do so shall be fined not more than ten dollars.

(b) If any person fails to return the certificate to the registrar of vital statistics, as required under subsection (a) of this section, the persons joined in a civil union may provide the registrar with a notarized affidavit attesting to the fact that they were joined in a civil union and stating the date and place of the civil union. Upon the recording of such affidavit by the registrar of vital statistics, the civil union of the affiants shall be deemed to be valid as of the date of the civil union stated in the affidavit.

Sec. 12. (NEW) (*Effective October 1, 2005*) The certificate required by section 11 of this act or an affidavit recorded pursuant to subsection (b) of said section shall be prima facie evidence of the facts stated in them.

Sec. 13. (NEW) (*Effective October 1, 2005*) All civil unions in which one or both parties are citizens of this state, celebrated in a foreign country, shall be valid, provided: (1) Each party would have legal capacity to contract such civil union in this state and the civil union is celebrated in conformity with the law of that country; or (2) the civil union is celebrated in the presence of the ambassador or minister to that country from the United States or in the presence of a consular officer of the United States accredited to such country, at a place within his or her consular jurisdiction, by any ordained or licensed member of the clergy engaged in the work of the ministry in any state of the United States or in any foreign country.

Sec. 14. (NEW) (*Effective October 1, 2005*) Parties to a civil union shall have all the same benefits, protections and responsibilities under law, whether derived from the general statutes, administrative regulations or court rules, policy, common law or any other source of civil law, as are granted to spouses in a marriage, which is defined as the union of one man and one woman.

Sec. 15. (NEW) (*Effective October 1, 2005*) Wherever in the general statutes the terms "spouse", "family", "immediate family", "dependent", "next of kin" or any other term that denotes the spousal relationship are used or defined, a party to a civil union shall be included in such use or definition, and wherever in the general statutes, except sections 7-45 and 17b-137a of the general statutes, as amended by this act, subdivision (4) of section 45a-727a, sections 46b-20 to 46b-34, inclusive, section 46b-150d of the general statutes, as amended by this act, and section 14 of this act, the term "marriage" is used or defined, a civil union shall be included in such use or definition.

Sec. 16. Section 7-45 of the general statutes is repealed and the following is substituted in lieu thereof (*Effective October 1, 2005*):

Each person making any certificate of birth, marriage, <u>civil union,</u> death or fetal death, or any copy of such certificate for the commissioner, or any sexton's report required by law, shall cause the same to be typewritten or printed in a legible manner as to all material information or facts required by the provisions of sections 7-48, 7-60 [,] <u>and</u> 7-62b, <u>and sections</u> 46b-25 and 46b-29 to 46b-30, inclusive, <u>or sections 8, 9 and 10 of this act,</u> and contained in such certificate. If the certificate is in paper format, such person shall sign the certificate in black ink, shall state therein in what capacity such person so signs, and shall type or print in a legible manner the name of each person signing such certificate, under such person's signature. If the certificate is in an electronic format, such certificate shall be authenticated by the electronic vital records system of the department. Any certificate not complying with the requirements of this section shall be returned by the registrar with whom it is filed to the person making the same for the proper correction.

Sec. 17. Subsections (a) and (b) of section 17b-137a of the general statutes are repealed and the following is substituted in lieu thereof (*Effective October 1, 2005*):

(a) The Social Security number of the applicant shall be recorded on each (1) application for a license, certification or permit to engage in a profession or occupation regulated pursuant to the provisions of title 19a, 20 or 21; (2) application for a commercial driver's license or commercial driver's instruction permit completed pursuant to subsection (a) of section 14-44c; and (3) application for a marriage license made under section 46b-25 or for a civil union license under section 8 of this act.

(b) The Social Security number of any individual who is subject to a dissolution of marriage decree, dissolution of civil union decree, support order or paternity determination or acknowledgment shall be placed in the records relating to the matter.

Sec. 18. Subdivision (7) of section 45a-106 of the general statutes is repealed and the following is substituted in lieu thereof (*Effective October 1, 2005*):

(7) For proceedings brought under section 46b-30 or section 10 of this act, the cost shall be twenty-five dollars.

Sec. 19. Subsection (c) of section 45a-676 of the general statutes is repealed and the following is substituted in lieu thereof (*Effective October 1, 2005*):

(c) For purposes of sections 45a-669 to [45a-784] 45a-684, inclusive, and section 46b-29 and section 9 of this act, any alleged inability of the respondent must be evidenced by recent behavior which would cause harm or create a risk of harm, by clear and convincing proof.

Sec. 20. Section 46b-150d of the general statutes is repealed and the following is substituted in lieu thereof (*Effective October 1, 2005*):

An order that a minor is emancipated shall have the following effects: (a) The minor may consent to medical, dental or psychiatric care, without parental consent, knowledge or liability; (b) the minor may enter into a binding contract; (c) the minor may sue and be sued in his own name; (d) the minor shall be entitled to his own earnings and shall be free of control by his parents or guardian; (e) the minor may establish his own residence; (f) the minor may buy and sell real and personal property; (g) the minor may not thereafter be the subject of a petition under section 46b-129 as an abused, dependent, neglected or uncared for child or youth; (h) the minor may enroll in any school or college, without parental consent; (i) the minor shall be deemed to be over eighteen years of age for purposes of securing an operator's license under section 14-36 and a marriage license under subsection (b) of section 46b-30 <u>or a civil union license section 10 of this act</u> without parental consent; (j) the minor shall be deemed to be over eighteen years of age for purposes of registering a motor vehicle under section 14-12; (k) the parents of the minor shall no longer be the guardians of the minor under section 45a-606; (l) the parents of a minor shall be relieved of any obligations respecting his school attendance under section 10-184; (m) the parents shall be relieved of all obligation to support the minor; (n) the minor shall be emancipated for the purposes of parental liability for his acts under section 52-572; (o) the minor may execute releases in his own name under section 14-118; and (p) the minor may enlist in the armed forces of the United States without parental consent.

Sec. 21. Subsection (b) of section 51-164n of the general statutes is repealed and the following is substituted in lieu thereof (*Effective October 1, 2005*):

> (b) Notwithstanding any provision of the general statutes, any person who is alleged to have committed (1) a violation under the provisions of section 1-9, 1-10, 1-11, 4b-13, 7-13, 7-14, 7-35, 7-41, 7-83, 7-283, 7-325, 7-393, 8-25, 8-27, 9-63, 9-296, 9-305, 9-322, 9-350, 10-193, 10-197, 10-198, 10-230, 10-251, 10-254, 12-52, 12-170aa, 12-292, or 12-326g, subdivision (4) of section 12-408, subdivision (3), (5) or (6) of section 12-411, section 12-435c, 12-476a, 12-476b, 12-487, 13a-71, 13a-107, 13a-113, 13a-114, 13a-115, 13a-117b, 13a-123, 13a-124, 13a-139, 13a-140, 13a-143b, 13a-

247 or 13a-253, subsection (f) of section 13b-42, section 13b-90, 13b-221, 13b-292, 13b-336, 13b-337, 13b-338, 13b-410a, 13b-410b or 13b-410c, subsection (a), (b) or (c) of section 13b-412, section 13b-414, subsection (d) of section 14-12, section 14-20a or 14-27a, subsection (e) of section 14-34a, subsection (d) of section 14-35, section 14-43, 14-49, 14-50a or 14-58, subsection (b) of section 14-66, section 14-66a, 14-66b or 14-67a, subsection (g) of section 14-80, subsection (f) of section 14-80h, section 14-97a, 14-100b, 14-103a, 14-106a, 14-106c, 14-146, 14-152, 14-153 or 14-163b, a first violation as specified in subsection (f) of section 14-164i, section 14-219 as specified in subsection (e) of said section, section 14-240, 14-249 or 14-250, subsection (a), (b) or (c) of section 14-261a, section 14-262, 14-264, 14-267a, 14-269, 14-270, 14-275a, 14-278 or 14-279, subsection (e) of section 14-283, section 14-291, 14-293b, 14-319, 14-320, 14-321, 14-325a, 14-326, 14-330 or 14-332a, subdivision (1), (2) or (3) of section 14-386a, section 15-33, subsection (a) of section 15-115, section 16-256, 16-256e, 16a-15 or 16a-22, subsection (a) or (b) of section 16a-22h, section 17a-24, 17a-145, 17a-149, 17a-152, 17a-465, 17a-642, 17b-124, 17b-131, 17b-137 or 17b-734, subsection (b) of section 17b-736, section 19a-30, 19a-33, 19a-39 or 19a-87, subsection (b) of section 19a-87a, section 19a-91, 19a-105, 19a-107, 19a-215, 19a-219, 19a-222, 19a-224, 19a-286, 19a-287, 19a-297, 19a-301, 19a-309, 19a-335, 19a-336, 19a-338, 19a-339, 19a-340, 19a-425, 19a-502, 20-7a, 20-14, 20-158, 20-231, 20-257, 20-265 or 20-324e, subsection (a) of section 20-341, section 20-341*l*, 20-597, 20-608, 20-610, 21-30, 21-38, 21-39, 21-43, 21-47, 21-48, 21-63, 21-76a, 21a-21, 21a-25, 21a-26 or 21a-30, subsection (a) of section 21a-37, section 21a-46, 21a-61, 21a-63 or 21a-77, subsection (b) of section 21a-79, section 21a-85, 21a-154, 21a-159, 21a-201, 21a-211, 22-13, 22-14, 22-15, 22-16, 22-29, 22-34, 22-35, 22-36, 22-37, 22-38, 22-39, 22-39a, 22-39b, 22-39c, 22-39d, 22-39e, 22-49, 22-54, 22-61, 22-89, 22-90, 22-98, 22-99, 22-100, 22-111o, 22-279,

22-280a, 22-318a, 22-320h, 22-324a, 22-326 or 22-342, subsection (b) or (e) of section 22-344, section 22-359, 22-366, 22-391, 22-413, 22-414, 22-415, 22a-66a or 22a-246, subsection (a) of section 22a-250, subsection (e) of section 22a-256h, subsection (a) of section 22a-381d, section 22a-449, 22a-461, 23-37, 23-38, 23-46 or 23-61b, subsection (a) or (b) of section 23-65, section 25-37, 25-40, 26-19, 26-21, 26-31, 26-40, 26-40a, 26-49, 26-54, 26-59, 26-61, 26-64, 26-79, 26-89, 26-97, 26-107, 26-117, 26-128, 26-131, 26-132, 26-138, 26-141, 26-207, 26-215, 26-224a, 26-227, 26-230, 26-294, 28-13, 29-6a, 29-109, 29-161y, 29-161z, 29-198, 29-210, 29-243, 29-277, 29-316, 29-318, 29-341, 29-381, 30-48a, 30-86a, 31-3, 31-10, 31-11, 31-12, 31-13, 31-14, 31-15, 31-16, 31-18, 31-23, 31-24, 31-25, 31-28, 31-32, 31-36, 31-38, 31-38a, 31-40, 31-44, 31-47, 31-48, 31-51, 31-51k, 31-52, 31-52a or 31-54, subsection (a) or (c) of section 31-69, section 31-70, 31-74, 31-75, 31-76, 31-76a, 31-89b or 31-134, subsection (i) of section 31-273, section 31-288, 36a-787, 42-230, 45a-450, 45a-634 or 45a-658, subdivision (13) or (14) of section 46a-54, section 46a-59, 46b-22, 46b-24, 46b-34, 47-34a, 47-47, 49-8a, 49-16 or 53-133, subsection (a) or (b) of section 53-211, or section 53-212a, 53-249a, 53-252, 53-264, 53-302a, 53-303e, 53-311a, 53-321, 53-322, 53-323, 53-331, 53-344 or 53-450, or section 4, 7 or 11 of this act, or (2) a violation under the provisions of chapter 268, or (3) a violation of any regulation adopted in accordance with the provisions of section 12-484, 12-487 or 13b-410, shall follow the procedures set forth in this section.

AN ACT CONCERNING CIVIL UNIONS

SUMMARY:

This bill authorizes same sex couples to enter into civil unions, granting them the same legal benefits, protections, and responsibilities as married couples. It incorporates civil unions by reference in most statutes that use or define terms indicating a spousal relationship. It establishes eligibility, application, and licensing criteria; specifies who can perform civil union ceremonies; and sets forth record-keeping requirements. The bill (1) restricts civil unions to couples over age 18, (2) exempts people authorized to perform civil union ceremonies from liability for failing or refusing to do so, and (3) requires town clerks to give civil union license applicants copies of the relevant laws. Otherwise, the bill's substantive provisions and penalties are identical to current marriage statutes.

The bill also defines "marriage" as the union of one man and one woman. It establishes circumstances under which the state will recognize civil unions performed in other countries.

*House Amendment "A" adds the definition of marriage.

*House Amendment "B" eliminates the authority of parents or probate court judges to consent to civil unions involving partners under age 18.

EFFECTIVE DATE: **October 1, 2005**

BENEFITS, PROTECTIONS, AND RESPONSIBILITIES (14 & 15)

The bill specifies that the rights it extends to civil union partners may derive under statute, administrative regulations or court rules, policy, common law, or any other source of civil law. Generally, these fall into the following categories:

1. family law, including marriage, divorce, and support;
2. title, tenure, descent and distribution, intestate succession, wills, survivorships, or other incidents of the acquisition, ownership, or transfer (during life or at death) of real or personal property;
3. state and municipal taxation;
4. probate courts and procedure;
5. group insurance for government (but not private-sector) employees;
6. family leave benefits;
7. financial disclosure and conflict-of-interest rules;
8. protection against discrimination based on marital status;
9. emergency and non-emergency medical care and treatment, hospital visitation and notification, and authority to act in matters affecting family members;
10. state public assistance benefits;

11. workers' compensation;
12. crime victims' rights;
13. marital privileges in court proceedings; and
14. vital records and absentee voting procedures.

Excluded Laws (§ 15)

The bill does not incorporate civil unions by reference in the chapter of the General Statutes relating to marriage procedures and formalities. But it includes new provisions setting out the same procedures and formalities for applicants and parties to civil unions.

Civil unions are also specifically excluded under the bill from the statute that states that "the current public policy of the state is now limited to a marriage between a man and a woman" (CGS § 45a-727a(4)).

Appendix 15-B

Provided Courtesy of Gay & Lesbian Advocates & Defenders (GLAD)

Connecticut Civil Unions

30 Winter Street, Suite 800, Boston, MA 02108-4720

GLAD's website is www.glad.org.

'Connecticut Civil Unions" is organized as follows:

- Introduction
- What Is A Civil Union?
- When Will Connecticut Civil Unions Be Available?
- What Is The Difference Between Marriage And Civil Unions?
- Who Can Get A Connecticut Civil Union?
- Do We Need A Connecticut Civil Union If Our Relationship Is Already Recognized Elsewhere'?
- How Do We Get A Connecticut Civil Union?
- What Are Some Things We Should Consider Before Entering Into A Connecticut Civil Union?
- What Protections Do We Gain From A Connecticut Civil Union'?
- Are There Any Limitations On Connecticut Civil Unions?
- What Does The Amendment In The Civil Union Law Defining Marriage As Between A Man And A Woman Mean?
- How Will A Connecticut Civil Union Affect My Children?

- Will I Be Able To Get Health Insurance Through My Employer For My Connecticut Civil Union Spouse'?
- Can A Connecticut Civil Union Couple File A Joint Tax Return'?
- If We Get A Connecticut Civil Union Will We Be Able To Get Married Later?
- How Do I Get Out Of A Connecticut Civil Union?
- What Legal Protections Can Same-Sex Couples In Connecticut Acquire Without Entering Into A Connecticut Civil Union?

Introduction

Connecticut has joined Vermont as the second state to allow same-sex couples to enter into a civil union, which provides all the rights, benefits and responsibilities that are granted to a spouse under state law.[4] In Vermont, the status of civil union was created for the very first time by the Vermont legislature in 2001 in response to a ruling by the Vermont Supreme Court that the exclusion of same-sex couples from marriage violated the Vermont state constitution. In Connecticut, without any compulsion from a court, the state legislature passed a law, "An Act Concerning Civil Unions," that was signed by the Governor on April 20, 2005 and became effective October 1, 2005.

Although GLAD sees this as a constructive first step toward full equality for same-sex couples in Connecticut, GLAD is still committed to achieving marriage equality in Connecticut through its lawsuit, Kerrigan & Mock v. Department of Public Health, filed in New Haven Superior Court in August 2004. GLAD represents seven loving and committed same-sex couples who seek to marry in Connecticut.[5] The Superior Court will hear arguments in early 2006.

While civil unions provide state-based legal rights similar to those of marriage, couples joined in them are more likely to face discrimination against their relationships by other states, and cannot make any claim to the 1138 federal rights associated with marriage. Also, the Connecticut

*4 California provides a registered domestic partnership system which is nearly as comprehensive.

5 GLAD's co-counsel in this matter include New Haven attorney Maureen M. Murphy, attorneys Kenneth Bartschi and Karen Dowd of Horton, Shields & Knox in Hartford and the ACLU of Connecticut.

Civil Union Law defines marriage as "the union of one man and one woman" which emphasizes the second class status being imposed on gay people and same-sex relationships.

Whether you should enter a civil union, and what it all means, are questions this publication is meant to address. Inevitably you will have questions to which there are simply no definitive answers at this time. In a moment of social change like the present, there are no guarantees and those who come forward and participate in the civil union process will be "pioneers" of a sort.

This document is intended to provide general information only and is not intended to provide guidance or legal advice as to anyone's specific situation. Moreover, this is a rapidly evolving area of the law; and, therefore, these questions and answers are based upon the information that is known to us as of this printing and that can change at any time. For guidance on your particular situation, you must consult a lawyer. You should not act independently on this information. The provision of this information is not meant to create an attorney-client relationship. You may call the GLAD Legal Information Hotline at (800) 455-GLAD (4523) or check our website www.glad.org for the latest information and to obtain lawyer referrals.

What Is A Civil Union?

A Connecticut civil union is not a marriage. It is a legal status, parallel to civil marriage at the state law level, in which the parties to the civil union "shall have all the same benefits, protections and responsibilities under [Connecticut] law ... as are granted to spouses in a marriage...." (Civil Union Law, Public Act 05-10, §§1(1), 14-15).

When Will Connecticut Civil Unions Be Available?

The new Connecticut law, "An Act Concerning Civil Unions," was enacted and signed by the Governor on April 20, 2005. It became effective on October 1, 2005.

What Is The Difference Between Marriage And Civil Unions?

First, there is a difference. Civil unions will provide state-based legal rights that normally come along with marriage, and that is a tremendous advance over where things stood previously in Connecticut.

However, marriage is more than the sum of its legal parts. Because it is a social, cultural and legal institution, access to marriage provides protections to the married family on each of those levels. The word is itself a protection because others understand that when you are married you are a family. For some, being married allows them to express externally the nature of the commitment they feel internally. Marriages receive widespread respect.

Beyond these intangible protections, there are some concrete differences. The word "marriage" is the gateway to the 1138 federal protections afforded married couples. Without that word, same-sex couples in civil unions have no claim for those legal protections. While those protections are presently withheld from married couples of the same-sex, we do not believe that discrimination will stand the test of time.

At the state law level, the Civil Union Law gives public officials the explicit right not to officiate at a civil union while there is no such explicit exemption in the marriage laws. Moreover, there are certain circumstances in which 16 and 17-year-olds may marry, but you must be 18 to join in a civil union (unless you are ruled an emancipated minor by a court). There are also almost certainly important details to be worked out particularly where state law interacts, or works in tandem, with federal law.

Finally, it will be harder to gain respect for one's civil union in other states – in whole or in part – than it would be for a marriage. While marriages of same-sex couples will face discrimination in some places, marriages are advantaged over civil unions because all states have a marriage-system (with rich histories of respect for marriages validly licensed elsewhere).

Who Can Get A Connecticut Civil Union?

As of October 1, 2005, a person is eligible to enter into a Connecticut civil union if that person:

1. is not a party to another civil union or a marriage;
2. is of the same sex as the other party to the civil union;
3. is at least 18 years of age (although a minor between ages 16 and 18 will be deemed to be over 18 for the purpose of

obtaining a civil union license if the minor has received a court order of emancipation)[6];

4. is not closely related by blood to the other party to the civil union (matching essentially the same restrictions applicable to marriage in Connecticut); and
5. Is not under conservatorship or guardianship or has the acknowledged, written consent of the conservator or guardian.

(Civil Union Law, Public Act 05-10, §§2-3, 9-10 and 19-20).

Do We Have To Be Connecticut Residents?

No. Although the new law does not speak directly to the question, there is no residency requirement for marriage in Connecticut and, by clear implication, no residency requirement for a Connecticut civil union. Therefore, non-residents should be able to readily obtain a civil union license in Connecticut provided they are otherwise eligible. For non-resident couples, the civil union must be celebrated in the town where the civil union license is issued.

Can We Get A Connecticut Civil Union License If We Are Already Married Or Have A Civil Union Or Have A California Domestic Partnership?

The new Connecticut Civil Union Law says a person is eligible to enter a civil union if "such person is: (1) Not a party to another civil union or a marriage." (Civil Union Law, Public Act 05-10, §2(1)).

In addition, the Connecticut civil union license process requires the applicants to disclose whether they are "single, widowed or divorced." (Civil Union Law, Public Act 05-10, §8). Presumably, this will require the applicants to indicate that they are currently married or in a civil union from another jurisdiction.

[6] This is different than the Connecticut law governing marriage. A person under 18 can marry in Connecticut if an acknowledged, written consent of a parent or guardian is filed with the registrar of vital statistics. If there is no parent or guardian resident in the United States, "the written consent of the judge of probate for the district in which the minor resides, endorsed on the [marriage] license, shall be sufficient." (Conn. Gen. Stat. §46b-30(b)). A person under 16 can many in Connecticut if "the judge of probate for the district in which the minor resides endorses his written consent on the license." (Conn. Gen. Stat. §46b-30(a)).

With this background, the question arises as to whether a couple can get a Connecticut civil union license if they are already married or have a civil union or have a California domestic partnership.

With the Same Person

The language in the Civil Union Law does not provide a clear answer. Being a "party to another civil union or a marriage," could mean simply whether you are in one of those statuses at all regardless of with whom. Alternatively, "another civil union or a marriage" may actually be a somewhat technical way of simply requiring that you not have "another spouse," someone other than the person you want to join in a Connecticut civil union.

The Connecticut Attorney General on September 20, 2005, issued a formal legal opinion paper to the Connecticut Department of Public Health in response to the following question from the Registrar of Vital Statistics:

"Whether after October 1st, a couple that has entered into a civil union, same-sex marriage, or domestic partnership out-of-state may legally enter into a civil union in Connecticut with the same partner"

In summary, the Attorney General responded that:

1. Couples with a Vermont civil union or a California domestic partnership will be treated in Connecticut in the same way as a couple with a Connecticut civil union, but CANNOT also enter into a Connecticut civil union;
2. Same-sex couples with an out-of-state marriage, e.g. from Massachusetts or Canada, CAN enter into a Connecticut civil union, but the state of Connecticut will not recognize their marriage as valid; and
3. Couples with a form of domestic partnership other than from California might or might not be able to enter into a Connecticut civil union depending upon a comparison of the specific provisions of the out-of-state domestic partnership law to Connecticut law.

The Attorney General's opinion also recognizes that the new Connecticut Civil Union Law expressly provides for the recognition of certain civil unions celebrated in a foreign country. Presumably, couples with such a foreign country civil union will also be UNABLE to enter into a Connecticut civil union.

It is important to remember that the Attorney General's opinion sets forth only his view as to "conclusions likely to be reached by our courts". These conclusions could ultimately be overturned by the courts. For example, GLAD believes that the Attorney General's opinion ignores long-established principles of Connecticut law that a marriage that is valid where celebrated is valid in Connecticut. However, as the new Civil Union Law begins to operate, we anticipate that all of the registrars will follow the Attorney General's opinion.

Here are the Attorney General's conclusions in the actual words of the opinion:

"Based on a reading of the Connecticut law and the United States Constitution we conclude as follows:

- The Connecticut General Assembly in Public Act No. 05-10 specifically approved civil unions for same-sex couples. Since this law articulates our State's public policy, civil unions performed under the laws of other States are valid in Connecticut under the Full Faith and Credit Clause of the United States Constitution.
- At present, our courts will conclude that Connecticut law and the Full Faith and Credit Clause of the United States Constitution require Connecticut to recognize Vermont civil unions and California same-sex domestic partnerships. Other out-of-state, legally authorized same-sex domestic partnerships may be recognized as civil unions in Connecticut depending on how specific provisions of the States' laws compare to ours.
- Same-sex couples whose civil unions and domestic partnerships are performed in other States and recognized in Connecticut already have a valid civil union in Connecticut that need not and cannot be repeated in Connecticut.
- The Connecticut General Assembly has specifically determined that same-sex marriages are contrary to Connecticut law. Because the legislature has determined that marriages in Connecticut may only be between a man

> and a woman, same-sex marriages performed under laws of any other State violate Connecticut's expressly articulated public policy and are not required by the Full Faith and Credit Clause of the United States Constitution to be recognized here.

Because same-sex marriages performed under the laws of another State are not valid marriages or civil unions in Connecticut, same-sex couples married under the laws of another State are allowed by Connecticut law to obtain a Connecticut civil union."

With a Different Person

It should be clear that a person cannot enter a Connecticut civil union if he or she is currently married or has a civil union or California domestic partnership to a different person.

The prior existing marriage or civil union or California domestic partnership must be ended before entering a Connecticut civil union. You should consult an attorney as to where and how this can be accomplished.

Once the Civil Union Law is in effect, Connecticut residents with a civil union will be able to dissolve that union in a Connecticut court. That process takes a period of time.

Termination of a California domestic partnership can take different forms and, in some cases, does not require a court proceeding. You should seek advice and consult California's informative brochure at www.ss.ca.gov/dpregistry/forms/sf-dp_termbrochure.pdf.

Failure to end the prior marriage or civil union or California domestic partnership before entering into a Connecticut civil union could result in criminal charges of bigamy.

Can We Get A Connecticut Civil Union License If We Have Already Registered As A Domestic Partnership In Some Municipality Or State Other Than California?

With the Same Person

It is GLAD's position that any non-California governmental domestic partnership status you have should probably pose no problem to entering a Connecticut civil union. However, as noted above, the Connecticut

Attorney General's opinion indicates that if an out-of-state domestic partnership would be recognized as a civil union in Connecticut, then a couple with such an out-of-state domestic partnership would not be allowed to enter into a Connecticut civil union. In the absence of any specific guidance as to any particular state or municipal domestic partnership, you should seek advice from an attorney.

With a Different Person

If you intend to enter a Connecticut civil union with someone other than the person with whom you presently have a state (other than California) or municipal domestic partnership, GLAD recommends that you consult an attorney to determine whether you should formally terminate the domestic partnership first. For a registered California domestic partnership, see the previous question.

Do We Need A Connecticut Civil Union If Our Relationship Is Already Recognized Elsewhere? Do We Need A Connecticut Civil Union If We Already Have A Civil Union From Vermont Or A Foreign Country or A California Domestic Partnership?

Although the answer to this question cannot be stated with complete certainty, it is very likely that, at least as of October 1, 2005, a Vermont civil union will be treated in Connecticut in the same way that Connecticut will treat Connecticut civil unions. This view has also now been adopted by the Connecticut Attorney General. In addition, because of this view and as noted above, the Connecticut Attorney General has opined that couples with a Vermont or foreign civil union, or a California domestic partnership CANNOT in any event enter into a Connecticut civil union. Only the courts can ultimately provide a definitive answer to these questions.

Do We Need A Connecticut Civil Union If We Are Already Married?

There is no clear answer to this question. Although it is GLAD's position that Connecticut should and will ultimately extend respect to marriages validly entered into by same-sex couples, that question has not been settled authoritatively by the courts, and the Connecticut Attorney General has now opined that Connecticut will not recognize an out-of-state marriage of a same-sex couple. Again, GLAD disagrees and the courts will ultimately need to settle this question.

Private entities, including employers, are not bound by the Attorney General's opinion and may freely accord out-of-state marriages the respect they are due.

As a result, GLAD believes that a Connecticut couple who is already married will have more certainty as to the availability to them of all the benefits, protections and obligations of marriage as provided under Connecticut law if they enter into a Connecticut civil union.

How Do We Get A Connecticut Civil Union?

Except as noted, this entire process is an exact mirror of the process for marriage in Connecticut.

Application for a License

In order to obtain a Connecticut civil union license, both parties must appear and make an application before the registrar of the town in which either: (1) the civil union is to be celebrated; or (2) either person to be joined in the civil union resides. (Civil Union Law, Public Act 05-10, §7). However, it would seem that parties may appear before the registrar separately since the law provides that "if the license is signed and sworn to by the applicants on different dates, the earlier date shall be deemed the date of application." (Civil Union Law, Public Act 05-10, §8).

The Law requires that the "license shall be completed in its entirety, dated, signed and sworn to by each applicant and shall state each applicant's name, age, race, birthplace, residence, whether single, widowed or divorced and whether under the supervision or control of a conservator or guardian." The parties' Social Security numbers must also be recorded even though they will not be made publicly available. (Civil Union Law, Public Act 05-10, §8).

The registrar must also provide the applicants with a copy of the Civil Union Law.

Connecticut has no blood test requirements to obtain a civil union license. Prior law, repealed in 2003, required testing for STD's and rubella prior to the issuance of a marriage license.

Finally, applicants should check with the appropriate town registrar as to any fee for obtaining a civil union license.

Celebration of the Civil Union

Measured from the date of application[7], the couple has 65 days to enter into a civil union. The same individuals authorized to legally join two people in marriage are authorized to join two people in a civil union. They may do so "in any town in the state." (Civil Union Law, Public Act 05-10, §4). (But note that, for non-resident couples, the civil union must be celebrated in the town where the Civil Union license is issued.)

Authorized officiants include: all judges and retired judges, including judges of other states who can legally marry people, family support magistrates, states referees, justices of the peace and all ordained or licensed members of the clergy from Connecticut or any other state. (Civil Union Law, Public Act 05-10, §4(a)).

The official issuing the license to a couple cannot then officiate at the civil union, and this prohibition includes any assistant or deputy to the issuing official. (Civil Union Law, Public Act 05-10, §4(b)).

A person authorized to officiate at a civil union may refuse to do so without fine or penalty. There is no comparable provision as to marriage in Connecticut. (Civil Union Law, Public Act 05-10, §6).

The Civil Union Certificate

The authorized officiant certifies on the civil union license "the fact, time and place of the civil union" and returns it to the registrar of the issuing town "before or during the first week of the month following the celebration of the civil union." If the officiant fails to comply, the civil union couple can file a notarized affidavit attesting to the same facts. Either the filed Civil Union Certificate or the affidavit is then legal evidence of the civil union. (Civil Union Law, Public Act 05-10, §§11-12).

What Are Some Things We Should Consider Before Entering Into A Connecticut Civil Union?

A civil union is an important commitment and should be considered carefully. Since a Connecticut civil union is designed to confer all of the

---

[7] If the parties appear separately before the registrar and therefore the license is signed and sworn to on two separate dates, "the earlier date shall be deemed the date of application." (Civil Union Law, Public Act 05-10, §8).

state law-based benefits, protections and responsibilities of marriage, entering into that status can affect many aspects of your public and private life. Moreover, because only Massachusetts, California and Vermont have any sort of comprehensive relationship recognition for same-sex couples, it is important to plan for the worst, i.e., that entities in other states will not respect the civil union, while hoping for the best.

Moreover, this is a rapidly evolving area of new law where some things are unclear and others are confusing and where we do not yet have a great deal of guidance as to the application and implementation of the law. Therefore, please remember that the information provided here is tentative and that circumstances may change rapidly. It is important to make an informed choice about whether to enter into a Connecticut civil union based on your relationship with your partner and the unique circumstances of your life. You should consult an attorney in your home state before entering a civil union.

In preparing to consult with an attorney, here are a few issues to consider:

- Entering into a Connecticut civil union may complicate matters if you are in the process of adopting a child or considering adoption in the future. Some foreign countries welcome single-parent adoptions but do not allow same-sex couples to adopt. This might also be true for some states in the United States.
- Being in a civil union could disqualify you from certain state government programs because your spouse's income and assets may be included with your own.
- The military provides that an "attempted marriage" to a person of the same sex is grounds for discharge under "Don't Ask, Don't Tell." The military may view a Connecticut civil union as the equivalent of a marriage for these purposes.
- Under Connecticut law, married persons are responsible for their spouse's debts such as medical bills, rent and the purchases of items that support the family or benefit the couple. Connecticut civil union spouses would undertake these same responsibilities.
- Under Connecticut law, a spouse generally cannot completely disinherit a spouse by leaving the spouse out of

her or his will unless the couple signed a valid prenuptial agreement. As a result, a spouse is entitled to a share of your estate. Connecticut civil union spouses would be subject to these same legal rules.

- Under Connecticut law, a civil union can be dissolved in Connecticut only if certain residency requirements are satisfied (see "How Do I Get Out Of A Connecticut Civil Union?'). Also, other states may or may not allow you to dissolve your civil union under those states' laws. With divorce in Connecticut, the court will determine property division, alimony, child custody and child support if the parties cannot agree on these issues themselves. Under Connecticut law, the court can consider any property owned by either or both of the parties as marital property subject to distribution in dissolution unless the parties enter into an otherwise valid pre-nuptial agreement addressing the question. Connecticut civil union spouses will divorce under the same legal system.
- An employer-sponsored domestic partnership plan may require you to be "single" in order to qualify. This could raise questions as to whether an employee in a civil union can participate. (If the plan only requires the employee to be "unmarried," an employee in a Connecticut civil union can forthrightly state that she or he is not married.)
- Once you are in a civil union, you have assumed a legal status that will have to be disclosed on forms and records in a variety of public and private contexts.

What Protections Do We Gain From A Connecticut Civil Union?

A Connecticut civil union gives you automatic inclusion within and under hundreds of Connecticut state laws that apply to married spouses, family and next of kin.

This is what the new law says:

Sec. 14. (NEW) (Effective October 1, 2005) Parties to a civil union shall have all the same benefits, protections and responsibilities under law, whether derived from the general statutes, administrative regulations or court rules, policy, common law or any other source of civil law, as are granted to spouses in a marriage ....

Sec. 15. (NEW) (Effective October 1, 2005) Wherever in the general statutes the terms "spouse," "family," "immediate family," "dependent," "next of kin" or any other term that denotes the spousal relationship are used or defined, a party to a civil union shall be included in such use or definition, and wherever in the general statutes [with some identified exceptions] the term "marriage" is used or defined, a civil union shall be included in such use or definition.

(Civil Union Law, Public Act 05-10, §§14-15).

Although the Civil Union Law does not spell out any specific benefits and responsibilities under those hundreds of Connecticut laws that will include civil union couples, the State Office of Legislative Research did an analysis of the bill and identified the following categories of laws that will include civil union couples:

- family law, including marriage, divorce, and support;
- title, tenure, descent and distribution, intestate succession,
- wills, survivorships, or other incidents of the acquisition,
- ownership or transfer (during life or at death) of real or
- personal property;
- state and municipal taxation;
- probate courts and procedure;
- group insurance for government (but not private-sector) employees;
- family leave benefits;
- financial disclosure and conflict-of-interest rules;
- protection against discrimination based on marital status;
- emergency and non-emergency medical care and
- treatment, hospital visitation and notification, and authority to
- act in matters affecting family members;
- state public assistance benefits;
- workers' compensation;
- crime victims' rights;
- marital privileges in court proceedings; and
- vital records and absentee voting procedures.

(**Office of Legislative Research, Bill Analysis, pp. 2-3**).

Also, on July 27, 2005, the State of Connecticut Insurance Department advised all property and casualty insurers to: (1) "become familiar with [the new civil union law], particularly sections 14 and 15," quoted above; and (2) "review their existing practices and ensure that as of ... October 1, 2005, they are in compliance."

Many private parties – e.g., businesses, employers, public accommodations, insurance companies, etc. – are subject to the state law prohibiting discrimination based on marital status, which as of October 1, 2005 will apply to the status of civil union as well as the status of marriage.[8] Of course, the non-discrimination law already prohibits sexual orientation discrimination and that will continue. (Employers with fewer than three employees are exempt from the nondiscrimination law as are private clubs and certain owner-occupied housing properties. Religious organizations are also sometimes exempt from the nondiscrimination law.)

(**Office of Legislative Research, Bill Analysis, p. 6**).

Family law attorneys highly recommend that couples consider entering into a prenuptial agreement before joining in a civil union to clarify what they consider to be the length of their relationship, the ways they wish their property to be divided (in the event that their wishes vary from usual dissolution laws), and other matters of particular concern to them.

Are There Any Limitations On Connecticut Civil Unions?

Yes. Although civil unions in Connecticut have been created to be essentially completely parallel to marriage for purposes of Connecticut state law, a Connecticut civil union is still not the same as a marriage and there are many benefits and rights that are available to married couples

[8] In many instances, the non-discrimination law will mean equal treatment for civil unions and marriages. However, because of federal law, there may be circumstances in which this non-discrimination protection will not be available to civil union spouses. For examples of where federal law may direct different treatment for civil union spouses, see employment-related health insurance below.

in Connecticut that same-sex couples joined in civil union will not be able to access.

The Federal Defense of Marriage Act (DOMA)

First and foremost, because of the so-called federal Defense of Marriage Act (DOMA) and because the federal government has a marriage-based system for benefits, the current federal government almost certainly will take the position that it is not obligated to recognize Connecticut civil unions and therefore is not required to extend to Connecticut civil union spouses the more than 1138 federal benefits, protections and responsibilities applicable to spouses in a different-sex marriage. This includes federal taxes, Social Security, immigration, veterans' benefits and many, many more.

While married couples will have a claim to end the federal government's discrimination against their marriages, couples in civil unions will not. Connecticut created a separate legal system for same-sex couples, and reinforced that "marriage" in Connecticut is presently limited to male-female couples.

Interactions between Connecticut Law and Federal Law

In addition, federal law interacts with Connecticut state law in many ways that have yet to be catalogued and considered in light of this new Connecticut Civil Union Law. Some of these will almost certainly treat same-sex couples differently than Connecticut married couples until corrective action is taken.

For example, a conflict in Connecticut tax law concerning the filing status on state income taxes has already been addressed by the Connecticut legislature (see "Can A Connecticut Civil Union Couple File a Joint Tax Return?"). Other issues like this can and may be resolved either administratively or legislatively over time. However, for the moment, we anticipate some areas of federal/Connecticut interaction that will create problems and inequality for civil union couples.

Respect for Connecticut Civil Unions Outside Connecticut

There is uncertainty as to how other states will treat a Connecticut civil union – when couples joined in a Connecticut civil union relocate, or simply travel outside of Connecticut, or when non-resident couples enter a Connecticut civil union and then return home.

It is GLAD's position that the legal status of Connecticut civil unions should be respected in all other states just as marriages enjoy a strong presumption of respect, but this will not happen immediately and a civil union is not a marriage.

To date, we have the experience of couples who have traveled to Vermont; entered into a Vermont civil union; returned home; and, in a small number of cases, sought to either dissolve their civil union or have the court respect their spousal status in some other context. The results have been mixed.

At the same time, all of these reported cases have involved non-Vermonters such that we have no experience of courts being asked to respect the civil unions of Vermonters who either have relocated or have traveled outside Vermont and required access to a non-Vermont court.

The recent California Domestic Partnership Law (AB205) expressly provides for the recognition of a legal status such as a Connecticut civil union. It is GLAD's position that Vermont will likely recognize a Connecticut civil union because Vermont has a civil union legal system and because the substantive core of the Connecticut Civil Union Law mirrors quite closely the core of the Vermont Civil Union Law.

In addition, the number of other states that have some statewide law or system addressing protections and benefits for same-sex couples is growing. Beyond Vermont and California, it currently includes: Massachusetts (marriage); New Jersey (domestic partnership statute with a series of important protections); Maine (domestic partnership statute with some benefits); and Hawaii (reciprocal beneficiaries statute with a series of benefits). Although it is GLAD's position that every state should respect a Connecticut civil union, it is reasonable to assume that respect might be more readily forthcoming in states which also extend a legal status to same-sex couples.

Social Respect

As a longstanding cultural and legal institution, marriage is a unique marker of family and commitment and enjoys a presumption of respect. As a new institution created only for same-sex couples, civil unions will not likely enjoy the same level of respect.

What Does The Amendment In The Civil Union Law Defining Marriage As Between A Man And A Woman Mean?

After the Civil Union Law had initially passed the Senate, it was amended in the House of Representatives to include an amendment denying marriage to same-sex couples. Specifically, Section 14 of the bill provides:

"Parties to a civil union shall have all the same benefits, protections and responsibilities under law, whether derived from the general statutes, administrative regulations or court rules, policy, common law or any other source of civil law, as are granted to spouses in a marriage, which is defined as the union of one man and one woman." (Civil Union Law, Public Act 05-10, §14).

The amended statute then returned to the Senate where it passed, as amended, and was subsequently signed by the Governor.

So, what is the effect of the "marriage amendment"?

First, while many rightly see this amendment as an "anti-gay" amendment that was intended to reinforce the denial of marriage to same-sex couples, it is also a correct statement about marriage eligibility under current marriage statutes. As the Connecticut Attorney General has indicated in another context, the definition reflects the current state of Connecticut law, i.e., only a man and a woman can get a marriage license.

Second, although it is a statement of the current law, that does not mean that this law cannot change. Right now, GLAD has pending in the Connecticut Superior Court an action challenging the constitutionality — under the Connecticut state constitution — of the exclusion of same-sex couples from marriage in Connecticut, Kerrigan & Mock v. Conn. Dept. of Public Health.[9]

The enactment of the Civil Union Law does not affect the legal status of that marriage litigation. The courts have been asked to determine whether same-sex couples are entitled to Connecticut marriage licenses, and the Connecticut Supreme Court will almost certainly rule on that question at some point in the future. GLAD's lawsuit was begun in

---

[9] GLAD's co-counsel in this matter include New Haven attorney Maureen M. Murphy, attorneys Kenneth Bartschi and Karen Dowd of Horton, Shields & Knox in Hartford and the ACLU of Connecticut.

August 2004 and is working its way to a hearing in the Superior Court on the constitutional questions in early 2006.

Third, the Civil Union Law does not address the question of respect for the out-of-state marriages of same-sex couples. Moreover, the simple definition of marriage as between a man and a woman does not answer the question of how Connecticut law will treat, for example, a Massachusetts marriage of two men or two women. Connecticut has a strong history of respect for marriages validly entered in another state or country.

The Connecticut Attorney General has recently opined that Connecticut will not recognize an out-of-state marriage of a same-sex couple. GLAD believes that the Attorney General's opinion is wrong and that Connecticut will ultimately extend respect to marriages validly entered into by same-sex couples. The courts will need to settle this question.

How Will A Connecticut Civil Union Affect My Children?

There is no more important question than establishing legal parenthood. This document can only provide general information. For you and your children, we cannot urge more strongly that you consult an attorney about undertaking co-parent adoption for any current non-legal parents — particularly in light of the information below.

As to legal status as parents, if both parties to the Connecticut civil union were parents before the civil union (e.g., through joint or second-parent adoption), both parties remain parents.

If one party to the civil union was not a parent before the civil union, the civil union will not change that. As a result of the civil union, he or she will likely be considered a stepparent, carrying whatever weight that status has in Connecticut. The sure way to become a legal parent in this situation is for the non-legal parent to adopt the child. Moreover, that adoption decree from the court is a legal judgment. As a result, it should be recognized broadly outside of Connecticut and has legal significance independent of the civil union.

If two people joined in a Connecticut civil union subsequently have a child, both parties may be legally presumed to be the legal parents of a child born to either of them. In Connecticut, a child born into a marriage is presumed to be the child of both the wife and the husband. By virtue of the Civil Union Law, that same presumption should extend to a child born into a civil union. Nonetheless, this is just a presumption and does not have the same effect as a court judgment. It is subject to being challenged and overturned.

In addition, the civil union could encounter a lack of respect in some states, so relying on the fact of the civil union alone to protect your children is not the best approach. Therefore, it is advisable to consult a lawyer and continue the practice of securing a second-parent adoption in order to obtain a decree of legal parenthood that should be recognized broadly outside of Connecticut, independent of the civil union.

Beyond these considerations, entering into a civil union will provide your children with every protection and benefit that the Connecticut government (not the federal government) extends to enhance the security and safety of children's lives.

Will I Be Able To Get Health Insurance Through My Employer For My Connecticut Civil Union Spouse?

Although a few things are clear, this is an area where the answers are still evolving; the situation is very confusing; and we are not sure where the law is headed. Therefore, the information provided can only be tentative; and you should make every effort to seek up-to-date information.

If you are employed by the State of Connecticut, a Connecticut county or a Connecticut municipality, your civil union spouse will be entitled to the same health insurance rights and benefits provided to married employees.

If you are employed by the federal government, the so-called federal Defense of Marriage Act (DOMA) means that health plans offered through the Federal Employees Health Benefits Program do not cover same-sex spouses of federal employees. It seems almost certain that the federal government will not provide spousal health insurance coverage to an employee in a Connecticut civil union.

If you are self-employed, you should be able to purchase coverage for your civil union spouse on the same terms as a self-employed married individual.

If you are a private sector employee, the picture is more complicated and evolving. First, your employer may not be required to offer health insurance and otherwise may not be required to offer spousal or family coverage.

Assuming your employer provides individual, spousal and family coverage, your employer is certainly permitted to extend coverage to civil union spouses if it is available. The issue is whether a private employer can be required to extend such coverage.

Most private employer health plans are covered by a federal law known as ERISA (Employee Retirement Income Security Act). Under ERISA, there are two types of health plans: insured plans and self-insured plans. Insured plans can be regulated by state insurance laws. It is GLAD's position that an insured plan in Connecticut, governed by Connecticut law, will not likely be able to refuse coverage to spouses of civil union employees if coverage is extended to spouses of married employees.

This position is supported by a letter issued on August 4, 2005, by the Connecticut Commissioner of Insurance in which Commissioner Cogswell states, "Health insurance companies providing group or individual coverage, which is subject to regulation by the State of Connecticut will be required to comply with [the new civil union law] effective October 1, 2005."

It is generally believed that self-insured plans can choose whether to extend or exclude coverage for same-sex civil union spouses. GLAD is exploring avenues for challenging employers with self-insured plans that refuse to extend health coverage equally to same-sex spouses whether in civil unions or marriages.

Under a federal law known as COBRA, private employers with 20 or more employees are required to continue group health coverage for departing employees and covered dependents for a set period of time following certain events. As COBRA rights come from federal law, employers can deny COBRA rights to the same-sex spouses of employees. However, employers are free to extend these benefits voluntarily if available in the insurance marketplace. Connecticut law may also provide coverage continuation benefits in certain circumstances and those laws would require treating civil union spouses the same as married spouses.

Another federal law with a major impact on health insurance is HIPAA. HIPAA allows dependents of a covered employee to enroll outside of the normal open enrollment period. Because of DOMA, employers in Connecticut almost certainly with not be required to grant this federal right to the spouses of civil union employees. However, if employers cover same-sex spouses, they may do this voluntarily. In addition, to the extent that Connecticut law extends certain special enrollment rights to married couples, those rights will extend to civil union couples as well.

As to tax consequences, when employers extend coverage to the spouses of married employees, that benefit comes tax-free to the employee. However, because of DOMA, if an employer extends coverage to the civil union spouse of an employee, the "fair market value" of those benefits is treated as income to the employee and added to the employee's W-2 at the end of the year. However, the value of those benefits should not be treated as income for Connecticut state tax purposes. Contact GLAD or a tax lawyer or accountant if you have concerns about how your employer is calculating the "fair market value" of this benefit.

Finally, complicated issues arise if Connecticut residents work in Connecticut for companies based in other states. The obligation to extend coverage to civil union spouses may depend on a variety of factors and is currently being evaluated by GLAD. Similar complicated issues arise for non-residents who obtain a Connecticut civil union and return home and seek spousal health insurance benefits from their non-Connecticut employer.

Can A Connecticut Civil Union Couple File A Joint Tax Return?

It seems clear that the IRS will not accept a joint federal income tax return filed by a same-sex couple whether they are married or joined in a civil union.

With respect to Connecticut income taxes, although the new Connecticut Civil Union Law, as initially passed, indicated that a civil union couple would be able to file taxes in the same fashion as a married couple, another Connecticut statute required that a resident's filing status for state income taxes (with a few exceptions not relevant here) must be the same as their federal filing status. Since federal law will require a Connecticut civil union couple to file separately as "single," Connecticut law would require the same, putting the Connecticut income tax law at odds with the Civil Union Law.

This conflict was resolved by the Connecticut General Assembly with the enactment of Public Act 05-03, §58 in July 2005 which states that for tax years commencing on or after January 1, 2006 Connecticut's income tax law would ". . . apply to parties to a civil union recognized under the laws of this state as if federal income tax law ... recognized such a civil union in the same manner as Connecticut law." In other words, beginning with the 2006 tax year, civil union couples will have the same options for filing their Connecticut state income tax return as married couples.

Given the newness of the civil union status in Connecticut and other potential undiscovered complexities involved, it is strongly recommended that you consult with a reliable tax advisor in preparing your taxes following a civil union.

If We Get A Connecticut Civil Union Will We Be Able To Get Married Later?

Although this question is not absolutely free from doubt, it is GLAD's position that there should be no impediment to you subsequently marrying the same person with whom you have joined in civil union when marriage is available to same-sex couples in Connecticut. Of course, when that eventuality occurs, the legislature might well act to clarify this question by, for example, creating a mechanism to convert existing civil unions to marriages. Again, this is an area of law that could change rapidly.

GLAD also does not see any impediment to Connecticut civil union couples subsequently marrying each other in Massachusetts. Massachusetts currently permits couples with Vermont civil unions to marry in Massachusetts if otherwise qualified to marry in Massachusetts. GLAD believes that is a correct view of the law and should apply generally.

The foregoing presumes that you are seeking to enter a particular relationship with the same person. While the law is not crystal clear, GLAD believes that if you enter into a Connecticut civil union with one person and then seek to enter into a marriage with a different person, you should not attempt marriage until the Connecticut civil union is dissolved. Regardless of whether you could succeed in obtaining a marriage license in those circumstances, the result would be having two legal spouses which might subject you to a charge of bigamy and which would certainly create untold complexities in sorting out marital obligations in a legal system that expects to deal with one spouse at a time.

How Do I Get Out Of A Connecticut Civil Union?

The Connecticut Civil Union Law parallels Connecticut marriage law, including the Connecticut law regarding the termination of a legal relationship. Therefore, Connecticut's dissolution and annulment laws should apply to a Connecticut civil union.

Although there is no residency requirement to enter a Connecticut civil union or marriage, there are residency requirements for obtaining dissolution of a civil union or a marriage in Connecticut. Specifically, in order to dissolve a civil union in a Connecticut court, you must satisfy one of the following requirements:

1. one party must have been a Connecticut resident for the 12 months preceding either the filing of the complaint or the issuance of the decree of dissolution; or
2. one party must have been a Connecticut resident at the time of the civil union and now has returned to
3. Connecticut with an intention, before filing the complaint, of permanently remaining in Connecticut; or
4. the cause for dissolution arose after either party moved into Connecticut.

(Conn. Gen. Stat. §46b-44(c)).

In summary, residency is a requirement for a dissolution in Connecticut although it can be satisfied in several ways. However, if both parties to the Connecticut civil union were non-residents when the civil union was celebrated, at least one party must be a Connecticut resident in order to obtain a dissolution. That residency must be for a year either before or during the dissolution proceeding unless it can be shown that the cause for dissolution came about after residency in Connecticut was established by one party to the civil union.

Although at this time there is no way to know for certain, if you are a resident of states such as Vermont, Massachusetts, and California which have a comprehensive system for recognizing same-sex relationships, it may also be possible to dissolve a Connecticut Civil Union there. For example, there has been at least one case in the Massachusetts probate courts where a Vermont civil union has been dissolved.

What Legal Protections Can Same-Sex Couples In Connecticut Acquire Without Entering Into A Connecticut Civil Union?

Because the Civil Union Law is new in Connecticut and because the establishment of legal statuses for same-sex couples is new throughout the country and taking different forms, this is a rapidly evolving area of the law where there are ongoing questions and considerable uncertainty as to where the law is heading. As a result, no one has sure answers to many important questions. Protecting your relationship and your family is obviously important and means that you should consult an attorney for advice on your particular situation. With or without a Connecticut civil union, there are a number of steps a Connecticut couple can take to safeguard their relationship:

1) Relationship Agreement or Contract: In 1987, the Connecticut Supreme Court ruled that an agreement between an unmarried heterosexual couple to share their earnings and the fruits of their labor was an express contract which could be enforced according to the ordinary rules of contract when the couple separated. Boland v. Catalano, 202 Conn. 333, 340-41, 521 A.2d 142, 146 (1987). There is every reason to believe that the same result will apply to the contract of a same-sex couple. While the court held that contracts could be oral or in writing, this ruling provides great incentive for couples to sort out their affairs in writing before a separation.

2) Document Designating a Non-Legally Related Adult to Have Certain Rights and Responsibilities: Connecticut adopted a new set of laws, in effect as of October 1, 2002, (Public Act 02-105), that allows an adult, known as the designator, to name another adult, known as the designee, to make certain decisions on her or his behalf, or giving the designee certain rights or responsibilities The protections this law provides fall far short of those associated with marriage, but they may provide some peace of mind for couples under a narrow set of circumstances.

- To make this designation, the designator must sign, date and acknowledge a document before a notary public and two witnesses. The designator can revoke the document at any time by destroying the document or by executing a new document. Public Act 02-105, § 3(b). The designation document must be honored in the following circumstances:

- In the Workplace: An employer must notify an employee of an emergency phone call concerning the employee's designee. Conn. Gen. Stat. §. 31-51 jj.
- In Court and Administrative Proceedings Involving Crime Victims: The designee of a homicide victim is granted employment protection for missing work in order to attend court proceedings. Conn. Gen Stat. § 54-85d. The designee is also entitled to request and receive advanced notice of the terms of plea agreements with the perpetrator, to make a statement in court prior to the sentencing of the perpetrator, and to make a statement at parole hearings of the perpetrator. Conn. Gen. Stat. §§ 1-1k, 54-91c, 54-126a. The designee, if wholly or partly dependent on the deceased person's income, may seek compensation from the Office of Victim Services. Conn. Gen. Stat. § 54-201.
- In Health Care Settings: With regard to end-of-life decisions, a doctor must attempt to determine the patient's wishes. If the patient's wishes are not written in a living will, the designee is among those with whom the doctor must consult regarding the removal of life support. Conn. Gen. Stat. § 19a-571(a). The doctor must record any such communications with a designee in the patient's medical record. Conn. Gen. Stat. § 19a-578(b). Before removing life support, the doctor must make reasonable efforts to notify the patient's designee. Conn. Gen. Stat. §19a-580. In addition, the designee has priority in making anatomical gifts on behalf of a deceased designator over all representatives or family members with the exception of a surviving spouse. Conn. Gen. Stat. § 19a-278c(a).
- In Psychiatric Hospitals: The designee is among the list of people who may consent to medical or surgical procedures for involuntarily committed psychiatric patients who are

unable to consent themselves. Conn. Gen. Stat. § 17a-543(b).

- In Nursing Homes: The act entitles the designee to:
  - receive advance notice of involuntary, non-emergency room transfer, including Medicaid patients' transfer into non-private rooms;
  - participate in any consultations prior to any contested transfer;
  - private visits with the patient; and
  - meet in the facility with family members of other patients.

Conn. Gen. Stat. § 19a-550.

Other documents, discussed below, allow same-sex partners to share financial, medical, and end-of-life decisions. The rights and responsibilities to which the designee is entitled under Public Act 02-105 overlap with some of those set forth in the documents discussed below. It is unclear how the law will handle these potential conflicts, and therefore any preference for who should carry out specific obligations should be clearly noted in all relevant documents.

3) Power of Attorney: Any competent person may appoint another person as his or her "attorney-in-fact" for financial matters and health care or personal matters in the event the one becomes incapacitated or disabled. Conn. Gen. Stat. § 1-42.

The law provides a "short form" which allows a person to check off the kinds of transactions he or she would want the "attorney-in-fact" to perform in his or her place. These include (A) real estate matters; (B) chattel and goods transactions; (C) bond, share and commodity transactions; (D) banking transactions; (E) business operating transactions; (F) insurance transactions; (G) estate transactions; (H) claims and litigation; (I) personal relationships and affairs; (J) benefits from military service; (K) records, reports and statements; (L) health care decisions; and (M) all other matters designated by the individual. See Conn. Gen. Stat. § 1-43(a).

Note that the "attorney-in-fact" may make health care decisions and thus serve as a voice for securing medical treatments already determined by the declarant. However, the power of the "attorney-in-fact" does not extend to decisions concerning engagement or withdrawal of life support.

That responsibility lies with a "health care agent" (see below) or a designee under Public Act 02-105, unless set forth in a living will.

It is not clear if the "attorney-in-fact" receives priority for visiting a person in the hospital, so it is important to state that you want such preference given in the power of attorney or another document.

The power of attorney can become effective immediately, or upon your disability (called a "springing" power of attorney, because it springs into being upon disability), and it can have a short termination date, long termination date, or no termination date. It should be witnessed by two disinterested individuals and notarized. The notary may also serve as a witness. The power of attorney must stay in possession of the "attorney-in-fact."

4) Health Care Agent: A person age 18 or over may appoint another person to act as his or her health care agent and thereby state his or her wishes regarding termination of life support, preferences for types of medical care, or limits on the agent's authority for end-of-life issues. Conn. Gen. Stat. §§19-575a, 578 — 579a. Absent appointment of a health care agent, doctors may determine the patient's wishes by looking at collateral statements the person has made and by consulting with others to whom the patient had communicated his or her wishes. Conn. Gen. Stat. §19a-571. It is the "health care agent's" responsibility to ensure those wishes are fulfilled. The designation can be revoked at any time by creating a new document or by a clear expression of revocation. A copy of the appointment of a health care agent must be given to a person's treating physician.

5) Appointment of Conservator: Before an individual adult becomes disabled or incompetent, he or she may also designate in writing one or more persons to act as a conservator of his person or estate or both for when the adult is found incapable of managing his or her own affairs. Conn. Gen. Stat. §45a-645. These documents must be treated with the same formality as wills. See generally Conn. Gen. Stat. § 45a-645 (b). The appointment of a conservator takes precedence over an attorney-in-fact or health care agent. Conn. Gen. Stat. §45a-650 (g). A person may also nominate a conservator in accord with the form provided by statute. Conn. Gen. Stat. §19a-575. Note that all nominations are subject to the scrutiny of the probate court at the time a person is deemed incapable or incompetent.

6) Will: Without a will, a deceased unmarried person's property passes to: (1) his or her children; (2) his or her family; (3) if next-of-kin cannot be located, to the state. If the person wishes to provide for others, such as his or her partner, a will is essential. Even if a person has few possessions, he or she can name in the will who will administer his or her estate. See generally Conn. Gen. Stat. §45a-433 – 45a-439.

In addition, if a person has children, he or she can nominate the future guardian and "trustee for asset management" of the child in the will. That nomination will be evaluated by the Probate Court.

7) Transfer of Car Ownership to Surviving Partner: Under Public Act 02-105, a car owner may designate, on the car's registration, a beneficiary to assume ownership of the car upon death of the owner. Conn. Gen. Stat. § 14-16.

8) Funeral Planning Documents: Upon death, a person's body is given to spouse or their next-of-kin. Conn. Gen. Stat. §45a-318. This can mean that a person's own partner has no right to remove the body, write an obituary, or make plans for a final resting place. To avoid that problem, you can create a document (witnessed and notarized) which designates the person you want to be able to have custody and control of your remains. Conn. Gen. Stat. §45a-318. (Some people include these instructions as part of a will, but since a will may not be found for days after death, it is preferable to give the instructions to the person you want to take care of matters as well as to family).

9) Summary: Some attorneys, particularly if a person is naming the same individual as responsible for his or her welfare, have wrapped together all of the above protections (except the relationship contract, will, and the designation under Public Act 02-105) into a document entitled: "Health Care Instructions, Appointment of Health Care Agent, Appointment of Attorney in Fact for Health Care Decisions, Designation of Conservator for Future Incapacity and Document of Anatomical Gift." It seems unlikely that the designation under Public Act 02-105 may also be incorporated into such a comprehensive document.

(NOTE: This document is intended to provide general information only and is not intended to provide guidance or legal advice as to anyone's specific situation. Moreover, this is a rapidly evolving area of the law; and, therefore, these questions and answers are based upon the information that is known to us as of April 2005 and that can change at any time. For guidance on your particular situation, you must consult a lawyer. You should not act independently on this information. The provision of this information is not meant to create an attorney-client relationship. You may call GLAD at (800) 455-GLAD for lawyer referrals and additional information.)

Appendix 17-A

Provided Courtesy of ACTEC

Engagement Letters: A Guide for Practitioners Representation of Fiduciaries

INTRODUCTION

These forms illustrate issues that should be addressed when the lawyer is about to undertake general representation of a fiduciary, whether it be an executor, administrator, or trustee. Representation of guardians and conservators is beyond the scope of this material as state laws typically set forth detailed requirements for representation of this class of fiduciaries. This Section comprises two checklists and two corresponding form engagement letters. The first set pertains to representation of an estate's executor or administrator, whereas the second pertains to the representation of a trustee. These letters are not designed to describe every situation in which lawyers represent fiduciaries and should be modified as appropriate for applicable state laws, rules of practice, and particular circumstances.

ESTATE ADMINISTRATION REPRESENTATION CHECKLIST

I. Who is the client?

A. Under the majority view, the named executor(s) or administrator(s) (hereinafter referred to for convenience as "the Executor") hires the lawyer and becomes the sole client.

B. Most courts hold that the fiduciary is the lawyer's client. A few courts and commentators suggest that "the estate" is the client, or primary client, of the lawyer. However, typically the discussion or analysis that follows such an assertion speaks in terms of duties owed to the fiduciary, the beneficiaries and even to the creditors. The practitioner should exercise special care to identify the client and anticipate and deal with potential or actual conflicts of interest. The form of engagement letter that follows does not attempt to deal with conflicts of interest but does both identify the client and identify those who are not clients, in accordance with the suggestions set forth in the *ACTEC Commentaries*.

II. Threshold issues

A. Does the lawyer have the experience, training and time to provide competent representation?

B. Does the lawyer have an impermissible conflict of interest, such as a client relationship with a party who is expected to have a claim against the estate?

C. If the lawyer has, or has had, a client relationship with a beneficiary, heir or creditor of the estate which the lawyer believes will not adversely affect the proffered representation, the lawyer must make disclosure and seek the informed consent of the former, present and proposed clients in accordance with ethical rules.

D. If the lawyer has a claim against the estate for prior services, is it appropriate for the lawyer to make disclosure to, and request consent from, the Executor?

E. If there are two or more Executors, is there anything to indicate that the interests are otherwise than mutual, or are there reasons to consult with the Executors and obtain their consents to multiple representation?

III. What should the engagement letter contain?

A. Statement as to the proposed client relationship, e.g., the representation is of the Executor in a fiduciary capacity and not of the beneficiaries.

B. Description of the services to be rendered and services not to be included. Avoid general, all-inclusive language that can give rise to more questions for interpretation by the Executor, and possibly by beneficiaries as well.

C. Explanation of how fees will be determined and billed, together with an explanation of how costs will be handled (e.g., third party invoices over a specified amount to be referred to the Executor for payment directly).

D. Explanation of lawyer-client communications privilege and potential conflicts of interest. Consider requesting the Executor to waive future conflicts (e.g., allowing the lawyer to continue to represent one or more co-Executors if split develops and co-Executor engages separate counsel and/or allowing the lawyer to disclose information to the court or the beneficiaries.)

E. Explanation of how the lawyer-client relationship may be terminated.

F. Consider suggesting that the Executor should feel free to consult other counsel before agreeing to the terms of engagement.

IV. Consider whether a copy of the engagement letter should be given to the beneficiaries (This step is required in some jurisdictions).

ESTATE ADMINISTRATION ENGAGEMENT LETTER

(Date)

Dear (Client):

The purpose of this letter is to confirm my representation of you as Executor of the Estate of ____________________ and to set forth the terms of engagement.

I appreciate your confidence and trust in engaging me as your lawyer. I will be primarily responsible for this representation [but other lawyers or paralegals in my firm will assist me. In any event, all questions should be directed to me to provide for continuity of communication].

1. Summary of Services to be Performed For You as Executor. I will provide those services that are necessary and appropriate to administer the estate under the law of ____________, commencing with the petition to probate the will and have you qualified as Executor. The normal services that will then be involved are the following [Optional language: The following list includes the types of services that may be provided]:

(a) Prepare and complete all notices of appointment of you as Executor and other notices with respect to creditors as are required by the laws of the State of ____________ and rules of court having jurisdiction of the estate.

(b) Assist you in preparing a complete inventory of all assets of any kind or nature which are subject to probate, and any nonprobate assets such as life insurance, retirement benefits, and other assets.

(c) Help you make a thorough search for all debts, obligations and contingent liabilities of the estate in order to determine the financial condition of the estate and advise you regarding other action which must be taken by you to secure, reinvest, or protect the assets and provide for the discharge of liabilities, including death taxes of the estate.

(d) Prepare and complete all interim reports to the Probate Court and the beneficiaries as required during the course of administration of the estate.

(e) Prepare all tax returns for the estate, including federal estate tax and generation-skipping tax returns, state inheritance tax, or any local or state property tax returns, as well as federal and state fiduciary income tax returns.

(f) Review and consider with you any post-death planning, such as alternative asset valuation options, use of disclaimers, funding of trusts as provided for in the estate plan, timing the distribution of assets that are beneficial to the estate and any beneficiaries, and election of income tax benefits to the estate and beneficiaries.

(g) Plan for the payment of all death taxes and the source of funds to be used in payment of any tax obligations, along with any elections for installment payment of taxes if available.

(h) Prepare a plan of distribution of assets held in the estate, either outright or to separate continuing trusts, for the beneficiaries.

(i) Prepare all reports, notices, consents, receipts, and accountings for closing the estate and your discharge as Executor.

(j) Counsel and advise on any related questions or matters arising out of the administration of the estate.

If there are other legal services that you wish me to perform for you as Executor, we should first consult together and supplement this letter agreement before commencing those tasks.

In that connection, you should understand that I represent you as Executor. I do not represent the beneficiaries of the estate, even though I will, from time to time, provide them with information about the administration of the estate. In appropriate circumstances, I may advise beneficiaries to obtain independent counsel as I do not represent them.

2. <u>Charges for Legal Services and Out-of-Pocket Costs</u>. I charge for services on the basis of the time devoted by me [and other professionals in my firm]. Current hourly billing rates are as follows [NOTE: In many jurisdictions, fees are set statutorily by the probate court]:

Partners $ ____________ to $ ____________

Associates $ ____________ to $ ____________

Paralegals/Estate Administrators $ __________ to $ __________

I will bill the estate on a periodic basis. Because income tax considerations and cash requirements often dictate the timing of fee payments, I will request payments when they will best serve the interests of the estate and its beneficiaries.

It is to be understood that my fees will be payable whether or not approved by the inheritance and estate tax authorities or by the Probate Court. Although it is usual and customary to look to estate assets as the source of funds with which to pay our charges, the responsibility for payment ultimately is yours [NOTE: This arrangement would be prohibited in certain states which have statutory fee legislation].

I will also bill the estate for out-of-pocket expenses, such as probate and filing fees, travel expenses, delivery charges, duplicating, express mail, faxing and toll telephone calls. I will expect reimbursement of such costs upon presentation of periodic disbursement bills.

3. Conflicts of Interest and Confidentiality. Any relationship between a lawyer and client is subject to Rules of Professional Conduct. In estates, ethical rules applicable to conflicts of interests and confidentiality are of primary concern because of the close relationship of the parties. I cannot overemphasize the need for complete and full disclosure to me at all times of all your acts and doings to avoid problems that may arise in these areas.

Apart from any applicable legal requirement to notify the beneficiaries that the will has been probated and the estate administration commenced, I consider it good practice to do so and to provide each beneficiary with a copy of the will. In doing so, I will make it clear that you, alone, are my client. Furthermore, I usually keep the beneficiaries advised as the administration of the estate progresses, for example by furnishing copies of the formal inventory of estate assets as soon as that has been formalized.

As a condition of this representation, I require that, notwithstanding normal rules of confidentiality, you authorize me to notify the probate court and creditors and beneficiaries of the estate, as the case may be, of any actions or omissions on your part that have a material effect on their interests in the estate, including acts or omissions that may constitute negligence, bad faith, or breach of your fiduciary duties [In many jurisdictions the attorney-client communications privilege might preclude this type of disclosure without the personal representative's informed waiver. Reference should be made to the law of the jurisdiction in which the estate proceeding is pending].

[IF THERE ARE MULTIPLE EXECUTORS]

While there is nothing at this point to suggest that any differences of opinion will develop between you, during the course of administration of the estate it is possible that issues may arise on which you do not agree. Ordinarily, under such circumstances, one lawyer could not represent all of the co-executors without being involved in a serious conflict of interest problem.

Conflicts of interest may arise in a number of different contexts, including whether and to what extent discretionary distributions should be made from the estate, the investment policy to be followed by the co-executors, and the payment of compensation to the co-executors. In the event that the co-executors should reach different conclusions concerning the management and administration of the estate, it might be best for each of you to have the benefit of independent counsel to avoid the possibility that my advice to one of you would be influenced in any way by my representation of one of the other co-executors. For now, I will represent all of you in the administration of the estate, with the understanding that each of you retains the right to obtain independent legal counsel at any time that it appears to you to be advantageous.

Although I do not anticipate that it will be necessary, if a conflict does arise between the co-executors, and it is impossible in my judgment to perform my obligations to each of you in accordance with the standards that I would maintain in representing any individual client, I will withdraw from all further representation of the co-executors and advise one or all of you to obtain independent counsel. In such event, I would submit a statement for legal services rendered up to the date of such withdrawal. [In some states, this will not be appropriate, and application would have to be made to the probate court for an award of a portion of the single statutory attorney's fee that will be awarded for ordinary legal services to the estate].

As a part of my representation, there will be complete and free disclosure to each of you of all information concerning the estate that I may receive from either of you in your capacity as co-executor. Such information will not be confidential between you, collectively, and me as your lawyer, irrespective of whether the information is obtained in conferences at which all of you are present, or private conferences with one of you, including conferences that may have taken place before the date of this letter.

[IF EXECUTOR IS ONE OF THE BENEFICIARIES]

Because you are a beneficiary of the estate, I must advise you that I only represent you in your capacity as Executor, and can only represent you as a beneficiary if there is no conflict of interest by reason of such relationship. For example, a conflict could arise in distribution of assets to you if one of the other beneficiaries should object to your individual ownership of partial interest in an estate asset; or by reason of the amount of compensation which you may claim. In the event of such a conflict, consideration may have to be given by you to the employment of independent counsel to represent your personal interests.

4. Termination of Engagement.

(a) You may terminate this engagement at any time by notice in writing to me. Upon receipt of such notice, subject to such court approval as may be necessary in the context of the situation, I will promptly cease providing any service to you. You will be responsible for paying for my services rendered up to the time I receive such notice and for such reasonable services that I provide thereafter in connection with the transfer of responsibility for the matters I am then handling to your new counsel [See notes above about applicability of this type of arrangement in statutory fee states].

(b) I may terminate this engagement by giving you written notice. Upon termination of my representation, you will be responsible for paying for my services rendered up to the time I terminate our engagement and for such reasonable services that I provide thereafter in connection with the transfer of responsibility for the matters I am then handling to your new counsel [See note above about applicability of this type of arrangement in statutory fee states].

If you have any questions about anything discussed in this letter, please let me know. In addition, you should feel free to consult with another lawyer about the effect of signing this letter.

If this letter meets with your approval, please sign the approval copy of this letter and return it in the envelope provided.

I welcome and look forward to the opportunity to be of service.

Yours very truly,

Date Approved ____________________

Signed: Executor

TRUST ADMINISTRATION REPRESENTATION CHECKLIST

I. Who is the client?

A. Under the majority view, the trustee should be and usually is the lawyer's client. However, a few courts and practitioners favor an entity approach. See Comments at (1)(b) of Estate Administration Representation Checklist.

B. Inter vivos trusts —

1. Typically, as part of an estate planning engagement, the lawyer serves as scrivener and then advises and assists both the settlor and trustee with respect to funding and otherwise setting up the trust; all parties likely proceed on the assumption, or with the tacit understanding, that the trustee will look to that attorney for ongoing advice.

2. In the case of the typical irrevocable trust, the settlor retains no ongoing legal or equitable interest, making it unlikely that any conflicts will arise that would preclude the lawyer's continued representation of the settlor for other purposes or matters while also representing the trustee.

3. A revocable trust is usually for the settlor's own benefit and remains fully subject to the settlor's control as long as the settlor remains competent to amend or revoke; however, if differences arise between the parties, the lawyer may have no alternative but to advise the trustee to obtain separate counsel, at least for the purpose of resolving the differences. When the settlor dies and the trust becomes irrevocable, the lawyer should confirm or formalize the representation of the trustee.

C. Testamentary trusts — Typically the lawyer who has represented the executor will, more or less as a matter of course, come to represent the trustee as well. The transition from estate to trust will be "seamless" in many cases, especially if exactly the same person serves in both fiduciary capacities. Nevertheless, an engagement letter is advisable to cover the points outlined below.

D. Co-trustees — Especially if unanimous action is required to bind the trust, the lawyer should be able to represent the co-trustees collectively, absent indications that differences exist between or among the co-trustees.

II. What should the engagement letter contain?

A. Statement as to the client relationship, i.e., the representation is of the trustee in a fiduciary capacity and no one else.

B. Specific description of the services to be rendered and, if appropriate, services not to be included. If there is a corporate or other professional fiduciary, the lawyer may simply indicate availability to perform those services the trustee may require from time to time.

C. Explanation of how fees will be determined and billed, together with an explanation of how costs will be accounted for. How to deal with principal vs. income issues. Further, will it be prudent for the trustee to pay fees on an interim basis, without court approval?

D. Explanation of lawyer-client communications privilege and potential conflicts of interest. Consider requesting the trustee to waive future conflicts (e.g., allowing the lawyer to continue to represent one or more co-trustees if split develops and a co-trustee engages separate counsel, and allowing the lawyer to disclose information to the court or the beneficiaries.)

E. Explanation of how the lawyer/client relationship may be terminated.

F. Consider suggesting that the trustee should feel free to consult other counsel before agreeing to the terms of engagement.

IRREVOCABLE INTER VIVOS TRUST ENGAGEMENT LETTER

(Date)

Re: Trust U/A John R. Doe dated 00/00/90

Dear Trustee:

As promised, I am enclosing a copy of the fully-executed agreement of trust for your records.

As you know, I have represented John Doe in connection with establishing this trust, which is irrevocable and in which he has retained no interest. Although I anticipate continuing to represent him for other purposes, I am able, and would welcome the opportunity, to represent you as Trustee upon the following terms:

(1) General Services. I will provide such advice and assistance in connection with the administration of the trust as may be appropriate and agreed to from time to time. In that connection, I would be pleased to discuss with you your duties and responsibilities as trustee and your obligation to the beneficiaries of the trust including any special circumstances with respect to beneficiaries that you should be aware of as trustee.

(2) Accounting Services. [Omit if a corporate trustee] I can provide, through a special custody account arrangement we have with XYZ Trust Company, full administrative services, including record keeping, bill paying, handling periodic or special distributions, and daily sweeping of principal and income cash into selected short-term investment funds. I will provide full particulars if this custody arrangement is of interest to you.

(3) Tax Advice and Return Preparation. I am also prepared to advise you on tax questions that may arise in the administration of the trust and to handle federal and state fiduciary income tax preparation and to deal with any property taxes that may be applicable.

(4) Investment Responsibilities. [Omit if a corporate trustee with investment services] I will advise you of your powers and responsibilities with respect to trust investments, but cannot provide investment advice as such.

Appendix 17-B

Provided Courtesy of ACTEC

Engagement Letters: A Guide for Practitioners Estate Planning Lawyer Serving as Fiduciary

INTRODUCTION

These forms address ethical issues which arise when a client asks the estate planning lawyer to serve as a fiduciary. These ethical issues should be disclosed and discussed with the client. These forms should be adapted to fit each specific factual situation and applicable state law.

There are two forms in this section. The first deals with appointment of the lawyer as executor of the client's estate while the second deals with the appointment of the lawyer as the trustee of a trust. There are a number of specific ethical issues in these settings, including full disclosure to and discussion with the client of the alternative possibilities for fiduciary appointment, relative cost effectiveness of each of the alternatives, bonding requirements and exculpatory language in the dispositive document which will have an effect on the standard of care to which the fiduciary will be held for liability purposes. Care must be taken with these subjects since the fiduciary will have been the scrivener.

ESTATE PLANNING LAWYER SERVING AS FIDUCIARY CHECKLIST

I. Does the lawyer or his or her law firm have a policy regarding lawyers serving as fiduciary? If so, what is the policy?
   a. Encourage?
   b. Discourage?
   c. Prohibit?

II. Does the lawyer have adequate support staff to permit the lawyer to perform fiduciary services efficiently and cost effectively?

III. Does the lawyer's professional liability policy include or exclude lawyers serving as:
   a. Personal representative?
   b. Trustee?
   c. Guardian or conservator?
   d. Attorney-in-fact

IV. What should the engagement letter contain when the client requests the estate planning lawyer to serve as fiduciary?
   a. Fact that client independently selected lawyer as fiduciary.
   b. Disclosure of potential conflicts of interest.
   c. Advantages and disadvantages of lawyer serving as fiduciary.
   d. Compensation to be paid lawyer as fiduciary and lawyer's law firm for legal services.
   e. Explanation of exculpatory language and available options with respect to its use.
   f. Explanation of bonding requirements, including cost of bond, customary practice and relationship to professional liability insurance.

V. Co-fiduciaries; advantages/disadvantages
   a. Two heads better than one
   b. Costs
   c. Checks and balances

LETTER NOMINATING LAWYER AS EXECUTOR

(date)

Dear (Client):

At our recent estate planning conference, you requested that I serve as the executor of your will. I am willing to undertake this responsibility. However, in accepting this responsibility, I want to explain certain ethical considerations to you and obtain your written waiver of potential conflicts of interest that could develop in connection with my service as your executor.

Responsibilities of Executor

The executor of your will is charged with the responsibility to collect, manage, and protect your assets; to pay your just debts and funeral expenses; to prepare and file federal estate and income tax returns; to pay the income and estate taxes required to be paid by your estate; to pay expenses of the administration of your estate; and to distribute your estate in the manner directed by your Will.

Your executor should exercise good judgment, prudence, common sense, diligence, fairness, honesty, have reasonable skill and have experience in the management of the types of assets which your estate comprises, or the good sense to obtain assistance in the management of those assets.

Others Who Could be Nominated as Executor

Others who might serve as your executor include your spouse, one or more of your children, a bank or trust company, an investment advisor, your accountant, a relative, a personal friend, or a business associate.

Potential Conflicts of Interest

I can serve as your executor if that is your desire. Several potential conflicts of interest may arise from my service as your executor. One of these conflicts of interest relates to the probability that my law firm will serve as legal counsel for me as executor.

A lawyer's independence may be compromised when he or she acts as both executor and lawyer for the executor. The normal checks and balances which exist when two unrelated parties serve separately as executor and lawyer for the executor are absent. Unless the Probate Court is asked to intervene, there may not be an independent, impartial review to determine if the executor is exercising an appropriate level of care, skill, diligence, and prudence in the administration of your estate, and there may not be an independent, impartial evaluation as to whether or not the fees and expenses charged by the executor and the fees and expenses charged by the law firm are reasonable.

There may be other potential conflicts that may arise which I have not anticipated at this time.

Compensation to the Lawyer Nominated as Executor

Both the executor and the lawyer for the executor are entitled to compensation for services performed on behalf of the estate. When a lawyer has been nominated as executor, he or she can receive compensation for performing services as executor and as the lawyer for the executor as long as he or she charges only once for services rendered and as long as the total compensation for serving as both executor and lawyer for the executor is reasonable.

When I am requested by a client to serve as executor, it is my practice to charge [describe basis for fees/commissions as executor]. In addition to an executor's fee/commission, I would also be entitled to reimbursement for out-of-pocket expenses, including court costs and fidelity bond premiums.

When I am requested by a client to serve as executor, it is my practice to engage my law firm to represent me in my capacity as executor. It is our firm's practice to charge [describe basis for fees as lawyer]. In addition to these fees, our firm would also be entitled to reimbursement for all out-of-pocket expenses.

[OPTIONAL ADDITIONAL PARAGRAPH]

It has been my experience that where I have been requested to serve as executor, the combination of my executor's fees and the legal fee charged by my law firm are less than the combination of an executor's fee charged by a bank or trust company and the legal fee charged by our law firm.

Waiver of Bond; Use of Exculpatory Language

It is common for a Will to include language relieving the executor from the normal obligation to post an executor's bond with the court for the faithful performance of his or her obligations as well as language absolving the executor nominated in the Will from liability for actions not involving negligence, fraud, or bad faith. For example, a Will typically provides that the executor is not to be charged with losses resulting from the action or inaction of the executor in the exercise of reasonable care, diligence, and prudence.

[CHOOSE ONE OF THE FOLLOWING]

1. Where the Will nominates the lawyer who prepared the Will as executor, there is a potential conflict of interest for the lawyer incorporating into the Will language that relieves the lawyer from the obligation to post bond or which absolves the lawyer from liability for his or her own actions. I normally include language that relieves the executor from the obligation to post bond and language which exonerates the executor from liability for decisions made in the exercise of reasonable care, diligence, and prudence.

2. In Wills where I am nominated to serve as an executor, I normally do not include any language that relieves the executor of the obligation to post bond or which exonerates the executor from liability for decisions made as executor. Absent such language, under the laws of this state, I may/would be obliged to post a bond for the faithful performance of my duties as executor and I am obliged to exercise the degree of care, skill, prudence and diligence that a prudent person would use in the management of his or her own affairs. [NOTE: The "prudent person rule" differs from state-to-state. Be sure the rule is correctly stated for the jurisdiction in which the document is being drafted.] I estimate the annual performance bond premium will cost approximately $____________ annually.

It is your choice whether or not to waive the requirements of an executor's bond and whether to include or exclude language exonerating me from liability as your executor. Please advise me of your decision.

Consulting Independent Counsel

Because I have a conflict of interest in advising you with regard to the decision to nominate me as the executor of your trust and the inclusion or exclusion of language relieving me of any potential liability, you should consider discussing these matters with another lawyer. [NOTE: Counsel should consider the implications of Fred Hutchinson Cancer Research Center v. Holman, 732 P.2d 974 (Wash. 1987) where the court held that an exoneration clause did not protect the scrivener fiduciary against liability: "As the attorney engaged to write the decedent's will, [defendant] is precluded from reliance on the clause to limit his own liability when the testator did not receive independent advice as to its meaning and effect." 732 P.2d at 980.]

Nominating the Lawyer as Executor

If, after consideration of these issues, you want to nominate me as your executor, I would like you to acknowledge and waive the potential conflicts of interest I have explained to you. Please review the statement of nomination below. After you have considered this decision carefully, I ask that you sign the consent which follows this letter to indicate your request that I serve as your executor. Please return a signed copy of the consent to me. If you have any questions about anything discussed in this letter, please let me know.

Sincerely yours,

NOMINATION

We have voluntarily nominated _______________ as executor in our Wills. He/she is also the lawyer who prepared these instruments for us. He/she did not promote himself/herself or consciously influence us in the decision to appoint him/her as executor. In addition, he/she has disclosed to us the potential conflicts of interest which might arise as a result of his/her serving as executor, as described above, including an explanation of the responsibilities of the executor, a list of others who might be nominated as executor, the fees and expenses to be paid to the executor, the likelihood that our lawyer's law firm will also serve as attorney for the executor, an explanation of the risks and disadvantages of such dual service, and an explanation of the decision regarding the inclusion or exclusion of exculpatory language in our Wills.

We direct that our Wills [______ include ______ not include] language relieving our lawyer from the obligation to post a bond for the faithful performance of his/her duties executing and [______ include ______ not include] language absolving the lawyer as executor from liability for losses resulting from decisions made in the exercise of reasonable care, diligence, and prudence.

Signed: HUSBAND Signed: WIFE

LETTER ACCEPTING NOMINATION OF LAWYER AS TRUSTEE

(date)

Dear (Client):

At our recent estate planning conference, you requested that I serve as the trustee of your trust. I am willing to undertake this responsibility. However, in accepting this responsibility, I want to explain certain ethical considerations to you, and obtain your written consent to potential conflicts of interest that could develop in connection with my service as your trustee.

Responsibilities of Trustee

The trustee of your trust is charged with the responsibility to manage, invest, reinvest and protect the trust assets; to prepare and file annual trust income tax returns; to pay taxes required to be paid by your trust and the expenses of the administration of your trust; and to distribute the trust income and assets in the manner directed by your trust agreement.

Your trustee should exercise good judgment, prudence, common sense, diligence, fairness, honesty, and have reasonable skill and experience in the management of the types of assets which your trust comprises, or the good sense to obtain assistance in connection with the management of those assets over the term of the trust.

Others Who Could be Appointed as Trustee

Others who might serve as your trustee include your spouse, one or more of your children, a bank or trust company, your accountant, an investment advisor, a relative, a personal friend or a business associate.

Potential Conflicts of Interest

I can serve as your trustee if that is your desire. Several potential conflicts of interest may arise from my service as your trustee. These conflicts relate to the probability that my law firm will also serve as legal counsel for your trust.

A lawyer's independence may be compromised when he or she acts as both trustee and lawyer for the trustee. The normal checks and balances which exist when two unrelated parties serve separately as trustee and lawyer for the trustee are absent. Unless a Court is asked to intervene, there may not be an independent, impartial review to determine if the trustee is exercising an appropriate level of care, skill, diligence, and prudence in the administration of your estate, and there may not be an independent, impartial evaluation as to whether or not the fees and expenses charged by the trustee and the fees and expenses charged by the law firm are reasonable.

Other potential conflicts may arise which cannot be anticipated at this time.

Compensation to the Lawyer Nominated as Trustee

Both the trustee and the lawyer for the trustee are entitled to compensation for services performed on behalf of the trust. When a lawyer has been nominated as trustee, he or she can receive compensation for performing services as trustee and as lawyer for the trustee as long as he or she charges only once for services rendered and as long as the total compensation for serving as both trustee and lawyer for the trustee is reasonable.

When I serve as trustee, it is my practice to charge [describe basis for fees/commissions as trustee]. In addition to this compensation, I would also be entitled to reimbursement for all out-of-pocket expenses.

It is also my practice to engage my law firm to represent me in my capacity as trustee. It is my firm's practice to charge [describe basis for fees as attorney]. In addition, my firm is entitled to reimbursement for all out-of-pocket expenses.

Waiver of Bond; Use of Exculpatory Language

When an individual fiduciary is appointed, it is not uncommon for a trust agreement to include language relieving the trustee from the obligation to post a trustee's bond for the faithful performance of his or her obligations and language absolving the trustee from liability for actions not involving gross negligence, fraud, or bad faith. Also, in many cases, a trust agreement will provide that the trustee is not to be charged with investment losses resulting from decisions made by the trustee if the trustee exercised reasonable care, diligence, and prudence in making investment decisions.

[CHOOSE ONE OF THE FOLLOWING]

1. When the trust agreement nominates the lawyer who prepared the trust agreement as trustee, there is a potential conflict of interest if the lawyer incorporates trust language that relieves the lawyer from the obligation to post bond or which absolves the lawyer from liability for his or her own actions. I normally include language that relieves the trustee from any obligation to post bond and language which exonerates the trustee from liability only for decisions made in the exercise of reasonable care, diligence, and prudence.

2. I typically do not include any language that relieves the trustee of any obligation to post bond or which exonerates the trustee from liability for decisions made as trustee. Absent such language, under the laws of this state, I may/would be obligated to post bond for the faithful performance of my duties as trustee and I am obligated to exercise the degree of care, skill, prudence and diligence that a prudent person would use in the management of his or her own affairs. [NOTE: The "prudent person rule" differs from state-to-state. Be sure the rule is correctly stated for the jurisdiction in which the document is being drafted.] I estimate the performance bond premium will cost approximately $__________ annually.

It is your choice whether or not to waive the trustee's bond and whether I include or exclude language exonerating the trustee from liability as your trustee. Please advise me of your decision.

Consulting Independent Counsel

Because I have a conflict of interest in advising you with regard to the decision to nominate me as the trustee of your trust and the inclusion or exclusion of language relieving me of any potential liability, you should consider discussing these matters with another lawyer. [Note: Counsel should consider the implications of Fred Hutchinson Cancer Research Center v. Holman, 732 P.2d 974 (Wash. 1987), where the court held that an exoneration clause did not protect the scrivener fiduciary against liability: "As the attorney engaged to write the decedent's will, [defendant] is precluded from reliance on the clause to limit his own liability when the testator did not receive independent advice as to its meaning and effect." 732 P.2d at 980.]

Consent to Appointing the Lawyer as Trustee

If, after consideration of these issues, you want to appoint me as your trustee, I would like you to acknowledge and waive the potential conflicts of interest I have explained to you. Please review the statement of consent below. After you have considered this decision carefully, I ask that you please sign the consent which follows this letter to indicate your request and consent to my serving as trustee of your trust and that you return a signed copy of the consent to me. If you have any questions about anything discussed in this letter, please let me know. In addition, you should feel free to consult with another lawyer about the effect of signing this letter.

Sincerely yours,

Signed: Lawyer

APPOINTMENT

We have voluntarily appointed __________ as trustee of our trusts. He/she is also the lawyer who prepared these instruments for us. He/she did not promote himself/herself or consciously influence us in the decision to appoint him/her as trustee. In addition, he/she has disclosed to us the potential conflicts of interest which might arise as a result of his/her serving as trustee, as described above, including an explanation of the responsibilities of the trustee, a list of others who might be appointed as trustee, the fees and expenses to be paid to the trustee, the fact that our lawyer's law firm will also serve as attorney for the trustee, an explanation of the risks and disadvantages of such dual service, and an explanation of the decision regarding the inclusion or exclusion of exculpatory language in our trusts.

We direct that our trusts [_______ include _______ not include] language relieving our attorney from the obligation to post a bond for the faithful performance of his/her duties and [_______ include _______ not include] language absolving the lawyer as trustee from liability for losses resulting from decisions made in the exercise of reasonable care, diligence, and prudence.

Signed: CLIENT

Appendix 17-C

Provided Courtesy of ACTEC

Engagement Letters: A Guide for Practitioners Spousal Representation

INTRODUCTION

These forms illustrate issues that should be addressed in discussing potential problems regarding confidences and conflicts of interest while representing spouses in an estate planning context and the manner in which these potential problems may be resolved.

There are two forms of letter reflecting fundamentally different approaches to the representation. The first form suggests a joint arrangement in which the lawyer is free to share all information in his or her possession with both spouses unless and until an event occurs that affects that representation, in which case the form sets out several different options for dealing with that event and its effect on the representation. Practitioners and their clients usually choose this method of representation.

The second form contemplates concurrent separate representation, which is tantamount to separate and independent representation of each spouse. In this mode, each client instructs the lawyer to hold all information he or she receives from either spouse in confidence so that the situation approximates as closely as possible that which would obtain if the spouses were represented by independent counsel. There is significant controversy as to whether this approach is viable in this context and others, although there are noted and respected practitioners who use it. In any event, it is recommended that, if this approach is attempted, the practitioner be aware of the potential pitfalls and proceed with caution.

SPOUSAL REPRESENTATION CHECKLIST

- I) Who is the client?
  - A) Options
    - 1) One Spouse
    - 2) Both Spouses
      - (a) Joint representation with full disclosure between lawyer and both spouses (see Joint Spousal Representation Letter)
      - (b) Separate representation of each spouse with no disclosure by lawyer to other spouse (see Concurrent Separate Spousal Representation Letter)
  - B) Issues the lawyer should consider before accepting the representation
    - 1) Having the scope of representation precisely defined.
    - 2) Determining what relationship existed previously or exists presently between the spouses and the lawyer and/or his or her firm.
      - (a) Is there any prior or existing client or adversary relationship between the lawyer or the firm and either spouse? If so, does the lawyer have any conflict in representing either of the spouses? If the lawyer or his or her firm has represented either of the spouses before, in what capacity (e.g., individually, as a corporate officer or director, as a fiduciary)?
      - (b) How well does the lawyer know the spouses or either of them?
      - (c) Other than the marital relationship, do the spouses have relationships with each

other (e.g., are they shareholders in a family corporation, partners in a family partnership, fiduciaries or beneficiaries of a family trust, etc.)?

3) Determining what duties, if any, the spouses owe to each other, and how these duties would affect the lawyer's representation and ability to carry out instructions (e.g., pre or post-marital agreements, contracts to make wills, rights under pension plans).
4) Determining what duties, if any, either spouse owes to third parties regarding financial or property arrangements (e.g., child support, parental support, obligations or rights to or from prior spouse and others by agreements, prior divorce decrees, or arising under compensation or retirement plans).
5) Determining what conflicts of interest exist or may exist between the two spouses, and how would they affect the representation (e.g., knowledge that the plan of one spouse might defeat the plan or adversely affect the interests of the other; knowledge that possible future actions by one spouse might defeat the plan or adversely affect the interests of the other; or knowledge that one's spouse's expectations or understanding of the other's intentions are not correct).
6) Determining how will fees be fixed and billed, and who will pay.

II) The lawyer's continuing role

A) Options

1) As counsel for both spouses in joint representation setting continuing indefinitely;
2) No continuing role following completion of initial task as spelled out either in engagement letter or termination letter;

3) Continued representation of only one spouse under appropriate circumstances.

B) Issues for consideration

1) In the joint representation setting, what disclosures do the spouses expect or consent to be made?

(a) Do the spouses consent to the disclosure of all confidences between them, do they prefer that all confidences be maintained, or are they willing to allow the lawyer to disclose to the other spouse only those confidences which the lawyer believes are relevant and material to the other spouse's planning (answers to these questions may lead to conclusion that representation really is separate and concurrent rather than joint)?

(b) Do the spouses agree to share documents or only information?

(c) If they have agreed to share documents, does this include existing documents, new documents, or both?

(d) How will the confidential information be used? How will disclosure, or lack of disclosure, affect each client?

2) Do the spouses authorize disclosure of privileged and/or confidential information to third parties, accountants, insurance advisors, etc.?

III) Resolution of future actual conflicts: Options

A) Withdrawal from representation of both clients

B) Retention of option to represent one client or the other as attorney decides (based on past relationship or other basis)

C) Commitment to represent one client or the other (based on past relationship or other basis)

IV) Documenting the representation

A) Is an engagement letter sent to the spouses prior to the first conference, or does the lawyer send out an engagement letter to the spouses after the first conference?

B) Does the lawyer review these issues with the spouses at the first conference following a checklist or memorandum filled in during the first conference?

C) Does the lawyer require that both spouses sign the engagement letter or memorandum or otherwise acknowledge the terms of the multiple representation?

D) Should the lawyer periodically review with the clients the engagement letter to confirm the clients' continuing assent to the terms of the joint representation during the term of the long term representation?

JOINT SPOUSAL REPRESENTATION ENGAGEMENT LETTER

(date)

Dear (clients):

You have asked me to [describe scope of representation]. I have agreed to do this work and will bill for it on the following basis: [Describe arrangements pertaining to fees, billing, etc.]. If I am asked to perform tasks not described in this letter, an additional engagement letter may be required for that work.

It is common for a husband and wife to employ the same lawyer to assist them in planning their estates. You have taken this approach by asking me to represent both of you in your planning. It is important that you understand that because I will be representing both of you, you are considered my client, collectively. Accordingly, matters that one of you might discuss with me may be disclosed to the other of you. Ethical considerations prohibit me from agreeing with either of you to withhold information from the other. In this representation, I will not give legal advice to either of you or make any changes in any of your estate planning documents without your mutual knowledge and consent. Of course, anything either of you discusses with me is privileged from disclosure to third parties.

[CHOOSE ONE OF THE FOLLOWING]

#1 If a conflict of interest arises between you during the course of your planning or if the two of you have a difference of opinion, I can point out the pros and cons of your respective positions or differing opinions. However, ethical considerations prohibit me, as the lawyer for both of you, from advocating one of your positions over the other. Furthermore, I would not be able to advocate one of your positions versus the other if there is a dispute at any time as to your respective property rights or interests or as to other legal issues between you. If actual conflicts of interest do arise between you of such a nature that in my judgment it is impossible for me to perform my ethical obligations to both of you, it would become necessary for me to withdraw as your joint lawyer.

#2 If a conflict of interest arises between you during the course of your planning or if the two of you have a difference of opinion concerning the proposed plan for disposition of your property or on any other subject, I can point out the pros and cons of your respective positions or differing opinions. However, ethical considerations prohibit me, as the lawyer for both of you, from advocating one of your positions over the other. Furthermore, I would not be able to advocate one of your positions versus the other if there is a dispute at any time as to your respective property rights or interests or as to other legal issues between you.

If actual conflicts of interest do arise between you of such a nature that in my judgment it is impossible for me to perform my ethical obligations to both of you, it would become necessary for me to cease acting as your joint attorney. Since [Bob] is a client of long standing, I may elect to/would continue to represent him and in that event [Mary] would have to retain another lawyer to represent her. However, I would not be able to continue to represent [Bob] if prior to my undertaking separate representation I learn that [Bob] has breached any understanding with [Mary] or has advised me that he intends to do so (such as changing his estate plan to her detriment) unless [Mary] is fully informed of the breach or the intended breach and fully understands your current circumstances. By signing her consent to this letter, [Mary] agrees to my continued representation of [Bob] should a conflict arise between you, subject to the conditions set forth in this letter.

[OPTIONAL]

Once documentation is executed to put into place the planning that you have hired me to implement, my engagement will be concluded and our attorney-client relationship will terminate. If you need my services in the future, please feel free to contact me and renew our relationship. In the meantime, I will not take any further action with reference to your affairs unless and until I hear otherwise from you.

After considering the foregoing, if you consent to my representing both of you jointly, I request that you sign and return the enclosed copy of this letter. If you have any questions about anything discussed in this letter, please let me know. In addition, you should feel free to consult with another lawyer about the effect of signing this letter.

Very truly yours,

CONSENT

We have read the foregoing letter and understand its contents. We consent to having you represent both of us on the terms and conditions set forth. We agree that you may, in your discretion, share with both of us any information regarding the representation that you receive from either of us or any other source.

Dated & Signed by each Spouse

CONCURRENT SEPARATE SPOUSAL REPRESENTATION ENGAGEMENT LETTER

Conflicts of interest and confidentiality are of paramount concern if a lawyer undertakes concurrent separate representation of spouses. Such representation should only be undertaken after careful consideration of all possible conflicts of interest.

(date)

Dear (clients):

It is common for a husband and wife to employ the same lawyer to assist them in planning their estates. You have taken this approach by asking me to represent both of you [describe scope of representation]. However, each of you wants to maintain your right to confidentiality and the ability to meet separately with me. I have agreed to do this work on this basis and will bill for it on the following basis: [Describe arrangements pertaining to fees, billing, and which of the parties, if not both, will be responsible for payment]. If I am asked to perform tasks not described in this letter, an additional engagement letter may be required.

I will represent each of you separately and will not discuss with either one of you what your spouse has disclosed to me. Each of you releases me from the obligation to reveal to you any information I may have received from the other that is material and adverse to your interests. Furthermore, I will not use any information I obtain from one of you in preparing the other's plan, even if the result is that the two plans are incompatible or one plan is detrimental to the interests of the other spouse. In short, the representation will be structured so that each of you will have the same relationship with me as if each of you had gone to a separate lawyer for assistance in your planning.

While I have agreed to undertake this representation on a separate and confidential basis, you should be aware that there might be disputes between you now or in the future as to your respective property rights and interests, or as to other issues which may arise between you. Should this occur, I would not be able to represent either of you in resolving any such dispute, and each of you would have to obtain your own representation.

After considering the foregoing, if you consent to my representation of each of you separately, I request that you sign and return the enclosed copy of this letter. If you have any questions about anything discussed in this letter, please let me know. In addition, you should feel free to consult with another lawyer about the effect of signing this letter.

Very truly yours,

CONSENT

We have read the foregoing letter and understand its contents. We consent to having you represent each of us on the terms and conditions set forth.

Dated & signed by each spouse.

Appendix 17-D

American College of Trust and Estate Counsel (ACTEC)

3415 South Sepulveda Boulevard, Suite 330
Los Angeles, California 90034
Telephone: 310-398-1888
Facsimile: 310-572-7280
Internet: www.actec.org

The American College of Trust and Estate Counsel is a professional association consisting of approximately 2,700 lawyers from throughout the United States. Fellows of the College are nominated by other Fellows in their geographic area and are elected by the membership at large. A lawyer cannot apply for membership in the College. Fellows are selected on the basis of professional reputation and ability in the fields of trusts and estates and on the basis of having made substantial contributions to these fields through lecturing, writing, teaching and bar activities.

The purposes of The American College of Trust and Estate Counsel ("College") are to maintain an association, international in scope, of lawyers skilled and experienced in the preparation of wills and trusts; estate planning; probate procedure and administration of trusts and estates of decedents, minors and incompetents; to improve and reform probate, trust and tax laws, procedures, and professional responsibility; to bring together qualified lawyers, whose character and ability will contribute to the achievement of the purposes of the College; and to cooperate with bar associations and other organizations with similar purposes. The College is a nonprofit mutual benefit corporation organized under the laws of the State of California. The College is not organized for profit and no part of its net earnings will inure to the benefit of any member or individual. On dissolution all assets of the College will be distributed to one or more organizations exempt from taxation under subsection 501(c)(6) of the Internal Revenue Code of 1986, as amended.

Appendix 17-E

Provided Courtesy of FindLaw, a Thompson Corporation Service

Intake Questionnaire: Initial Meeting with Probate Lawyer

DISCLAIMER

The following form is provided by FindLaw for informational purposes only and is intended to be used as a guide prior to consultation with an attorney familiar with your specific legal situation. FindLaw is not engaged in rendering legal or other professional advice, and this form is not a substitute for the advice of an attorney. If you require legal advice, you should seek the services of an attorney.

If you are a responsible family member of a deceased person who died without a will or have been named as the "executor" or "personal representative" in a deceased person's will, it is advisable that you seek the counsel of an experienced probate lawyer to help you through the probate process. In order to do the best possible job, your attorney needs information about the deceased, the deceased's estate plan, and the deceased's assets and liabilities. At your first meeting with your attorney, you should be prepared to provide, as applicable, the following information:

NAMES AND ADDRESSES

- Your Name(s):
- Mailing Address
- Telephone Nos.:
  - (Work)
  - (Home)
  - (Mobile)
- E-mail Address:
- Your Relation to the Deceased:

IDENTITY OF DECEASED

- Name of Deceased:
- Deceased's Date of Birth:
- Deceased's Social Security Number:

ESTATE PLAN

- Did the Deceased have an existing Will(s)? [] Yes [] No
  - (If yes, provide your attorney with a copy)
- Did the Deceased have an existing Trust(s)? [] Yes [] No
  - (If yes, provide your attorney with a copy)

FAMILY INFORMATION

- Was the Deceased's married? [] Yes [] No
  - If yes, what is/was the name of the Deceased's spouse?
- Is the Deceased's spouse still living? [] Yes [] No
  - If no, when and where did the deceased spouse die?
- Deceased's Children:
  - Name:
  - Date of Birth:
  - Indicate Whether Adopted or from a Previous Marriage:
- Have any children received an advance on their inheritance or are any children financially indebted to the deceased? [] Yes [] No
- Any deceased children? [] Yes [] No
  - If Yes, Name of Deceased Child:

- o Did this deceased child leave any children? [] Yes [] No
- o Deceased's Grandchildren, if any:
  - ▪ Name
  - ▪ Date of Birth
  - ▪ Parents
- Other Pertinent Family Information or Explanation of Above Items:

PERSONAL REPRESENTATIVE

- Does the will or any other communication from the Deceased indicate who should be Personal Representative ("executor") of the Deceased's estate? (The Personal Representative is responsible for probating the will, paying debts, collecting the assets, and settling the estate.) [] Yes [] No
  - o If so, who?

SAFE DEPOSIT BOX

- Did the Deceased have a safe deposit box? [] Yes [] No
  - o If so, where?
  - o Does anyone else have access to the box?

PROFESSIONALS

- Did the Deceased have an attorney? [] Yes [] No
  - o If Yes to the above, please give name and address:
- Did the Deceased have an accountant? [] Yes [] No
  - o If Yes to the above, please give name and address:
- Did the deceased have a financial planner, investment advisor or insurance agent? [] Yes [] No
  - o If Yes to the above, please give name and address:

INFORMATION REGARDING THE DECEASED'S ASSETS

- Estimated net worth of estate:
- To the extent possible, collect information and documents regarding the Deceased's accounts held at financial institutions:

- To the extent possible, collect information and documents regarding the Deceased's investments:
  - [] Cash or money fund accounts, or certificates of deposit with stock broker firms
  - [] Stocks, bonds, and mutual funds where the broker holds the certificates and sent the Deceased periodic statements showing the account balance
  - [] Mutual funds where the Deceased dealt directly with the issuing company rather than through a stock broker
  - [] Stocks and bonds (other than U.S. Savings Bonds) where the deceased held the certificates in your possession
  - [] U. S. savings bonds
  - [] Treasury bills or other government securities
  - [] Limited partnerships
  - [] Oil and gas royalty or working interests
  - [] Oil and gas mineral rights in land
  - [] Other securities [describe]
  - [] Individual retirement accounts (IRAs), Keogh, or other individual plans providing tax deferment for deposits and income.
- Retirement plans:
  - [] Employer-provided profit sharing, retirement, or other benefit plans:
- Real estate:
  - [] Individual retirement accounts (IRAs), Keogh, or other individual plans providing tax deferment for deposits and income.
  - [] Personal residence located in state of:
  - [] Other property. How many different parcels of real estate did the Deceased own, other than his/her personal residence?
    - In what state(s) are these parcels located?
    - Was the Deceased purchasing any of the above properties on a contract for deed? [] Yes [] No
    - If Yes, provide details:

- Complete this section if the deceased was engaged in business.
    - o Do you own a business, or are you a partner in a business? [] Yes [] No
    - o If Yes, complete the following:
        - [] Business is organized as a corporation.
            - How many corporations?
            - How many corporations are subchapter S corporations?
        - [] Business is organized as a partnership.
            - How many partnerships?
        - [] Business is a sole proprietorship. How many different firms?
- Receivables: If any money is owed to the Deceased, as payments on contracts, where the Deceased sold a business, as payments on obligations secured by real estate, or where the Deceased loaned money to someone and held a note, indicate each type of indebtedness:
    - o [] Promissory note(s) secured by real estate.
    - o Amount(s) owed:
    - o [] Installment contract(s) of sale of personal property.
    - o [] Amount(s) owed:
    - o [] Unsecured promissory note(s). Amount(s) owed:
- Life Insurance Policies: For life insurance policies insuring the Deceased, indicate the name of the insurance company, the face amount of the policy, and the type of policy.
    - o Type of Insurance
    - o Company
    - o Face Amount
- Annuities: Please indicate the name of the annuitant and the type of annuity. Do not list annuities under which no benefits are payable after the death of the annuitant.
    - o Regular annuities payable for guaranteed minimum term or amount:
    - o Tax-deferred annuities:
- Personal property other than automobiles, trucks, boats, and trailers

- o [] Household furniture and appliances
- o [] Collections, art, antiques, valuable jewelry
- o [] Automobiles
- o [] Boats
- o [] Recreational vehicles
- o [] Motor home
- o [] Business machinery and equipment
- o [] Personal equipment and tools
- o [] Farm or ranch machinery and equipment (other than general tools)
- o [] Livestock

LIABILITIES

- (Make a list of known liabilities or debts of the deceased.)

QUESTIONS

- (Make a list of pertinent questions to ask your attorney.)

Appendix 18-A

Provided Courtesy of ACTEC

Medicaid Estate Planning: A Review of the Ethical Considerations of Practicing Medicaid Estate Planning in the Area of Elder Law

Many elderly Americans are in fear of being impoverished as a result of having to pay for long-term health care after becoming too frail or sick to care for themselves. Many middle income Americans, who do not qualify for public welfare assistance, are worried that their personal and family finances will be depleted by having to move into a nursing care facility. Wealthy Americans are not faced with this problem; the middle-income Americans are the segment of the population who are becoming inundated with the costs of long term care.[1] Financing the cost of long-term care poses the problem for middle class individuals who have incomes and resources too high to qualify for Medicaid, yet not high enough to cover the cost of their long term care needs.[2] These factors come together to raise questions regarding how these individuals can plan for long term care; some options are to deplete their assets completely on long-term health care until they can qualify for Medicaid, and this is known as "spend down;" to finance long-term care insurance in some way, or to transfer just enough of their assets in ways which are legal and acceptable thereby qualifying for Medicaid and retaining their assets for themselves and their families.

There are a few different ways in which individuals can finance long-term care. Medicare, which is a federal assistance program for the elderly and disabled, will fund long-term care in certain limited circumstances. Normally, individuals have to provide for long-term care expenses out of their personal savings and other assets. If there are no personal savings or assets to draw from, the costs of long-term care may be paid by Medicaid - a health-care program that covers acute medical and long-term care costs for those with limited financial resources. "Medicaid, however, provides for only about half of those individuals below the poverty level."[3] Many elderly people are "house rich but cash poor."[4] Assuming these people do not need institutionalized nursing home care, a number of home-equity conversion tactics may be used in order to generate income to cover the costs of long-term care.[5] Long-term care can also be an insurable event. Insurance can make personal savings last longer, thereby delaying, or even preventing, the need for financial-planning strategies.[6]

Adding to the increasing worry about long-term care for the elderly are developments in medical science, technologies, and treatments which have allowed individuals to live longer and that means individuals have longer periods of time for which they may have to plan for long-term care. The fastest growing segment of the population is people who are sixty-five years old and older. This is due to the resulting increase in life expectancy, and this creates the problem that the elderly will need greater amounts of financial assistance in caring for and supporting themselves.[7] Faced with limited options for financing the increasing costs of healthcare, our elderly population is relying heavily on the Medicaid program.[8] "The Medicaid system faces a serious financial crisis, and the need for a clear policy on long-term care financing is urgent. There is concern at both the federal and state levels over where public responsibility for long-term care ends and private responsibility begins."[9]

The Medicaid program was enacted in 1965 as a combined federal-state effort designed to make health care available for needy individuals, whether they fall into the "medically needy" or the "categorically needy" categories. Medically needy individuals are not necessarily low income individuals with little or no assets, but they cannot afford the cost of long-term health care. Categorically needy are those individuals who are low income and have little or no assets to use towards their health-care needs, long term or not. The Medicaid program provides federal financial help to states that choose to reimburse certain costs of medical treatment for needy persons.[10]

The practice of structuring an estate so an individual can become eligible for public benefit programs such as Medicaid is known as Medicaid estate planning. This is where assets are transferred and sheltered so as to qualify the individual for Medicaid without depleting her life savings. Medicaid estate planning is not the same as Medicaid "spend down." Spend down is the practice where a Medicaid applicant spends down his or her income and assets on medical expenses so he or she can become eligible for Medicaid. Medicaid estate planning is the practice of divesting one's resources on things other than health care costs, such as giving money to family members or buying new cars, for the purpose of appearing to be impoverished in order to become eligible for Medicaid.[11]

After the Medicaid program was enacted, the legal practice of "Medicaid Estate Planning" arose. This is a legal practice that involves the utilization of the complex rules of Medicaid eligibility to help one become eligible for Medicaid benefits. Some people have compared Medicaid estate planning to the way one uses the Internal Revenue Code to her advantage when preparing taxes. Individuals attempt to shelter or divest their assets, with the guidance of an attorney who practices in this area, to qualify for Medicaid without first depleting their life savings and other assets. "Serious concern arose over the widespread divestiture of assets by mostly wealthy individuals so that those persons could become eligible for Medicaid benefits."[12] Is it an abuse of the system to have wealthy individuals, those who can afford to finance long-term healthcare without depleting all of their assets, divesting their assets in such a way that enables them to qualify for Medicaid benefits? In other words, should wealthy individuals have the right to give away their wealth to those of their choosing in order to draw from a welfare program for their long term healthcare thereby placing the burden of the cost of their long-term care on society?

There are several commonly used techniques in financial planning which estate planners use in Medicaid estate planning. Individuals can invest money is assets which are considered exempt under the Medicaid rules, transfer assets directly to children or others tax free, or set up Medicaid trusts in order to shelter assets and still be eligible for Medicaid benefits. Finally, couples can change their wills and title their property to prevent the Medicaid recipient from being disqualified from Medicaid through inheritance. These estate planning techniques can help to assure that an individual is eligible for Medicaid benefits in her future.[13]

In this way, Medicaid estate planning involves structuring the client's estate so that eligibility for Medicaid may be established and maintained for that person's future.[14] In 1988, Congress passed 42 U.S.C. § 1396(p)(c), ("§1396") which requires a period of ineligibility for Medicaid benefits if the applicant transferred assets for the purpose of obtaining benefits.[15] Basically, the formula is the total amount of assets that were transferred during the "look-back period" of 36 months, divided by the average monthly cost of services as determined by the state of residency. The term "look-back period" refers to the length of time from the date of the Medicaid application so as to scrutinize all asset transfers made by the applicant in order to determine the applicant's Medicaid eligibility date.

Margaret Peebler, an 87 year old widow with no living children or siblings, who was in need of 24 hour care for the rest of her life, had assets totaling the amount of $14, 824.22.[16] She had no insurance to cover long term care and, under her current amount of assets, she could not qualify for Medicaid. Her attorney advised her to transfer some of her assets away so that she could meet the requirements for Medicaid, which in turn resulted in a 3 month period of ineligibility for her. The statute, 42 U.S.C. § 1320a-7b(a)(6), states that, "Whoever for a fee knowingly and willfully counsels or assists an individual to dispose of assets (including by any transfer in trust) in order for the individual to become eligible for medical assistance . . . if disposing of the assets results in the imposition of a period of ineligibility for such assistance . . . shall . . . be guilty of a felony and upon conviction thereof fined not more than $25,000 or imprisoned for not more than five years or both . . .."[17] This is precisely what Peebler's attorney did, and it is clearly against the law because it is in direct opposition to the rule. Peebler brought an action for relief seeking a judicial declaration that 42 U.S.C. § 1320a-7b(a)(6) is unconstitutional.[18] However, this case was dismissed for lack of standing because plaintiffs (Peebler and her attorney) had not been indicted, arrested, threatened with arrest, or even granted an "advisory opinion" concerning the application of this rule; therefore there was no genuine case or controversy.[19]

"Attorneys and Congressmen have engaged in debate over whether Medicaid estate planning is ethical, economical, and legal." An attorney has a fiduciary duty to her clients to do what is best for them, and, in many situations which arise in the area of Elder Law, that includes advising them of Medicaid estate planning. The question of whether Medicaid estate planning is illegal under the current Medicaid laws must be debated by the Legislature.[20] The Legislature is better able to assess the whole fiscal situation regarding Medicaid demands and benefits usages; better able to poll the population to see what the people want to have happen; and better equipped to investigate the actual impact of Medicaid estate planning on society thereby focusing their inquiry on public policy.

Medicaid does not allow a person to gift or transfer away all of her income or assets in order to be eligible for Medicaid. These transfers are considered to be Medicaid fraud and can result in criminal penalties and an applicant's disqualification from Medicaid eligibility altogether. In the past twenty years, Congress has tightened the loopholes in order to prevent elders from spending down their assets to allow them to qualify for Medicaid.[21] However, some loopholes are still in place; therefore, Congress must not have desired a complete shut down of Medicaid estate planning or it would have been explicitly stated otherwise.

Starting with the Omnibus Budget Reconciliation Act of 1980 ("1980 Act"), Congress enacted laws to prevent transfers of assets and income for Medicaid qualification reasons; if the only purpose to the asset transfers was to enable the individual to qualify for Medicaid, this Act limited his ability to do that. The law gave the states the ability to deny Medicaid coverage to applicants who transferred assets below their fair market value within a look-back period of twenty-four months before applying for Medicaid. Also, if Medicaid fraud was found, the 1980 Act also allowed states to impose a penalty of ineligibility for 24 months for the applicant.[22] In a situation like this, if the applicant had transferred away all of his assets and was in need of immediate long-term care, he would find himself in serious financial difficulty since he was disqualified for Medicaid benefits for the first 24 months. Beyond that, the problem of actually finding a bed for him would be at issue as well.

Next, Congress tightened the rules further by enacting the Tax Equity and Fiscal Responsibility Act, ("1982 Act"). This Act allowed states to consider whether an applicant had transferred not only available assets but also exempt assets within 24 months prior to applying for Medicaid. It also authorized the first "estate recovery rule" which allowed states to recover Medicaid expenditures from people who had committed Medicaid fraud by allowing states to impose liens on the applicant's home.[23]

One particular problem some courts had to grapple with regarding the 1982 Act was the question of what Congress meant by the word "estate" and which assets were to be considered part of the estate. An example of how the "estate recovery rule" has been implemented is found in Belsh v. Hope, Jr.,[24] where the California courts enforced recovery of Medicaid benefits as allowed under 42 U.S.C. § 1396p(b)(1)(B), in such a way as to permit recovery from heirs and joint tenants alike. However, when hardship is involved, California makes allowances across the board, regardless of whether an heir or joint tenant is involved. Under these circumstances, California's statute does not apply at all when the recipient passes a residence to a surviving spouse or minor or disabled children. If enforcement of the statute would cause substantial hardship, the Department has authority to waive its claim in whole or in part.[25] "Allowing states to recover from the estates of persons who previously received assistance furthers the broad purpose of providing for the medical care of the needy; the greater amount recovered by the state allows the state to have more funds to provide future services. Furthermore, if a person has assets available to pay for the benefits, then the state should be allowed to recover from those assets because that person was not fully entitled to all benefits."[26] These rules clearly further public policy. So, while California does exercise its right to recovery, it has policy in place which allows it to waive its claim in cases where recovery would cause undue hardship to the heirs or joint tenants of the estate.

The Medicare Catastrophic Act of 1988 ("1988 Act") drastically changed the eligibility requirements for applicants with spouses and tightened the existing asset transfer rules. This Act required that all states adopt the previously optional asset transfer restrictions in the Omnibus Budget Reconciliation Act of 1980 and extended the look-back period for asset transfers from twenty-four months to thirty months prior to the application for Medicaid benefits. This meant that applicants could not transfer available assets within the thirty month period prior to applying for Medicaid. Amendments to this act also prevented an applicant from transferring assets to his spouse who transferred them to someone else at that point.[27]

Other Congressional attempts to prevent applicants from transferring their assets to qualify for Medicaid were included in the Omnibus Budget Reconciliation Act of 1993 ("1993 Act") and the 1997 Balanced Budget Act ("1997 Act"). These Acts implemented steps to further tighten loopholes in the Medicaid eligibility rules by restricting the applicant's ability to plan effectively to avoid the Medicaid eligibility rules and by imposing criminal penalties for such transfers. These rules were tightened because of claims of widespread abuse of the Medicaid program.[28]

The 1993 Act lowered the fair market value transfer rules, imposed a greater penalty ineligibility period, and put more restrictions on shelters in trusts, jointly held property, and bank accounts. The 1993 Act also expanded the existing rule that prevented the transfer of assets for less than the fair market value of that asset and expanded the definition of assets to include transfers of property and income. This keeps applicants and their spouses from transferring property to qualify for Medicaid and from transferring income by way of trusts or other outright transfers. The 1993 Act also extended the look-back period from 30 months to thirty-six months, and if an applicant tried to shelter assets through recoverable trusts, the look-back period was extended to sixty months.[29] So at this point, if an applicant wanted to engage in Medicaid estate planning, he would need to be able to see far enough into the future to be able to make a decision to divest himself of his assets more than three full years before he was going to require long-term care, and if he chose to shelter his assets through a recoverable trust, then he needed to know five full years in advance.

"The 1993 Act also expanded estate recovery rules so that states can recover amounts expended for nursing home care, home and community based services, and related hospital prescription drug services."[30] The 1993 Act requires that states institute programs for recovery of the costs of Medicaid payments for nursing home care or long-term care from the estate of an individual receiving benefits after the age of fifty-five.[31] Apparently, these provisions were a result in the ineffectiveness of the previous estate recovery programs which had been optional.[32]

There are many different types of assets and property that can be recovered. These include property not only from the probate estate of the former Medicaid recipient, but also from the applicant's real and personal property.[33] Additionally, the state recovery program can also obtain other assets which the former Medicaid recipient had an interest in at the time of death whether or not they are included in the probate estate.[34] Basically, the state can recover any assets that belonged to the former Medicaid recipient in order to reimburse the state for its expenditures, but these rules are subject to limits and exceptions.

One way the state recovery programs are limited is by an ineligibility period for certain assets transferred for less than fair market value.[35] Another way is that the regulations provide a grace period during which asset transfers for less than fair market value can not be recovered by the State.[36] Finally, these estate recovery rules can be suspended for several reasons: The recovery of Medicaid costs for a former recipient who has a surviving spouse is suspended until after the death of the individual's surviving spouse.[37] Further, recovery can also be suspended if the Medicaid recipient is a child under the age of twenty-one, blind, or disabled.[38] Finally, the recovery can be permanently suspended in cases where recovery would cause undue hardship.[39]

Through the 1997 Act, because of the rising Medicaid budget and the problems with Medicaid estate planning, Congress imposed criminal penalties on those who counseled an applicant to divest assets resulting in the applicant's ineligibility for Medicaid, and this is where the attorney who practices in Elder Law and engages in Medicaid estate planning comes in. In 1996, congress passed a provision which made it a crime to "knowingly and willfully dispose of assets in order . . . to become eligible for Medicaid, if disposing of such assets results in the imposition for period of ineligibility for such assistance."[40] So, if an attorney or an accountant assessed the client's situation, advised that client to divest enough assets so as to leave the client with just enough money to pay for the period of ineligibility, the giving of this particular advice would be against the law.

A provision which became known as the "Granny Goes to Jail Clause" made it criminal for one to divest her own assets for the purpose of qualifying for Medicaid eligibility within the look-back period if diverting those assets resulted in the applicant becoming ineligible for Medicaid assistance.[41] The law was debated and amended rather quickly to prevent an applicant from incurring criminal penalties for transferring assets.[42] As a result of this Act, however, if an attorney knowingly counseled an individual to get rid of her assets within the look-back period and as a result, the individual became ineligible for Medicaid, then the attorney could be criminally penalized; this criminal provision has been hotly debated, and the meaning of the statute has not been fully defined.[43]

While the rules were tightened, the 1993 Act did contain recognized exceptions of certain asset and income transfers, and it is these exceptions to which an attorney can guide her client in preparing her to qualify for Medicaid. These exceptions include the right to prove affirmatively that transfers were not made for the purpose of qualifying to Medicaid; the option of correcting fraudulent transfers, and the option of retrieving wrongly transferred assets. There are also certain assets transfers which are exempt such as: the transfer of an applicant's home to her spouse, dependant child, or a sibling with an equity interest in the house; spousal transfers that are made for the sole purpose to benefit the spouse; outright inter vivos transfers or transfers to a trust for the benefit of a disabled dependent; or transfers that will cause undue hardship.[44]

All of these Acts resulted in a set of new Medicaid disqualification rules; applicants must be very careful in estate planning if the goal is to prepare for Medicaid eligibility. There are risks involved, and it is important to be aware of the strict rules that can result in ineligibility or criminal penalties if a mistake is made.[45]

An example of how the trust situation was handled is found in Ahern v. Thomas, Commissioner of Social Services,[46] where the court found that the principle of the trust that Mildred F. Ahern created could not be considered as an available resource in the calculation of her eligibility for Medicaid benefits, even though the amount held in principle exceeded $600,000. "The amount of principal and income of a Medicaid qualifying trust considered "available" to an applicant "is the maximum amount of payments that may be permitted under the terms of the trust to be distributed to the grantor, assuming the full exercise of discretion by the trustee or trustees for the distribution of the maximum amount to the grantor. . . ."[47] The court stated, "[T]he provisions of the trust instrument that address the obligations of the plaintiff's estate do not provide the trustees with either authority or discretion to make payments "to the grantor" . . . [c]onsequently such provisions do not provide a basis for including trust principal in the calculation of the plaintiff's eligibility for Medicaid (sic). Because the trust instrument does not provide the trustees with authority or discretion to distribute trust principal "to the grantor" . . . the principal of the trust is not a resource "available" to the plaintiff and it therefore cannot be included in the calculation of her eligibility for Medicaid (sic) benefits."[48] The dissent stated, "The majority of the court allows a wealthy plaintiff – with assets in excess of $600,000 – to take advantage of a program established to care for the medical needs of the poor."[49]

This is precisely the argument that opponents of Medicaid estate planning make, and with good cause. In this case, Ahern wanted to leave her money to her children, but they were not dependent children and were, presumably, perfectly capable of supporting themselves. So, she was legally able to impinge on a government welfare benefit system to pay for her care, a cost which is directly transferred to society, so that she could leave her considerable assets to her children. This is clearly a question of public policy: should we burden society for the benefit of a few? Worth taking note of is the fact that the court did not label her "categorically needy" but did label her "medically needy:" "Under the Medicaid (sic) act, states have an additional option of providing medical assistance to the "medically needy" — persons who, like the plaintiff, lack the ability to pay for their medical expenses but do not qualify as "categorically needy" solely because their income exceeds the income eligibility requirements of the applicable categorical assistance program."[50] Individuals who are categorized as "medically needy" become eligible for Medicaid if the state decides to cover them by incurring expenses in an amount sufficient to reduce their incomes below the income eligibility level set by the state in its Medicaid plan.[51] It is not hard to understand why some believe that the Medicaid system is being taken advantage of. On the other hand,

Ahern's desire to leave her assets to her children is a desire that many Americans who have saved their money share.

Attorneys who practice elder law may find themselves unsure about their ethical and professional obligations when advising their clients about Medicaid estate planning issues.[52] "Elder law attorneys are very sensitive to ethical and professional duties because they work with elderly clients when they are the most vulnerable and are easily influenced by others.[53] Attorneys have a fiduciary duty to do what is best for their clients within the parameters of the law. This makes it a legislative function to resolve the issues at hand on a policy level.[54] The Model Rules of Professional Conduct ("Model Rules") require lawyers to discuss the goals of representation, communicate with the client, and represent the needs of the client in a competent and diligent manner.[55] The Model Rules are not binding on the states, but most states have adopted substantial portions of the Model Rules or equivalent rules.[56] In light of these rules and their application to the area of Medicaid estate planning, the attorney owes the duty to her client to inform her of her option to use Medicaid as a way to finance long term care, to communicate to her Medicaid estate planning techniques, and to diligently represent the estate planning needs of the client. The lawyer must then select the best means available to accomplish the goals of the client her estate plan.[57] Additionally, the lawyer has a duty under the Model Rules to inform the client as to the status of her case and to provide the client with any and all pertinent information.[58]

Regarding the duty to represent the client's goals, in the context of Medicaid estate planning, the lawyer has the duty to directly communicate with the client about his goals and options with regard to planning for long term care. This basically breaks down to the duty to inform the client of her option to use Medicaid to finance long term care and inform the client of the means that can be utilized in order to organize her estate with that goal in mind. Once this information has been imparted to the client, the lawyer must work in a diligent manner to achieve the client's goals if the client chooses to prepare her estate in order to make her eligible for Medicaid.[59] This is particularly important when looking at middle-income clients who have just enough money to render them ineligible for Medicaid, but whose health is deteriorating in such a way that they will need to be cared for in a nursing home type of facility, and whose assets will, in no way, carry them through. This scenario is further complicated when one spouse is ailing but the other is still able to live on his/her own and will need to depend upon the assets for his/her support, hence the reason for the spousal exception. Add dependent children into the mix, and Medicaid estate planning can be crucial for these people even though they do not technically qualify as "categorically needy" or low income.

The client has the authority to make the decisions regarding the goals of the representation, but the lawyer has a duty to consult and communicate with the client about the means used to achieve these goals.[60] The lawyer also has a duty to inform the client of the risks involved in Medicaid estate planning, particularly regarding the risk of asset divestment and financial autonomy. These risks might include divesting the assets and then never actually needing a nursing home; the difficulty in finding a Medicaid funded facility with an available bed and the differences in the quality of care provided to Medicaid residents in comparison to paying residents, and the moral, social, criminal, and political consequences of Medicaid estate planning.[61]

Model Rule 1.1 requires that the attorney competently represent the client. The rule states, "Competent representation requires the legal knowledge, skill, thoroughness and preparation reasonably necessary for the representation."[62] In terms of Medicaid estate planning, competency means that the attorney must be competent in estate planning tools in order to accurately represent the client's needs. It also requires that the attorney be able to use and employ the Medicaid estate techniques in the most reasonable manner to achieve the client's goals.

Medicaid divestment is a very technical area of practice. The rules governing eligibility for benefits change frequently, and there are several ways to qualify for Medicaid if that is the client's goal. A lawyer who is not entirely familiar with all aspects of this practice should not agree to represent a client in this type of case unless the lawyer is prepared to associate with another lawyer who is qualified in this area.[63] "The attorney who provides services in this area must have a high degree of competence and command specialized skills and knowledge. He must know the tax laws, rules for Medicaid eligibility, how to sift through the maze of issues presented by the Social Security Administration or the state department of social services, and the ins and outs of estate and trust work. Medicaid is a social safety net that is provided to individuals after they spend-down their available assets. In this as well as in many other asset transfers, one must be concerned about fraudulent transfers which compromise the rights of creditors or other third parties. Trusts can be arranged in a manner to take care of the person when he is no longer capable of self-determination. In addition, trusts aid in the disposition of one's assets at the end of life. All this must be done within the parameters of appropriate estate planning and the rules of the tax code."[64]

Model Rule 1.3 requires lawyers to act with diligence. Acting with diligence is, "Pursuing a matter on behalf of a client despite opposition, obstruction or personal inconvenience to the lawyer, and may take whatever lawful and ethical measure are required to vindicate a client's cause or endeavor."[65] This rule may also mean that an attorney has to sacrifice some of her own ethical and moral considerations in order to diligently represent her client.[66]

Medicaid estate planning has been viewed as ethically controversial. The primary issue is whether people of some means, generally middle-income or high-income Americans, should be allowed to rid themselves of enough of their assets to qualify for what is, essentially, a medical welfare benefits program. To help find some resolution, one might compare Medicaid estate planning to tax planning. "Tax planning and Medicaid estate planning are essentially analogous and should be considered equally legitimate tactics that a lawyer can employ in representing the needs of the client."[67] In each of these areas, the rules are used in such a way that the client can pay less money to the government and keep more for himself and/or his family. Nobody really questions the idea of tax planning.

In Helvering v. Gregory,[68] the defendant organized a shell corporation in order to purchase another corporation because the purchase offered his company reduced tax consequences. Without the use of a shell corporation, the purchase of the corporation outright would have caused him to incur large amounts of taxes. The court had to address the question of whether this practice was legitimate. The Second Circuit held that the practice of planning in such a way to reduce tax payments was legal.[69]

One could arguably draw the comparison between tax planning and Medicaid estate planning. While Medicaid planning is criticized as being unethical and contrary to the legislative intent to provide Medicaid benefits for the truly needy, others defend it arguing that the right to transfer assets is an integral part of "America's wealth transmission system."[70] Since Congress made Medicaid estate planning possible, attorneys should employ the techniques available to represent their clients in a diligent and competent manner.[71]

In her article, Jan Ellen Rein supports Medicaid estate planning: "America's wealth transmission system accommodates a property owner's desire to transfer assets remaining at death to loved ones. However, a curious deviation from this time-honored tradition appears in policy discussions and legislation in the context of wealth retention and transmission by elders stricken with disabilities requiring long-term care. Research suggests that wishful thinking, misinformation and self-deception account for this deviation from accommodation to censure of attempts by the disabled elderly to preserve sufficient assets for lifetime security and modest transfer at death."[72] This article was written during ongoing debates about the Republican balanced budget proposal, which was vetoed by President Clinton, which would have altered Medicaid dramatically, particularly Medicaid's provisions for long-term care. She has strong view points, and they are also valid view points. It has been a long standing tradition in our history for Americans to leave their accumulated wealth to whomever they choose. The question is, do we, as a society, take on the burden of caring for those who could otherwise provide for themselves by allowing them to draw Medicaid benefits?

In addition to an attorney's ethical duties toward her client, she also has separate professional ethical obligations as a member of the bar. One of these obligations is to avoid professional misconduct. Model Rule 8.4 states that it is professional misconduct for an attorney to "commit a criminal act that reflects adversely on the lawyer's honesty, trustworthiness or fitness as a lawyer in other respects" or "engage in conduct involving dishonesty, fraud, deceit or misrepresentation."[73] Under the 1997 Act, it constitutes fraud if an attorney counsels her client to divest her assets for the purpose of qualifying for Medicaid if such transfer results in the person becoming ineligible for Medicaid benefits, and this only happens if the applicant transfers her assets within the look-back period. As a result, an attorney can lawfully and ethically inform her client about Medicaid estate planning and not be committing fraud as long as the attorney does not counsel her client to transfer assets within the look-back period. Therefore, while an attorney has an ethical obligation not to counsel her client in any way which would result in her ineligibility for Medicaid, an attorney also has an obligation to inform her client on the lawful and non-criminal aspects of Medicaid estate planning.[74]

The ethical obligations of the attorney are not fully defined under the 1997 Act. Former Attorney General of the United States, Janet Reno, informed Congress that the Department of Justice will not enforce the criminal provisions imposed by the 1997 Act.[75] The validity of the 1997 Act's criminal provision has been contested and found deficient on constitutional grounds in New York State Bar Assoc. v. Reno.[76] In an action for a preliminary injunction, the New York Bar Association challenged the statute arguing that it violated the First and Fifth Amendments.[77] The Bar argued that the Act was in violation of the First Amendment because it unconstitutionally restricted free speech and is overly broad and that it was in violation of the Fifth Amendment because it is vague. Based upon these arguments, the court found that the statute was deficient on constitutional grounds.[78] As a result, the validity and enforcement of the statute are not clearly understood.[79] "Despite the debate over the constitutionality of the criminal provision, a attorney must be aware that there are criminal penalties for counseling a client about Medicaid if it renders an applicant ineligible for such benefits. However, the Model Rules still obligate an attorney to inform her client about Medicaid estate planning within the parameters of the law."[80]

"In light of the duties imposed on lawyers by the Model Rules and by the fiduciary duty that the lawyer owes to her client, the lawyer has an ethical duty to inform her clients of Medicaid estate planning within the parameters of the law. If the client chooses to employ such techniques in the scope of the representation, the lawyer has a duty to abide by the client's goals. While an attorney must be aware of the criminal penalties imposed by the 1997 Act, the attorney must use Medicaid estate planning techniques to represent the client and attain her goals. It is, therefore, not the professional responsibility of the lawyer to stop the use of Medicaid estate planning, but the responsibility of the legislature to choose to curtail the use of Medicaid estate planning for ethical policy reasons."[81]

"In addressing ethical concerns related to Medicaid estate planning, ultimately, professional ethics and personal ethics must be distinguished."[82] Attorneys should advise their clients about Medicaid estate planning and diligently pursue such estate planning tactics if that is what the client chooses in preparation of her estate for Medicaid eligibility, as long as it is done within the parameters of the law. Personal ethical considerations against the use of Medicaid estate planning should not to be addressed at the attorney client level because it is the attorney's job to represent her client's interest according to the law. Instead, personal ethics must be debated by the legislature as a policy tool to prevent the use of Medicaid estate planning because it is the legislature who must make these kinds of public policy laws.

"In determining whether or not to close the loopholes in the Medicaid rules, the legislature must weigh personal and policy considerations. [T]he legislature must consider all relevant interests in deciding to close all existing loopholes in addition to ethical concerns. For example, the legislature should consider the government's interests in providing long term care treatment to poor Americans. It should weigh the interests of every American having the right to pursue Medicaid eligibility. Furthermore, the legislature needs to consider whether more restrictive laws should be enacted to contain the costs of Medicaid by restricting Medicaid eligibility for long term care. In the past, most of the changes in the current Medicaid laws were driven by budgetary policy concerns instead of ethical and equitable issues. The past revisions of the Medicaid rules were driven by policy efforts to develop stricter rules and enforcement mechanisms for policing fraudulent transfers."[83]

A possible result of federal and state efforts to set forth legislation preventing Medicaid estate planning might be that it forces the elderly to give greater consideration to purchasing long-term care insurance.[84] Tax credits for long-term insurance are available at the state and federal level; however, they do not appear to be incentive enough for many people to purchase a policy.[85] There is the possibility of relief in the form of public-private partnerships, a solution which includes the private insurance companies and the government where the state provides incentives to buy a long-term care insurance policy in exchange for asset protection in the event that the individual's long-term care costs exceed her benefits.[86]

"Resolving ethical dilemmas in an elder law practice involves a reconception of zealous advocacy, because the interests of the client may be difficult to discern and the goals of representation do not always involve an easily quantified, win-lose outcome."[87] In looking at the ethical concerns related to Medicaid estate planning, it seems clear that attorneys, regardless of their personal feelings on the matter, should inform and advise their clients about the avenues available to them through Medicaid estate planning. Further, the attorney has an obligation to diligently pursue these estate planning tactics should the client choose to prepare her estate in contemplation of Medicaid eligibility so long as the attorney stays within the parameters of the law. It is the job of the legislature to form the policies regarding Medicaid estate planning; this is the avenue through which the people may speak. Until then, the attorney's primary duty is to represent the client in a competent and diligent matter in reaching the client's goals: it would seem like malpractice to do anything other than that until and if the legislature speaks.

[1] Laura Herpers Zeman, Estate Planning: Ethical Considerations of Using Medicaid to Plan for Long-term medical Care for the Elderly, 13 Quinn. Prob. Law Jour. 187.

[2] Eleanor M. Crosby and Ira M. Leff, Response to the conference: Ethical Considerations in Medicaid Estate Planning: An Analysis of the ABA Model Rules of Professional Conduct. 62 Fordham L. Rev. 1503 (1994).

[3] Erick J. Bohlman, Financing Strategies: Long-Term Care for the Elderly, 2 Elder L.J. 167, 168 (1994).

[4] Pocket Guide to Money, Consumer Rep., Oct. 1992, at 637, 637

[5] Id.

[6] Bohlman, 2 Elder L.J. at 168 citing Susan E. Polniaszek, Insurance to Pay for Long-Term Care, in Financing Long-Term Care for the Elderly 143, 143 (Peter J. Strauss ed., 1993).

[7] Zeman, 13 Quinn. Prob. Law Jour. at 188.

[8] Kristen A. Reich, Note: Long-term Care Financing Crisis – Recent Federal and State Efforts to Deter Asset Transfers as A Means to Gain Medicaid Eligibility, 74 N. Dak. L. Rev. 383 (1998).

[9] Id.

[10] Thompson v. Dept. of Children and Families, 835 So. 2d 357, 359 (Fla. 4th Dist. App. 2003).

[11] Zeman, 13 Quinn. Prob. Law Jour. at 205

[12] Id.

[13] Id. at 205.

[14] Id. at 190.

[15] Peebler v. Janet Reno, Attorney General of the U.S., 965 F. Supp. 28, 29 (D. Or. 1997)

[16] Id.

[17] 42 U.S.C.A. § 1320a-7b(a)(6) (West 2003)

[18] Id.

[19] Peebler, 965 F. Supp. at 30.

[20] Zeman, 13 Quinn. Prob. Law Jour. at 190.

[21] Id. at 197

[22] Id. at 198

[23] Id.

[24] Belsh v. Hope Jr., 33 Cal. App. 4th 161 (Cal. App. 4th dist. 1995),

[25] Id. at 172

[26] Id.

[27] Zeman, 13 Quinn. Prob. Law Jour. at 199.

[28] Id.

[29] Id.

[30] Id. at 202 citing 42 U.S.C.A. 1320a-7b(a)(West 1992 & Supp. 1997)

[31] Id. citing 42 U.S.C.A. 1396p(b)(1)(B)(West 1992 & Supp. 1997)

[32] Id. at 203

[33] Id. citing 42 U.S.C.A. 1396p(b)(4)(A)(West 1992 & Supp. 1997)

[34] Id. citing 42 U.S.C.A. 1396p(b)(4)(B)(West 1992 & Supp. 1997)

[35] Id. citing 42 U.S.C.A. 1396p(c)(1)(A)(West 1992 & Supp. 1997)

[36] Id.

[37] Id. at 204 citing 42 U.S.C.A. 1396p(b)(2)(West 1992 & Supp. 1997)

[38] Id.

[39] Id. citing 42 U.S.C.A. 1396p(b)(3)(West 1992 & Supp. 1997)

[40] 42 U.S.C.A. 1320a-7(a)(6).

[41] Zeman, 13 Quinn. Prob. Law Jour. at 201.

[42] Id.

[43] Id.

[44] Id. at 200

[45] Id. at 202

[46] Ahern v. Thomas, Commissioner of Social Services, 248 Conn. 708 (1999).

[47] 42 U.S.C. § 1396a(k)(1)(1988)

[48] Ahern 248 Conn. at 742

[49] Id. at 752

[50] Id. at 714

[51] Id.

[52] Zeman, 13 Quinn. Prob. Law Jour. at 215

[53] Bohlman, 2 Elder L.J. at 168

[54] Zeman, 13 Quinn. Prob. Law Jour. at 216

[55] Model Rules of Professional Misconduct Rule 1.3 (1996) [hereinafter "Model Rules"]

[56] Zeman, 13 Quinn. Prob. Law Jour. at 217

[57] Id. at 217

[58] Model Rule 1.4

[59] Id.

[60] Model Rule 1.2
[61] Zeman, 13 Quinn. Prob. Law Jour. at 217
[62] Model Rule 1.1
[63] See Model Rules, supra note 55, at rule 1.1 cmt.
[64] Steven H. Hobbs & Fay Wilson Hobbs, The Ethical Management of Assets for Elder Clients: A Context, Role, and Law Approach, in Ethical Issues in Representing Older Clients, 62 Fordham L. Rev. 1411 (1994).
[65] See Model Rules, supra note 55, at rule 1.3 cmt.
[66] Zeman, 13 Quinn. Prob. Law Jour. at 219
[67] Id. at 219
[68] Helvering v. Gregory, 69 F.2d 809, 810 (2d. Cir. 1834).
[69] Id.
[70] Jan Ellen Rein, Misinformation and Self-Deception in Recent Long-Term Care Policy Trends, 12 J.L. & Pol. 195, 207 (1996).
[71] Zeman, 13 Quinn. Prob. Law Jour. at 220
[72] Rein, 12 J.L. & Pol. at 196.
[73] See Model Rules, supra note 55, at Rule 8.4
[74] Zeman, 13 Quinn. Prob. Law Jour. at 221.
[75] New York State Bar Assoc. v. Reno, 999 F. Supp. 710, 713 (N.D. N.Y. 1998).
[76] Id.
[77] Id.
[78] Id.
[79] Zeman, 13 Quinn. Prob. Law Jour. at 222.
[80] Id.
[81] Id.
[82] Id. at 223
[83] Id.
[84] Brian E. Barriera, Using a CRAT (Charitable Remainder Annuity Trust) to Pay for Long-Term Care Insurance, 24 Est. Plan. 99, (1997).
[85] Id.
[86] Janice Cooper Pasaba & Alison Barnes, Public-Private Partnerships and Long-Term Care: Time for a Re-Examination?, 26 Stetson L. Rev. 529, 537 (1996).

[87] Joseph A. Rosenberg, Adapting Unitary Principles of Professional responsibility to Unique Practice Contexts: A Reflective Model for Resolving Ethical Dilemmas in Elder Law, 31 Loy. Chi. L.J. 403 (2000).

About the Author

Julie Jason is a money manager, author, and columnist who began her Wall Street career as a securities lawyer after earning a master of laws degree from Columbia University School of Law in 1975.

She is president and co-founder of Jackson, Grant Investment Advisers, Inc., a registered investment adviser serving affluent individuals and their families. The firm specializes in the unique needs of people who acquire important sums of money through once-in-a-lifetime events such as pension distributions, 401(k) rollovers, inheritances, divorce settlements, and lifelong savings. Managing these assets requires a far different level of attention, care, and skill than casual stock picking. When Ms. Jason assists her clients in coordinating financial and estate planning issues, she works with her client's attorneys and accountants.

Ms. Jason is a proponent of investment education and investor protection. She serves as an arbitrator and mediator for the National Association of Securities Dealers (NASD) and teaches and writes to educate the lay person about investment and financial matters. Ms. Jason's column, called "Road to Security," appears weekly in the Sunday business sections of the Stamford Advocate, the Greenwich Time, and the Norwalk Advocate.

Her books include:

- You and Your 401(k): How to Manage Your Returns for Maximum Results (*Simon & Schuster* 1996),
- The 401(k) Plan Handbook (*Prentice Hall* 1997),
- J.K. Lasser's Strategic Investing After 50 (*John Wiley & Sons* 2001),
- Julie Jason's Guide to Connecticut Probate: What Every Connecticut Family Needs to Know About Probate (*Author House 2006*), and
- The AARP Crash Course on Creating Retirement Income (*Sterling Publishers, 2007*).

Ms. Jason encourages readers to contact her with questions and comments. Her telephone number is (203)322-1198 and her email address is Julie@JacksonGrant.us. Jackson, Grant Investment Advisers, Inc. is located at Two High Ridge Park, Stamford, CT 06905.

Message from the Author

If you are a regular reader of my column or my books, you know that I enjoy hearing from my readers. By all means email me with comments and questions that I may be able to answer in my column.

If you are a member of an association or group and would like me to speak to your group about probate or investing, let's see if we can arrange that.

Likewise, let me know if you would like to learn more about our portfolio management services for families.

My telephone number is 203-322-1198. My email is Julie@JacksonGrant.us.

Watch for my next book, *The AARP Crash Course on Creating Retirement Income* (Sterling Publishers). In the meantime, email me with questions you would like to see answered on how to invest for your retirement.

Printed in the United States
85884LV00010B/89/A

9 781425 960155